IS THIS WHAT YOU WANT?

"Our aim is nothing less than to create a world system of financial control in private hands to dominate the political system of each country, and the world economy as a whole. Freedom and choice will be controlled within very narrow alternatives . . ."

— Carroll Quigley, CFR, (1996)

If you do not wish to become a serf in the New World Order, *The Satori And The New Mandarins* is must reading.

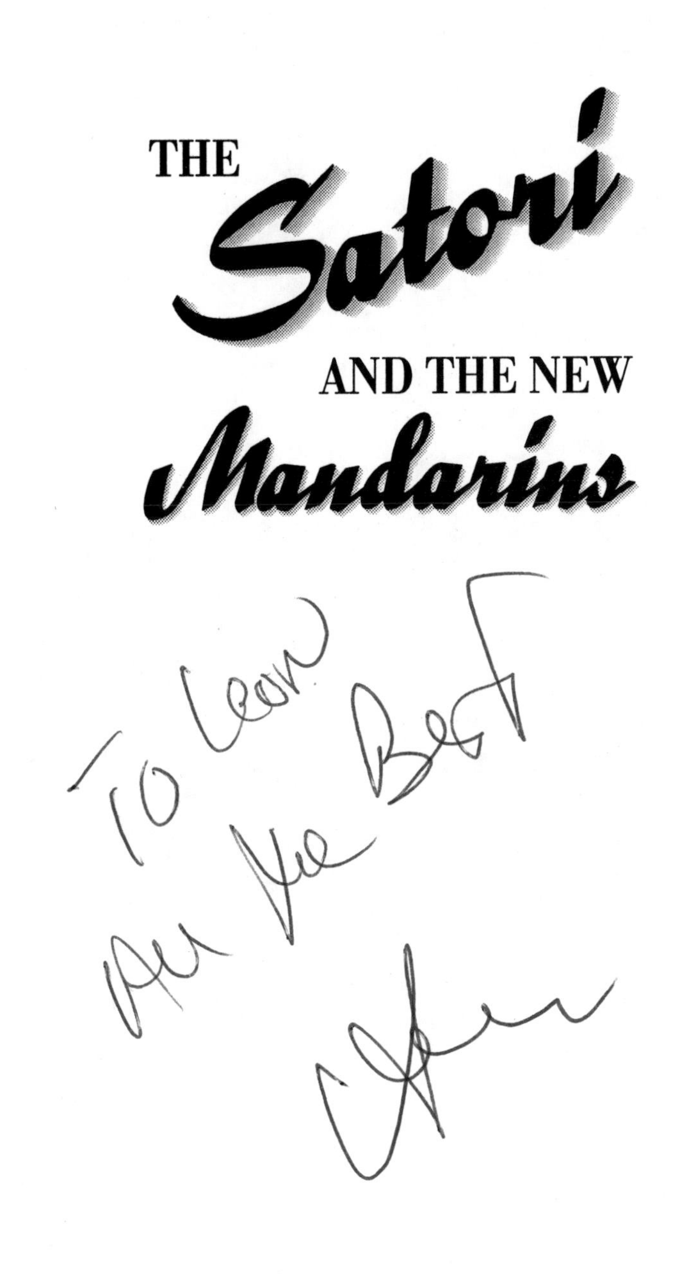

THE Satori AND THE NEW Mandarins

BY

ADRIAN H. KRIEG

HALLBERG PUBLISHING CORPORATION

Nonfiction Book Publishers – ISBN 0-83719

Tampa, Florida 33623

ISBN Number 0-87319-044-4

Library of Congress Catalog Card Number 97-077068

Cover design and typography by Michael X Marecek

Printed in the USA. First printing January 1998.
For information concerning Rights & Permissions or other questions
contact:

HALLBERG PUBLISHING CORPORATION
P.O. Box 23985 • Tampa, Florida 33623
Phone 1-800-633-7627 • Fax 1-800-253-READ

DEDICATION

*This book is dedicated to the over one hundred and twenty million citizens of the world murdered by their own governments in the 20th century. *This includes Wounded Knee, Oklahoma City, Waco and Ruby Ridge.*

**Death by Government* by R.J. Rummel

CONTENTS

Foreword XI

Introduction XV

Chapter 1 – Manipulation 27
- Dialectic Process 30
- The Political Class 32
- Mexico & NAFTA 34
- Russia 40
- Angola 43
- Healthcare 46
- Quik Shot Dialectics 49

Chapter 2 – Labyrinth from Above 53
- Political Systems 56
- The Greens 60
- Playing the Populace 68
- Societal Relations 73
- Gaia, The New God 77
- Gender Bender 83

Chapter 3 – Politics & Conflict 87
- Kulturkampf 95
- Gun Control 101
- Education 109
- Who Are The Mandarins 113
- Americana 114
- Mantle of Charlemagne 117
- Japan 121
- Wildcards 123
- 4th Generation War 126
- The New World Army 134

Chapter 4 – The Machine 139
- Financial Monopoly 151
- Following the Money 153

CONTENTS (Con't.)

Chapter 5 – Foundations 157

Chapter 6 – The Mandarins 171
- The Council on Foreign Relations 174
- The Order 191
- Trilateral Commission 203
- The Bilderbergers 218
- Super Mandarins 233

Chapter 7 – What You Can Do 237

Appendices . . .
- A) Coffin letter to Senator Dodd 249
- B) Nazi Gun Law of March, 1938 250
- C) Nazi Gun Law of November, 1938 251
- D) U.S. Gun Control Act of 1968 252
- E) CFR Membership List 253
- F) Trilateral Commission Membership List 294
- G) The Bilderbergers "Membership" List 314
- H) Patents of Dr. Adrian Krieg 322

Bibliography 327

Index 331

FOREWORD

As you read this book, you will realize that the most important aspect of any information, be it from radio, TV, magazines or books, is the qualification of the source of that information.

It is for this reason that we decided to begin this book with a full review of the author's background.

You will note that he has wide experience in international affairs, both as a successful businessman and as a government advisor. He has travelled widely doing business in Europe, Asia, Mexico and South America. Throughout his career he has played an important role in his industry, having contributed several books, over 100 technical articles, and in addition, designed and licensed many new products for use in his industry.

In short, Dr. Adrian H. Krieg is a thinking man who likes to analyze problems and search for workable, common sense solutions. And, may I add, as an engineer, he understands how one very small gear can manipulate a mammoth machine.

Read Dr. Kreig's "curriculum vita" and you will know why we chose to publish his findings as stated in *The Satori and the New Mandarins.*

Charles M. Hallberg, *Publisher*

Dr. Adrian H. Krieg CfMgE
Curriculum Vita
Updated July 1997

Personal particulars:
Born St. Gallen Switzerland 1938
Dual National, Fluent in English and German

Education:
HS Pembroke Academy. NH class Valedictorian
Elmhurst College/University of Mex./
San Miguel De Allende Campus
CCU California Coast University
SME Society of Manufacturing Engineers/Certified
Manufacturing. Engineer.
Rectified 1996.
World University/Cultural Doctorate Manufacturing Science.

Special:
ASW American Welding Society Speakers Bureau since 1985
Vice Chair AWS Committee Fume & Ventilation 1985-until
disbanded
Recipient NATTCO Award 1983 - Best New Welding
Product of 1983-AWS
z 48- 1 Committee (standards for welding safety ANSI & AWS)
AWS & ASM & SME consultants directories.
Thomas Award for advertising 1983
AWS Silver Certificate
Académie Européenne des Sciences, des Arts et des lettres
1989
Eli Whitney Entrepreneur of the year (certif. of recognition)
CT District Export Council 1982-1992 (appointed by Sec.
Commerce)
Rolex award 1987

Memberships:

American Nuclear Society	(ANS) Ret. 1997
American Welding Society	(AWS)
American Society for Metals	(ASM)
Society of Manufacturing Engineers	(SME) Certified
Society of Pipe Engineers & Designers	(SPED)
Nuclear Suppliers Assoc.	(NSA) Ret. 1997
American Arbitration Society	(AAS) Ret. 1987
World Affairs Council	Ret. 1990
CT World Trade Assoc. Advisory board	Ret. 1993

U.S. Dep. of Commerce:

CT & RI District Export Council	1980-1992
Co-Chair CT Strike force for Fair Trade	1990
Legislative Committee	1989-1992
Finance Committee	1989-1991

Published:

Plate Bending Machines, (FMA)

The Problems with Welding Fumes and what to do about them, (Widder)

Marketing your Product through Distribution Channels (Krieg)

Distributor Marketing, (Widder)

The Satori and the New Mandarins, (Hallberg)

Over 100 technical articles in the world press 1962-1997

Business Experience

CEO of: Widder Corp./Rovic Manufacturing Co./Nugget Realty Corp./Mamaroneck Depot Plaza Corp./A. Krieg Consulting Inc./ Consumable Trading Inc.

Secretary: Vicktor J. Krieg Inc.

Past and present board of Directors: Widder Corp./Rovic Manufacturing Co./Nugget Realty Corp./ Mam. Depot

Plaza Corp./ Panox Trading Inc./Widder UK ltd./Colonial Bankcorp./CT World Trade Asoc./Widder RSA Pty.Ltd./ FM Reg. School Board CT District Trade Council./AWS Fume Committee.

Trademarks Presently Licensed:

WIDDERVAC
WIDDER
VERSIFLAME
WIDDER BLADES

Licensed Products:

Welding Fume Nozzle
Oxy-Fuel orbital Pipe Cutters
Remote Controlled Power Tools
Plasma Orbital Pipe Cutter
Water-Jet Orbital Pipe Cutter
Saw Blades
Magnetic Pipe holder
Pipe Cutting Robot
Portable Power Hacksaws
Remote Controlled Cylinder Actuator
Interactive Guidance System
Saw Blade Holding Device

Designed, in use, but un-patented Machine Tools:

Hydraulic Lay Shaft Drill
Hydraulic 3 Axis Bore Plug Drill
Fuel Channel Cutter (BOOR)
Neutron Window Cutter
Fuel Pool Lighstantion Cutter
Fuel Pool Rack Cutters

Patents:

In excess of 25 U.S. and foreign patents issued. (See Appendix H)

INTRODUCTION

As you read the title of this book you undoubtedly asked yourself several questions. The title, although it may appear so, is not at all cryptic. "Satori" is the author's designation for the ruling elite. The word has its origin in feudalistic Japan and means "the hidden organizers." The "Mandarins" were the people and organizations which attended to day-to-day operations for the Satori, and, it is in this sense that the words "Satori" and "Mandarin" are used in this book.

Any book dealing principally with a conspiratorial view of history, even when written by a renowned professor such as Carroll Quigley, *The Anglo-American Establishment*, is subject to ridicule by the very power elite, and their servants, which represent the backbone of that conspiracy. All conspiracies are by their very nature a secret to be held only by the conspirators, who will go to any lengths to hide their nefarious plans and schemes. Due to this, it is often necessary to bring a strong case of circumstantial evidence to bear as it is very difficult to obtain hard evidence. However, as conspiracies age they leave behind evidence whereby not only their intent, but also their organizations, leave themselves open to public scrutiny. Prominent evidence has come to light not only in the United States but worldwide in one nation after another. The conspiracy has never, in all its existence, altered its course of World Domination. To accept 20th century history as pure happenstance is to play ostrich. When governmental, national, international, and multinational corporate policies are all directed at a single goal, one must come to the realization that there is a guiding hand behind the scenes directing events. In my opinion, it strains credibility to deny that fact.

A difficult and perhaps exasperating task has been what to name the conspiracy, without linking it to some historic organization. They do not name themselves, as their nature is to deny their existence. Many of the Mandarin organizations are well known, even if rarely spoken of. No affiliation of organizations with a total membership of about 5,000 could possibly be monolithic. This makes it considerably more difficult to prove their presence and avails them an easy rebuttal to any conspiratorial accusation.

Countless readers will, at this juncture, find it difficult to ascribe our national and international political, monetary, and economic problems to that of a conspiracy seeking total world control. Yet readers should be aware that hundreds of historians, Prof. Quigley of Georgetown University among them, have come to that exact conclusion. I have attempted in this book to check all facts to the best of my ability, and wherever possible to name my source. I must state that in some instances sources preferred to remain anonymous, and in such cases I have omitted the source.

In order for the reader to understand the nature of the beast it is necessary to have a basic grounding in 19th century Hegelian philosophy. At the turn of the last century, a formidable group of German philosophers came into prominence on the continent. This group included Fichte, Hegel, Nietzsche, Wundt, and several others.

Their ideas were "old world" and contrasted sharply with those of John Locke, the English theologian and philosopher whose concept that all men were given the right to Life, Liberty and Property by God, not the State, had gained political power in Great Britain and became the cornerstone of the United States Declaration of Independence. To comprehend just how radical a departure this new concept was from that of philosophers from Plato to Hegel, let me quote Hegel:

> *"The State is the general substance, whereof individuals are but mere accidents."*
>
> *"The State alone possesses rights."*
>
> *"The State incarnates the divine idea upon earth."*

Hence, in order to once again enslave mankind and return to feudal times, when only the elite rulers had rights, they devised a method they termed the Dialectic Process, commonly referred to as the Hegelian Philosophy.

What Hegel and his cohorts concluded was that in order to facilitate the changes they sought, two opposing thought structures must be brought to prominence, and out of the confusion brought on by these opposing thoughts a new and different paradigm would develop. It is of the utmost importance that the reader clearly understand this concept because it is at the root of how change in our society is instituted by the Satori. The Hegelian dialectic is the principal vehicle used by the conspiracy to orchestrate change within our system and is so manipulated by them as to insure the desired outcome. Example: First, the desired outcome of the dialectic is generated. Second, two radically opposite concepts are structured and presented to the public. Third, the two opposing radical views are moderated so as to become the planned Satori outcome. By playing the citizenry like marionettes, one against the other, through the vehicles of *Class Envy, Racial Strife, Political Separation, Kulturkrieg and Gender Conflict,* we are separated and played against each other. Through these dialectics, and out of this division, the Satori hope to achieve their New World Order. This method of operation makes the exposure of the conspiracy all the more difficult. They in fact use it to divide and conquer. Through it they say, "Look we represent no planned outcome, there is no uniform structure. There are basic fundamental differences between us and to say that we represent the membership of a conspiracy is a delusionary figment of the radical right's imagination." You must understand now and forever that the Satori no longer favor conservative, liberal, socialist, or capitalist dogma. To the Satori all these are simply a means to an end. These people have been at this for generations, and make no mistake about it, they are not stupid. Hegelian philosophy was prominent in Germany at the turn of the last century, from there it went to England, and then gradually to America. The Satori have been using it since about 1830 with considerable success. The root of Satori rests in Germany, where from 1700 until the First World War, Germany was preeminent in philosophy, music, engineering, science and mathematics.

It is unfortunate that we in our busy lives, with a continuously (for over 20 years) declining standard of living, and in most cases in two working parent households, remain unaware of this dialectic. We do not think of these matters as events unfold. We are kept too busy feeding ourselves and paying exorbitant taxes to actually follow the ball. We do not look behind the false news of black church burnings (a fabricated lie, more white churches were burned, and no racial motivation could be found) which create racial tension allowing the government the opportunity to make more laws restricting all people's individual liberties. We are played like a fine instrument: rich against poor, women against men, theists against atheists, infirm against healthy. The list is endless. All of these dialectic issues are orchestrated from above. World conspiracy is a fact, not a theory. It is well documented in hundreds of books, documents, and as this text will show, in the actual statements made by members of the very conspiracy whose existence they deny. While most philosophic tenants are theoretical in nature this one is not; it is a constant and has been so for decades. Without control of the media — news, entertainment, radio, and television — all the efforts of the Satori would come to naught, being exposed by those very people. It is an apparent and provable fact that the major world news and entertainment sources march to the beat of the same drummer. The Satori, through their Mandarins, have infiltrated not only the primary information services, but also academia, law, government, investment banking, entertainment, and to some degree organized religion. The lowest participation of Mandarin infiltration is in the manufacturing sector, with only 12% participation. A fine example of Mandarin presence is the first term Clinton cabinet. All cabinet members were Mandarins; not one came from a real life job, and they represented a group of academicians, lawyers, and government functionaries. It should be obvious to you that the Satori do not care if you are black, white, liberal, or conservative, Christian or non; they control all and frankly do not care which group you belong to.

A large portion of their control is through financial manipulation. Countless billions of dollars are redirected to achieve the Satori desired outcome. This is carried out through the diversion of your taxes and through foundations.

It is an unfortunate fact that more then half of the Mandarins have no idea of the master-plan nor that one exists. They are not aware that they are the instruments of our and their own ultimate enslavement to a new type of feudalism. These new Mandarins, like the mandarins of old in China, do their masters bidding, with the conviction that they are serving societies best interest.

There are two basic political paradigms of political thought which are at the center of current exploitation by the Satori.

> The first is the socialist paradigm, i.e. *our lives can be improved in a positive manner through the subsidation of individuals who act socially in an undesirable manner, and through the penalizing of good social outcome individuals.*

What in essence this means is that we should reward those who do not work by subsidizing their incomes through confiscatory taxation on producers (this is also true of nations). This represents a static vision as a manner of addressing social ills. It has never worked, it will never work.

> The second is the market paradigm, i.e. *society's social problems are best solved by rewarding desirable social outcome.*

In other words, if we reward, the good society will endeavor to obtain rewards by doing good. This represents the dynamic approach to solving social ills. Bear in mind that the Satori are on both sides of the issue, but favor the socialist redistribution approach because it is easier to control. All this is more Hegelian dialectic, divide and conquer as it were. Today we live in a society world-wide that has made a cult out of victimization. Our entire school systems, kindergarten through university, have been subjugated into a Satori-inspired socialist cabal which teaches our young that the state is responsible to cure all societal ills befalling the citizens of the Republic. This obnoxious cult permeates all western academia. Our children are being taught by our educators that in our society we must cherish misfortune and reward stupidity, while penalizing competence and achievement.

The great Roman general and historian Cicero made the following observation, "The first law for the historian is that he should never utter an untruth." To expand on that, historians should not alter the reality of history through the acts of linkage, omission, or alteration. With the advent of Dr. Joseph Gobbels, the father of modern propaganda and minister of information under the Nazis, the reporting of events and historic expression took on an entirely new perspective. The practice of historic and current event information manipulation through the process of propaganda reached a pinnacle during the Second World War on both sides. This makes it very difficult to separate fact from fiction in Second World War history. It is an indisputable fact that throughout major portions of 20th century, historians — through the manipulation of information, laziness, and an intent to tout a populist line, or for fear of peer pressure — have altered the factual history through these procedures. This will certainly be borne out by any multilingual student of the subject. This practice has permitted tainted historic reporting for decades. One of the best examples of this are the facts relating to the American Civil War. Most history text books in American schools teach that slavery was the cause of the Civil War. Nothing could be further from the truth. There were actually riots in New York City and Milwaukee in opposition to the war. Slavery was a topic introduced after those riots in an effort to popularize the confrontation. The reason for the American Civil War was totally economic. The Satori wanted to re-introduce the central bank (today known as the Federal Reserve) vetoed by President Jackson and to do so they used the tariff issue. While the North was industrialized, the South was agrarian. The South imported the majority of their industrial products from England, and the North wanted that business at a higher price than that charged by the British. The North instituted high tariffs, thus forcing the Southern states to purchase their products from them. The South, faced with competition from other agrarian producers, had little choice but to withdraw from the Union, as provided for in the U.S. Constitution. The North objected to the South's decision and the Civil War ensued. This was the cause of the Civil War — slavery had absolutely nothing to do with its beginning. It is in this manner that we all develop a false perspective of events. The Satori use such created distortions of reality to their decided advantage. Through the manipulation of historic facts, the omission of information, and the process of linkage, they deceive us all. Linkage is the process of taking unrelated items and linking them to create a false impression. An example: Adrian Krieg of the "radical political right" in association with Hitler, Hitler being the name of someone universally despised. A good example of recent historic manipulation concerns the Waco massacre, instituted by the Satori as an object lesson for those of us who would resist paying income tax. The media did an exemplary job of disseminating false information provided by the government: 1) An enormous weapons cache (the actual number of guns at the compound was below Texas state average of gun ownership). 2) A drug factory producing a variety of illegal drugs (no drug producing factory was in existence at any time). 3) Child molestation was reputed (the only government witness was in California at the time of the reputed act in Texas). 4) The only four deaths on the government side were of four BATF agents, recently transferred to the BATF from the Arkansas State Police where they had been assigned as bodyguards for then-governor Clinton. The destruction of the federal office building in Oklahoma City is but another example. General Partin, a retired Air Force general and the leading expert in the United States on this type of explosion, proved beyond any reasonable doubt that the government scenario of the explosion was a fabricated lie and published an extensive expose of it in *The New American* in 1995. To further my case, of 19 BATF employees assigned to work in that building, only one was slightly injured, the rest were all out of the building at the time of the explosion. What I am showing you is that there is a great deal more to current history than you might suspect.

I admonish the reader to keep his eye on the ball and to consider the facts that you will be informed of in this text. Most of this information is available, but not in any organized logical manner or in any single book. Some information was difficult to obtain, some came from secret or hidden sources. Some was in the public domain in research libraries, other information was published in magazines or newspapers. More than 80% came from such sources, the rest through personal interviews. Bear in mind that the information had to be developed in reverse order. First a list of Mandarins had to be produced and only then would the pyramid of the command and control structure become apparent.

It is a sad and difficult task to inform my many conservative and Republican friends that their chance of winning the immediate battle against the Satori is nominal at best. There is no doubt that I am firmly encamped within the compound of the Republican constitutionalist minority, who in my opinion are on the moral and ethical high ground. The problem we have as conservative protectors of our God-given rights is that the Satori lead a coalition firmly ensconced in education, government, police, the military and the judiciary. Like 4th generation war (later on in the text), constitutionalists are fighting a foe who is hidden from public scrutiny. This army of Satori is well financed out of public coffers and foundations, and already controls the media, thus the dialogue. We are fighting a defensive action instead of an offensive one and are thus perpetually handicapped. Unless constitutionalists, monotheists, conservatives and libertarians take the offensive, the war is all but lost. Historically, conservative thinkers have almost always been passive. It is not conservatives who instill violence and social unrest; that legacy belongs solely to the political left. I give you Karl Marx, Benito Mussolini, Adolph Hitler, Mao Ze Tung, Fidel Castro, Joseph Stalin. Leftist each and every one. Our media worldwide have people believing that society must fear the "radical right" or the "right wing extremists" yet they cannot point to a single instance of any organized "right" assault on anyone or anything. Societal problems universally come from leftist theology: communism, socialism, secular humanism, pedophilia, radical feminism, naziism, fascism are all from the left.

It is an eminent fact of social behavior that the right is invariably defensive while the left is always aggressive. I do not mean to state that the right does not at times strike out, but this act is in almost all instances a reaction to a leftist act.

It is also a fact that the left, more often than not, is the winner in any ideological conflict because they have defined the language as well as the issues. The left postulates a position that is considered lunatic by all. They are opposed by the right who exposes their position as radical. The left then relents in their position by 20% and claims to now be centrist. The right has lost another one — by default — to Satori dialectic.

This book is about America and the world in the 1990s. In fact, this text may be viewed as contemporary history. It covers occurrences from the turn of the last century and attempts to project what the author believes will occur in the near future. You may agree or disagree with the basic tenants of this work. No one is forcing you to read it. If, however, the topic and ideas interest you, by all means continue on. It is my contention that all history, particularly in this century, has been manipulated and controlled by a small, select group of individuals to suit their own ends. To put it bluntly, I believe in a conspiratorial view of history. This fact I hope to impart upon you by providing evidence of it.

It is my further contention that the founding fathers of the American Republic did not have in mind what has taken place on the world stage. Indeed, a review of the Federalist Papers, the U.S. Constitution, and the American Bill of Rights more than confirms that fact. We have turned our backs on our own heritage, our history and culture. Our educational institutions defile western culture and civilization. The very fact that we have publications like *Culture Wars* and *The Barnes Review of History* is sufficient impetus to give rise to reflection.

A young man of my acquaintance worked for some time to earn adequate funds to return to college for a BS degree. He had already obtained an associates degree in a technical field. For his degree, he was required to take two semesters of sociology. This cost him $400 per semester. When I spoke to him, he was very angry, and justifiably so, as his instructress was a communist. He had to pay his hard earned money to listen to some clap trap moron expounding on the utopian wonders of state centralized control of the economy and what a great guy Marx was. The subversion of our youth through state controlled education is a process of the Satori and one of the tentacles of their many-headed hydra.

It is my hope that you will learn from this book, and, if nothing else, it will lead you to begin asking questions so that you will become sufficiently interested in politics to become involved. It is only with your participation and those of your neighbors that we can ever hope to turn the tide and bring our republic back from the brink of absorption into the "New World Order."

"Nothing in politics ever happens by chance."

— Franklin Delano Roosevelt

CHAPTER ONE

MANIPULATION

For as long as I can remember I have been a history buff. Beginning with recorded history right through today I have read more books then I care to remember. In my own library I have over 100 history texts in English, as well as in German. This study of history has lead me to the conclusion that events don't just happen, they are planned. This is particularly the case when you investigate the method of finance of great events throughout this century. An old axiom admonishes us to "follow the money." If there is but one indisputable fact, it is that history repeats itself. As a logical consequence, through its study, we can prevent repeating the errors of our forefathers. It is a sad fact that the belief in chance history, as propagated by most historians, prevents us from ever speaking to this very important fact. By negating the very fact of how past events were centrally orchestrated we cheat ourselves from any logical correction of past errors. The entire world at the end of this century is at the crossroads between a future of incredible expansion and a feudalistic centrally controlled nightmare. It is my belief that we, as a civilization, have the opportunity to reach goals so wonderful as to make all previous human history appear insignificant. Unfortunately, if we follow the lead of the Satori we shall enter a second dark age of a feudalistic society in which we will all become uneducated serfs in the service of a ruling elite, the Satori. The way to the future is our choice. It is not the option of the Satori, for they do not yet rule. The outcome of your future and that of your children is in your hands, it depends on the citizenry of the world, and the notion of self rule and personal achievement. If we choose to be lazy and accept the socialist and controlled concept of government rather than the free market concepts as developed by the great republics of this century, we will lose.

Always remember the Hegelian dialectic. Two different political systems have been in conflict for all of the second half of this century: communism/socialism vs. capitalism. Out of this the Satori hope to produce their "New World Order," a feudalistic world government run by the Mandarins for the Satori. This term "New World Order" is in fact quite old, and you can read it in texts by Napoleon, in Hitler's *Mein Kampf* 1933, and it appears in Mussolini's *Lebensgeschichte* 1927 (Hesse & Beck Leipzig). Remember that the Satori do not care about the two principal confrontational political systems because under the dialectic, the new correlation will not be either but a replacement of both, which is a feudal system.

Our joint decision is in fact a simple one: do we want to govern ourselves or do we want to be ruled by the Satori?

The difference between socialism and capitalism is that socialism is a lie. Socialism promises what it can not possibly deliver. Like a Ponzi scheme, it continuously promises more and more services provided by government, when that very government has only one income, the taxes it collects from you. Capitalism, on the other hand, promises nothing and tells people to be self reliant. Socialism is very popular in academia, and many governments, particularly in the west, are staffed by socialist Mandarins. The reason for this is that it represents a very appealing sales tool for politicians who dupe the naive populace into believing that they can get something for nothing.

One of the touted tenants of the socialist/communist line is that the means of production belong to the people, i.e. the state, and not to the "captains of industry." Well, one must wonder where these idiots have been keeping themselves. Perhaps they have not heard of the stock market, bonds, or any of the capital markets. The people, if they choose, do own the means of production in a free society. Interestingly all of the ideas of this cabal of BS come not from the people but from a select group of individuals who never in their collective lives had a proper job. I give you Karl Marx, Engler, Bertrand Russell, Ted Kennedy, Bill & Hillary Clinton, Robert Reich, Laura D'Andria Tyson, all of them from academia or inheritors of the labors of their fathers. People gainfully employed in productive occupation have no time for such rubbish.

The aforementioned dialectic is only one of many that are used by the Satori in an attempt to bring about the new feudalistic empire they wish to build. Some additional examples of the dialectic are:

Race	Black	vs.	White
Green	Producers	vs.	Environmentalists
Sex	Male	vs.	Female
Sex	Heterosexuals	vs.	Homosexuals
Guns	Constitutionalists	vs.	Confiscators
Religion	Christians	vs.	Everyone else
Greed	Rich	vs.	Poor
Culture	Western Civilization	vs.	All others

These are but a few examples — there are hundreds more. How many can you think of?

Every one of these issues is contrived. There are differences and disagreements to be sure, but they do not exist in any violent form, they are in fact purposely expanded for the sole reason of expanding the regulation of our lives by government. In every one of the aforementioned groups you will find violent extremists whose sole purpose is to create hostility and confusion between factions so as to allow the Satori plan to proceed unnoticed. When you follow the financing of all these groups of extremists the money trail always leads to the same end. Foundations and government are the major financiers of hate. It is with all this in mind that we begin the first part of this book — the primary operating dialectics in use by the Satori.

DIALECTIC PROCESS

Let us assume that you wish to control the dialogue in a future debate. To accomplish this, you must first control the language and second the issues. You know what your ultimate objective is. It has been well formulated by you and your associates. In order to achieve your desired goal, you must first create the language which will allow you to shape public opinion. Have you ever noticed how all the major issues in our present society seem to come up with their own new set of words and expressions . . . Cop Killer Bullet . . . Assault Rifle . . . Healthcare Reform . . . Free Trade . . . Free Choice . . . etc. This, in effect, is the first part of the process by which language is created in a manner benefiting the desired outcome. The second part is to create two opposing factions that can then be utilized to achieve the previously determined outcome. Thus position A & B are put in place. Again, clearly understand that the two publicly debated opposing positions are not the desired outcome. The actual desired outcome is what was previously decided upon. Next, position A (usually the liberal side of the issue) is made public. This position is represented by a very extremist assertion, so extreme in fact that the majority of the citizenry will outright reject it. I give you Hillary's Healthcare proposal which would have governmentalized 14.7% of the economy. Then position B is introduced slowly: Kennedy/Metzenbaum Healthcare Reform. You are now given the opportunity to support a total disaster, or a partial one. As the debate continues, pro and con, the political parties become polarized in their positions. The public debate has been totally co-opted by one side and the free market position is not even within the sphere of the debate. Freedom cannot win. It is not on the agenda.

By dominating all sides of the debate, the outcome of the Satori is always assured.

THE DIALECTIC:

The predetermined result desired is . . . position X

Debate radical positions . . . A vs. B

. . . B vs. C

. . . C vs. D

Agree to compromise . . . . position X.

Note: In the foregoing dialectic process, it is important to include only those positions requiring government action, regulation or supervision. The laissez faire, private property, unregulated and unsupervised by government positions, must be excluded. In fact, the word capitalism *was invented by the socialists to replace words such as private property, free exchange and free market, etc., with an "ism" to which they could ascribe sinister, nagative meaning.*

The debate is continuously moved toward the desired outcome position of X, through the structuring of issues and language. The outcome desired by the Satori is totally pre-programmed. If you are able to structure the language, the debate, and the questions, you are always assured of attaining your desired outcome. Through their control of all those factors they were able to institute, even with an opposition of over 80% of the public, such very unpopular issues as NAFTA, GAT, WTO, and EC. In America, opposition to NAFTA alone was 87%. As you will recall, every single Mandarin in North America was pressed into service for NAFTA. The USDC (Department of Commerce) spent $14 million while the Mexican government brought in $30 million in payola for the media and politicians.

Not one congressman or senator in our entire legislative branch read the treaty,[1] and both houses, in a lame duck session, passed the treaty.

[1]The treaty was not published until 3 months after ratification by congress.

THE POLITICAL CLASS

A large problem that exists in the world today is that we are, as societies, ruled by Mandarins. I will utilize America as a primary example but point out to the reader that exactly the same situation is present in all of the western societies, and even more so in Japan. In America it can be argued that we live under a judicial tyranny. Judges appointed for life daily vacate electoral mandates by the people. In the EC, Brussels-based Mandarins do the same

To understand the political class more clearly we must again look to the money trail. In the United States real income since the presidency of Harry Truman has declined by 17%. Federal revenue is derived 2% from the poor and 22% from the wealthy. This means that the middle class pays 81% of the tab. This creates a position whereby the Mandarins clearly understand that the only way to increase revenue is to increase taxes on the middle class. Thus under Reagan, Bush and Clinton, there were back to back large, larger, and enormous tax increases. This clearly poses a problem in that the middle class will not vote for people who continuously increase their tax burden. Thus the use of judicial mandate, where life-appointed judges make law interpretations that drastically increase the tax burden.

To understand the political class, let us draw some examples: Tipper Gore, the wife of our current VP, has a larger staff (65 people) then did Harry Truman as VP, and she's not elected to a damn thing. Not to be outdone, our congress now employs 30,000 people, a 10,000% increase since the Truman administration. The pension program for congress is a guarantee of millionaire status for the rest of their lives. Take the following: Senator Pat Schroeder, darling of the left, contributed a total of $45,000 to her pension plan, but has a vested interest of $0.5 million. Dan Rostenkowski, the congressman who was indicted on 18 counts of fraud, is getting a pension of $114,000 per year, even while languishing in a federal penitentiary. In fact, his total fine was less then one year's pension payment. To stay in power the political class must provide something in return, and they do. Examples are 154 different job training programs offered by Washington which are administered by 14 different agencies and cost the taxpayers an estimated (by CBO) $25 billion. Political crime has mushroomed to a 30-fold increase since 1970. Last, but not by any means least, the national debt has sky-rocketed by $1.3 trillion since the beginning of the Clinton administration. The deficit has grown $60 billion in excess of the reported numbers because Social Security taxes have been looted from the SS Trust Fund and replaced with worthless Treasury IOU's.

All of this is an outgrowth of Satori policies. The Mandarins who are in fact working for the Satori are bought and paid for by the taxpayers.

This then, brings us to one of the basic concepts of Satori management. If you will observe, the following actions are brought about by the creation of the political class. First, there is an institutionalized class of citizens who no longer owe their allegiance to a republic, but rather to a system — the Satori system. Second, through the control of the political process and the picking of all major candidates for office the desired outcome is assured. Third, by availing the Mandarins of generous pensions for very limited service they attain allegiance. Fourth, if voted out of office they become lobbyists (pimps for special Satori interests) earning even more then they did as elected officials.

All this demonstrates the vested interest that the Mandarins have in supporting the status quo. In order to keep you from understanding exactly what is going on, the Mandarins continuously bring new dialectics into the game thereby creating government by crisis. The average citizen keeps his eye on the nonexistent political turmoil rather then the people manipulating events to create yet another dialectic.

MEXICO & NAFTA

No finer and clearer example of the Satori at work can be found in all of world history than the 1996 Mexican bail-out. To completely understand the events let us examine in detail the people and events and, most importantly, the flow of funds from the United States to Mexico to Satori Wall Street banks.

Having lived in Mexico for a long time I am personally familiar with the life-style and culture of Mexico and its people. I truly love the Mexican people, but the government is quite a different matter.

Some historic background information will be helpful to understand the events better. American manufacturers with whom the Satori have considerable investments, as well as outstanding loans, have been experiencing market share losses on the North American market for decades. Most of these losses have been to Pacific Rim nations. Nowhere is this more evident than with Japan, the largest industrialized economy on the pacific rim, with whom the United States have an enormous trade deficit. Beginning in the 1970s, US auto manufacturers began experimenting with a process that came to be known as the Maquiladora process. What they did was to ship parts to Mexico for assembly at in-house captive factories and ultimately return to the US. By agreement with the Mexican and American governments there would be no tariffs in either direction. (Interestingly the USDC, in reporting export statistics, counts parts shipped to Mexico for Maquiladora assembly as exports, but does not count assembled items as imports). No labor union, no social security, no EPA, no clean air act, no pensions, no OSHA. At an average salary of $1.15 per hour versus American labor costs (auto industry) of $32.00 per hour. This process, which expanded to include all American automobile manufacturers, rapidly grew to many other industries. Products made in this manner were comparable in price with Japanese products made in Korea and other Pacific Rim nations. The financing for the Maquiladora plants came from the Mexican government and Wall Street.

Mexico has had social and economic problems ever since the last revolution. A dominant portion of this is directly attributable to massive corruption in the entire Mexican body politic. Mordita, the process of kicking back 10% of your salary to the person who hired you, is a practice not only common in government but also in the private sector. Furthermore, elections are a sham. The winner is always of the PRI that has been in power since the revolution at the turn of the last century.

During the Bush administration severe financial strain was developing in Mexico. The problem became so acute that the Mexican government advised NY bankers that they would have to cease payment of interest as well as principal on all outstanding loans. They were in fact broke. The Satori could not allow such a default of their assets and thus events were set in motion for the American taxpayer to cover the losses. NY banks, which comprise the controlling interest of the Federal Reserve System and are completely Satori operated, instructed the Bush administration to purchase pesos by the billions. It was hoped that this act would prop up the faltering pesos and the Mexican government as well. Continuous additional peso purchases throughout the Bush administration and well into the Clinton administration accomplished nothing except the decline of the value of the pesos held by the US Treasury. Total peso purchases by this time had reached the sum of US $5 billion. Mexico, during this interim period, paid interest due but not one centavo of the principal.

As the Bush administration came to a gradual end, a lame duck congress with the acquiescence of both political parties passed the now infamous NAFTA accord. NAFTA (the North American Free Trade Agreement) was the pinnacle achievement of the Bush administration on behalf of the Satori. Shortly after that, in the Clinton administration, another $6 billion in pesos was sopped up by the treasury, labeled as "The Peso Protection Fund." Directly after that the IMF (International Monetary Fund) which is 87% funded by American Taxpayers, in violation of its rules that limit the size of financial transactions, kicked in another $7.5 billion. These funds went to Mexico, the payments were endorsed and returned to Wall Street bankers credited to outstanding interest payments past due. This was for previous loans by NY banks to the tune of $48 billion. This was, and remains to this day, the largest single loan in IMF history. Another $18 billion was borrowed from NY banks only to be immediately returned to the same banks that made the loan and applied to past due interest. Please note that not one cent had, by this time, been paid toward principal. Then the proverbial . . . hit the fan when Mexico, which had strenuously promised not to, devalued the peso by 50%. This in effect meant that all the pesos held by the IMF and the US Treasury had instantly been devalued by 50%. This reflects a loss to US taxpayers of $54 billion. Robert Rubin was, at this time, a member of the Clinton Cabinet. He had previously been employed on Wall Street by the very firm who held the largest share of Mexican paper: Goldman Sacs. In fact, Goldman Sacs had outstanding loans to Mexico in the amount of $5.7 billion.

Now think back to the time before NAFTA. America had an annual $6 billion trade surplus with Mexico at that time. Do you remember the debate? It was along partisan lines; Republicans favored the NAFTA agreement and the Democrats opposed it. Do you remember the bail-out? Republicans opposed and Democrats supported. Do you remember the NAFTA vote for ramification? A large portion of congress which was controlled by the Democrats had just been ousted; and the new members were to be sworn in in a few days. The sitting Republocrats all voted for the Satori NAFTA agreement, and retiring members were given wonderful high paying lobbying jobs.

How was NAFTA sold to the American and Canadian people? There had been only minimal opposition to the Canadian/American deal. The economics and culture of Canada and America have sufficient similarity as to make them easily compatible. Furthermore pay scales, benefits of employment, as well as government regulations and labor laws are very similar. This, however, is not the case with Mexico. Besides language, culture, social structure, government, and tradition, Mexico's per capita income is vastly different. Average Mexican blue collar industrial pay scales are at $1.15 per hour without overhead. In Canada and America this figure is well over $20.00. Counting overhead, Mexico is at about $1.45 and the US & Canada at $35.00. This would be a hard sell! While American opposition was at 87%, Canadian was at almost 90%.

In an unprecedented effort the USDC went all out. Secretary Ron Brown pulled out all the stops. He, together with Clinton, spent $514 million on advertising and a road show that, together with a Mexican delegation, flew to every major city in the US. The media and local politicians were lavishly entertained, nothing was spared. The Mexican government in dire financial difficulty, nevertheless, was able to find $30 million which it spent in Washington and Ottawa on media and government in the form of "incentives."

The way of least resistance was to sell the US/Canada deal first, have it legislatively approved, and then add the Mexican deal in last. This is exactly how the Satori did it.

You must be aware that the premium social/political thrust of the Satori in the latter half of this century has been their slogan "Free Trade." This in effect is the underlying premise of the entire NAFTA agreement. It is also what is behind the EC in Europe. "Free Trade" is an oxymoron. It is in fact impossible. Like socialism it sounds so fair and good. It is a Satori captive expression. It is a lie meant to further their aims and aspirations. In order for trade to be free between competing economies, and not hurt either party, they must be on a level playing field. Mexico and their two northern neighbors are no more on a level playing field than are Greece and Germany in the EC.

Some of the differences between them on the North American continent are Religion, Income, Productivity, Social Structure, Employment Benefits, Government Regulations, Language, Climate, Food, Population, Age Average and Education.

What has this ghastly agreement meant to Americans? We have lost upwards of 4 million manufacturing jobs to Mexico in the last 10 years. New American jobs are primarily in the service sector at lower wages. Average middle class income has plummeted since FDR but the acceleration of this process since the inception of NAFTA by Bush and Clinton has been dramatic. In virtually all American and Canadian families it takes two full time jobs to make ends meet. In other words the NAFTA agreement is accomplishing exactly what the Satori intended it to do: it is lowering the American standard of living while increasing it in Mexico. That exact same thing is taking place in Europe where the standard of living in Northern EC member states is going down while in Southern ones it is going up. Note the inevitable unemployment consequences. A level playing field in the EC as well as NAFTA states is under construction. As the Mexican population is about 67 million and that of the other two members is about 265 million, and taking into consideration the per capita income variations, we can project that the per capita income in the United States and Canada will have to be reduced by about 38% in order to make the playing field level.

Satori, who have no national allegiance to any nation state, frankly don't care one iota about the citizens who will be adversely affected by this cabal. They do not care about you or any others affected by their schemes. Their god, you see, is money and power. On every international transaction, on every national bank transaction, on every international loan, on every stock transaction . . . they turn a profit. Their allegiance is to each other and to the system (see section on finance.)

This now brings us to the important question of why the Satori want free trade: NAFTA, EC, GAT, WTO, and all those odious international agreements. The answer to this is really quite simple. The principal occupation among the Satori is international banking, investment banking — in a word — finance. They earn their money not the old fashioned way — working for it — they make their money by interest on loans, fees for transactions, interest fees, mortgage, collection fees, and service fees.

Let us clearly understand what the object of the Mexican policy by the Satori is all about. NAFTA and the Mexican bailout are both symptoms of the Satori "free trade" initiatives. WTO is an international treaty which supersedes all signatory nation's constitutions and is staffed by Mandarins working exclusively for the Satori. All the alphabet soup of international treaties and organizations relating mostly to international trade as well as the EC are designed but for one purpose and one purpose only: to create a one world government with the Satori at its helm.

The profit center for the Satori is international trade. The vehicle to achieve that objective is the policy of free trade. The object of the whole exercise is to bring the developed nations down and the developing nations up, in order to have a level playing field. Once that objective is attained, the creation of a world government with a feudalistic type of society which is controlled by a one world government whose masters are the Satori will become a reality. Forget all those wonderful sounding cliches like "world peace" and "free trade." The object is not peace or trade, it is nothing less than world domination.

RUSSIA

The socialist USSR collapsed, as do all totalitarian states, and without doubt due to Ronald Reagan's American military expansion and High Frontier, which, when they attempted to duplicate caused their financial collapse. (The effort caused an already strained command and controlled central economy to self destruct). Western political, social, and economic policy toward the remaining Russia appears, at first, to be chaotic and nonsensical. This is exactly the desire of the Satori who are utilizing the situation to further their schemes with a new dialectic. Until the breakup of the Soviet empire, the main dialectic on the world stage was between capitalism and socialism. There were, as we all clearly understood, two distinctly different socio-political systems that were in constant conflict. Today a change has been achieved, primarily due to the dialectic aforementioned. One of the systems collapsed and out of it we have a new dialectic . . . or do we?

Today, although a reformer is the head of the Russian state, the Duma is controlled by the communist party. Free market reformers in Yeltsin's government have been purged. A civil war with one of the republics was lost. Yeltsin has made every effort to distance himself from free market reforms, and from the west. He was only able to win re-election by a small margin and through massive western funds which were, for the most part, used to bribe voters. Yevgeny Primakov, a former KGB intelligence chief and radical supporter of anti-western terrorism, was made foreign minister. While all this is occurring, Russia is steadily expanding their nuclear weapons program and turning out nuclear submarines like sausages.

In the meantime, the American government, at the direction of President Clinton, has committed in excess of $20 billion in US aid to Russia, who is not even able to give an account of where and how those funds are being used. The worst part of this effort is that the majority of these and other western funds have gone to the former ruling and corrupt communist apperatniks and the Russian Mafia who have used those very funds for the sole purpose of expanding their political clout. All this goes under the title . . . *If They Won't Join You . . . Buy Them*. Of this failed foreign policy one U.S. Senator, Bill Bradley of NJ, said, "Not only do we fail to influence the course of Russian reform, we actually create an anti-American backlash . . ." In another quote from the Toronto Star, S. Handelman states, "The US has provided about $335 million in a fund to encourage free enterprise and most of it has gone into the pockets of Russian bureaucrats."

Consider now what happens when the IMF, or the Deutsche Bundesbank, or the American government transfers funds to Russia. Governments are not transfer agents, banks are. What happens every time a multi-national corporation opens an office in Russia? That's right — you're beginning to get it. Monies transferred go through the Satori-controlled banking system, and they take their cut. As goods are made and sold, more money is conveyed, and all these transactions, whether they make or lose money, the producers make more profit for the Satori.

It can be stated quite clearly that the only people making any hay out of the West's entire Russian policy are banks, gangsters, and crooked politicians. With the banks being either owned or controlled by the Satori and the politicians being Mandarins, it's easy to figure out the reasoning for the course. What we can surmise is that there is an appearance of change, but that it is really a mirage. In actuality what we have is the consolidation of Satori power in Russia. Poland has already at this time freely re-elected the communists who destroyed that once great nation. Who are the winners in all this? More nations, more trade, more borrowing, more corruption, and of course more profit to the Satori.

The establishment of large trading blocks are from Satori perspective more manageable. The first was what is now the EC, the second NAFTA, the third will be a Pacific Rim association, the fourth will be Russia with some of their previous empire. This will separate the world into four major, manageable trade blocks. The contest among them will be the spoils of minerals in southern Africa and the oil of the Middle East.

"NAFTA represents the single most creative step towards a New World Order."

— Henry Kissinger
LA Times Syndicate 8/93

ANGOLA

The jewel of the socialist colonial Portuguese empire is an excellent example of the Satori dialectic hard at work. Luanda, the capitol, was a splendor of colonial grandeur, but today in 1996 the elevators no longer work. Remember that Portugal was not socialist at the time of its empire, which stretched from Chinese Macao to Brazil and Angola. In those early years Portugal was a world leader, a vibrant outward looking expansionist state.

Today Luanda is not even an acceptable ruin. Social, political, and structural decay are the new hallmarks of Angola. If climate, natural resources, and location were the criteria of wealth and development, Angola would be the Rhur and silicon valley (all rolled into one) of Africa. A civil war between UNITA and the communist government supported by Cuban troops with Russian and Chinese weapons has taken its toll. UNITA, with a free market concept and the backing of South Africa, not only fought the communist government and its Cuban surrogates to a standstill, they controlled more than half of the country. In 1994, a protocol was signed between UNITA and the government. The peace process is moving forward at a very slow pace.

This nation with more natural resources than 80% of all other nations of the world, is at present in an economic state that defies human conception. Inflation is at a level which makes barter the most common media of property transfer. An item that sells for the equivalent of $5 in any of the G7 nations sells for one million kwanzas. Parking a car without a guard is impossible. Police routinely set up road blocks not to catch criminals but to supplement their income with thievery. Imports from Portugal in 1995 topped $400 million. The largest single import item is beer, and this is in a nation which should be exporting beer. Electric power is sporadic at best. Children walk the streets hawking everything from toilet paper to cigarettes. Imports widely outpace exports, which is just plain crazy considering local resources available. Cultural life, which was an important and integral part of Angola for generations, is now nonexistent due to poverty. Finally, working foreigners and Angolans who have any financial acumen live in enclaves protected by towers and guards toting machine guns.

The world is separated for reasons only known to God into regions of incredible raw material wealth and total absence of same. One region of the world which is incredibly wealthy in raw materials is Southern Africa. The story goes that when God created the world he gave oil to the Middle East and everything else to Southern Africa. Angola has virtually every valuable resource known in abundance. If logic were the prevailing factor in human development and civilization, then all the world's industrial development would be in Southern Africa. This factor certainly has not escaped the attention of the Satori, whose agents have been deliberately exploiting the region for generations. The first major conflict for control of the region was the Boer war, a particularly nasty conflict by which the British attained power over South Africa, the southern neighbor of Angola. As previously noted, the distribution of raw materials around the globe is, to say the least, unequal.

The world's greatest treasure troves of raw materials are in Southern Africa, Siberia, Alaska, the Middle East, and to a lesser degree portions of South America and Mongolia. Of all of these, Southern Africa has not only the largest deposits but the most amenable climate for their exploitation. The war over who controls the geographic locations containing raw material is the history of mankind. International bankers whose funds are required for the exploitation of those raw materials are acutely aware of this important fact. Since the discovery of Southern African mineral wealth around the turn of the previous century, the region has been nothing but a free-for-all among competing political national interests: the Belgians in the Congo, the Dutch and then the British in South Africa and Rhodesia

(Zimbabwe). The colonial powers are now gone but their influence, culture and the national boundaries they established remain. With that, one way or another, ownership of the natural resources remains with the same interests as before because the indigenous populations lack the education, knowledge, or ability to exploit them.

The Satori, by their acts, have created long term problems in the region which will not go away for generations. Their first act was to separate the African continent into nation states possessing boundaries and divisions. These West European concepts were completely foreign to the nomadic bronze age peoples of Africa. Such concepts were at least 500 years ahead of African development. The tribal culture of Africa has never adapted to this division of land into nation states, hence the continual warfare across the entire African continent. Their second act was to impose Western culture (civilization) on a society that was still in the bronze age. I am not commenting on the value of any culture versus any other one. What I am trying to point out is that the Satori have for hundreds of years exploited the difference between these cultures for their own profit.

We can see by this that the region was purposely destabilized. Two great dialectics have been brought into play. First, the creation of nation states where none previously existed, a materialistic system vs. a nomadic existence. Second, a cultural dialectic pitting Western culture against an indigenous one. This has served its masters well and has brought about a situation by which the continued exploitation of Angola is ensured. The financiers of the entire situation will continue to profit at the expense of the populace. The reader may say that the aforementioned facts were not orchestrated by anyone but were inborn in the developmental process. Even if this were the case, the fact remains that throughout the entire recorded history of Angola, the same group of individuals profited from it. This fact is not disputable.

HEALTHCARE

Who can possibly forget the effort of the Clintonistas at nationalizing the entire healthcare industry. The effort was so extreme as to give pause even to many political liberals. It would have, in one swift movement, nationalized 14.7% of America's private sector economy: hospitals, clinics, drug producers, nursing homes for the aged, doctors, chiropractors, every one of them controlled by a gigantic new state bureaucracy. All would undoubtedly be run and managed by that troop called the Hillary Healthcare Committee. This illegal and unconstitutional secret task force spent $25 million unaccounted for tax dollars without any reasonable recommendations, auditing of expenses, or even an effort to justify the exercise. The immediate result was a dialectic of whether or not to nationalize healthcare. The dialogue and language had been established, and thus the outcome was assured. The actual effort was structured to present a position so extreme as to turn the majority of the citizenry against it, and then to offer the actually desired plan as a reasonable alternative. Manipulation of public opinion was left to the Satori-controlled media. Every single free market alternative was undermined by the media, being portaged as extremist and right wing. Free market positions were preempted by first offering two varying socialist alternatives, and secondly by attacking free market alternatives as extreme. The major free market alternative of MSAs (medical savings accounts) were restricted by company size, deposit limitation by year, number of accounts to be allowed, and state insurance departments who have, to date, not issued any licenses to carriers for MSAs. The two alternatives sponsored by the Satori became the primary objects of discussion, and all other alternatives were dropped from the public dialogue.

It is through this type of manipulation of the public dialogue that we as a world society move ever closer to the "New World Order." As you can clearly see, once the dialogue, positions, and language have been established, the outcome can be planned and the desired end product assured. In this manner we move ever further in the direction of Satori planned world government. If we allow this situation to continue, we will have lost. Clearly understand that the Satori completely control the dialogue on both sides of all issues, the politicians are paid for and the major media is controlled. It is a sad revelation that the majority of these individuals are not aware that they are controlled or directed, and would even refer to this position as crazy. Consider the last four head-of-government elections. Did you vote for the candidate whom you originally supported, or did you wind up voting for what you considered the lesser of two evils? The candidates, as in the last American presidential election, represented an alternative that was not to the liking of the electorate. It resulted in the lowest voter turnout in 50 years. The choice was between Tweedledumb and Tweedledee.

The health care debate is a prime example of this. As you will recall, the entire Hillary fiasco was dropped — or was it? Out of the turmoil and confusion came the Kennedy/Kassenbaum bill. This legislation mysteriously appeared out of nowhere, completely intact. The odious legislation accomplished a large amount of the Hillary plan, and it passed the senate 100 to zip.

So long as patriots worldwide continue to support major two-party systems they will lose. The same group of people, through institutionalized operating procedures and leadership control will be calling the shots. The only way we can save our Republic is to start an alternative political party in which "We the People" will control the issues brought to the forefront. It is my belief that such a third party would be able to gain plurality. The American Reform (Perot) Party, is an insider organization. Perot, the founder, is a consummate creature of Washington, and over 80% of his conglomerate derives its business from government contracts. I have been told that an agreement was made between Clinton and Perot, that if Hillary's healthcare initiative was successful Perot's firms would get the computer business generated by the plan, and that is why he ran for the presidency both times. The Reform Party is, in my opinion, a Satori creature meant to prevent the formation of a viable third party. The Satori have thus preempted the inevitable opposition to the two party structure before it was even articulated.

Why do the Satori want this type of legislation? The reason is obvious. Any legislation that centralizes power in Washington, New York (UN), Brussels, or London is the desired goal of the Satori. The centralization of power is how people are better controlled by a centralized establishment.

The amalgamation of national structure into large trade blocks and eventually world government is the final and only plan of the Satori. Fractionalized national entities are, from their perceptive, uncontrollable and hence to be eliminated. In the second half of this century, in every sphere of influence — be it government, business, religion, or foundations — the ever present spectre of mergers and consolidation into larger, easier to manipulate entities is an indisputable fact. The larger the structure of an organization, the more difficult it becomes to oppose it. Collectivization creates a more powerful establishment which in turn, suppresses individual freedom and liberty. The end result of all this centralization of power will inevitably lead to a feudalistic, centralized, international new world order controlled by the Satori.

QUIK-SHOT DIALECTICS

Clinton & Congress

No sooner had Clinton been elected to his first term with his own party's majority, than we heard of the terrible congressional gridlock in both houses of Congress. How a minority party could stall all action was not once explained. The media diatribe about Republican obstruction continued unabated for two entire years. Our president whined incessantly about all the wonderful plans he had and how the evil Republicans were blocking his every effort to better America. These improvements, among others, were socialized medicine, a $16 billion "Economic Stimulus" package of political pork, and such fine efforts as AmriCorps, a politicized underclass to work for Clinton reelection. That was the 103rd congress. In those two years we had 51 filibusters.

The 104th congress saw a dramatic change in that the Republicans took control of both houses. Listening to the media, however, you might have missed the entire election. In the two successive years there were 71 filibusters by the Democrat minority. Clinton, who had made all these wonderful promises, instead vetoed welfare reform (twice), medical reform, entitlement reform, social security reform, medicare reform, regulatory reform, and a balanced budget (twice). Not to be outdone by Clinton, all this prompted Senator Kennedy to single-handedly obstruct every effort at healthcare reform in the senate.

Judicial Tyranny

We are in the midst of a cultural Jihad carried out by the American judiciary, and the Supreme Court against the wishes of "We the People" who pay their exorbitant salaries. The warfare has attained a level where the people must begin seriously to consider the impeachment of several members of the supreme court (starting with Kennedy). This is constitutionally possible by the houses of congress. Examples of this tyranny are as follows: the people of California vote overwhelmingly to limit immigration and services available to immigrants, a judge overrules the people's vote. The people of Colorado vote to eliminate special privileges for homosexuals, a judge overrules the people. In Virginia the supreme court rules that VMI must accept females into what is primarily a combat infantry school, overruling the school and the people, as well as the state.

On a daily basis judges ignore the constitution they swear to uphold and base their decisions not on constitutional law, but on the court prescedent established by them. To then add insult to injury they inform us that the framers had actually meant it that way. The message to the people is this: the people don't matter, your vote does not count, we don't care about the 10th amendment, we — the life appointed judiciary — know better and will administer the state as we see fit. These judges work their magic for the Satori who long ago figured out that what can't be accomplished by willing politicians (due to election cycles) can be instituted by the courts. These tyrants are destroying our heritage while stripping us of our God-given rights.

The Black Church Fire Hoax of '96

As reported by the Wall Street Journal by Michael Fumento, "the entire black church fire reportage is nothing more then a huge scam by the elite to create yet another distraction for the people." This is part and parcel of the so often played Black vs. White dialectic. Here are the actual facts. In 1994 there were 520 fires involving churches, versus 1,420 in 1980. A dramatic decrease of over 100%. There is no empirical evidence of any form of conspiracy in fires at black churches. Only a very small handful of black church fires were set by whites (less than 3%). In fact, a substantial number of black church burnings were by blacks.

Where then, did all this misinformation come from? The ultra-left Center for Democratic Renewal. The NFPA (National

Fire Protection Association) reported that 1994 is the year with the lowest amount of church burnings they have on record. Furthermore, in every year on record, more white churches were burned than black. Did the Satori-inspired hoax work? You bet it did. In Greenville, Texas, Khallid Muhammad and the Black Panthers arrived carrying AK 47s and began chanting, "Its time to send whitey to the cemetery." In the congress, immediate legislation was drawn up. It passed the Church Fire Bill allocating funds to be utilized to rebuild black churches which had burned down. Whatever happened to the much touted "Separation of Church and State" doctrine which the left routinely brings up (which, of course, cannot be found in the constitution). The legislation also increased federal police, made a new class of crime federal, and further helped with the centralization of power in the hands of the Satori.

> *"When the tyrant has disposed of foreign enemies by conquest or treaty, and there is nothing to fear from them, he creates conflict in order that the people may require a leader."*
>
> — Plato

Global Government

Propaganda experts continuously devise false issues, such as the "ozone hole" and "global warming" to justify UN Global Government.

Their propaganda has been successful as proven by laws against freon, etc., and global warming headlines, even though Nobel prize winning climatologists state: "Human activities do not cause global warming."

L.A. Times Syndicate, *10/24/97*

CHAPTER TWO

THE LABYRINTH FROM ABOVE

Oh, if we could but see the labyrinth from above we could cease our endless and confused wandering therein. We are all trapped in an international Cretan labyrinth of Satori construction, and the capital problem with those therein contained is that they are unaware that they are in it and, therefore, are unable to find their way out. It sometimes appears that the entire international citizenry is walking in a dazed state of ignorance within the maze.

Be assured that one strong criticism of this book will be that, "the author sees a conspiracy in everything." This will obviously be a criticism directed at the author from travelers within the maze. Only by detached observation from a historic perspective is it possible to see which direction must be taken in order to find one's way. In this part of the book I will give some common examples of how we are manipulated. Please remember this is not only taking place in the nation where you live, but everywhere, simultaneously. Globalization is the plan. The New World Order is the name. The Hegelian dialectic is the instrument of operation. And the Satori are the puppet-masters.

It is difficult, if not impossible, to precisely date the beginning of the conspiracy. I do not, in this volume, plan to expose any actions prior to the turn of the 20th century. I firmly believe that the time in history from 1900 to 1997 is more then sufficient to develop the required evidence. The present roots most certainly rest in the French Revolution, Germany, and Napoleonic France. It is my feeling that occurrences prior to 1900 have limited consequence upon our present history and on matters about to develop.

An interesting and ever present Satori presence is that of the great banking houses of England and America, which in many cases, act as the paymasters for the Satori. One of these dating to the early part of the 20th century and which is still active in both the UK and the US, is Kuhn & Loeb. They have vigorously denied it, but they were the principal financiers of the Bolshevik revolution.[1] Their American operation, together with their British affiliates, met Trotsky's payroll even to the extent of providing personnel from the USA as well as Europe. Recall that at the outbreak of the First World War, Lenin was in Zurich, Switzerland. I have personal knowledge of this because he was a tenant in an apartment owned by my grandfather who evicted him for non-payment of rent. (On top of being a plagiarist, a lousy economist, and a murderer, he was also a deadbeat). In any event, Germany had a considerable interest in getting Lenin and Trotsky back into Russia. The Russians were allied with the French and the British against Germany, and the return of those two miscreants to Russia would almost assuredly cause a civil war in Russia. This would free German forces on at least one front. The revolutionary troublemaker Lenin would neutralize the Russian army and sue for an independent peace with Germany.

This brings us to the interesting and only superficially reported fact that England was almost bankrupt at this time, the war, which was in a veritable stalemate, had taken its toll in money and lives. Trotsky was in Newfoundland which was firmly in British hands. The King's cousin, the absolute ruler of Russia, would have been unhappy had the crown released Trotsky to return to instigate revolution. England was in the midst of negotiations with Kuhn & Loeb for a loan of Sterling £100,000,000. One of the requirements placed on the crown for the loan was allowing Trotsky to be repatriated to Russia.[2] Kuhn & Loeb, a Jewish banking house, felt that Russian Jews would

[1]*The Rotten Heart of Europe*
[2]*The Creature from Jeckyll Island*

be better off under the rule of two Jews than under the Czar's. This appears evident also because of Rotschild's involvement. Little did they know. In any event the loan was processed, Trotsky and Lenin returned to Russia to murder, maim, and rape the country into a state it has not been able to overcome in over 80 years.

The Balfour declaration was another Satori inspired maneuver . It promised a Jewish homeland for all Jews in Palestine. The fact that the land was not owned by the British, and had been settled by Arabs for well over 1,000 years was conveniently overlooked. Now before you call me anti-Semitic, I am only reporting facts with which you should be acquainted. The Balfour declaration was authored by none other then the British Home Secretary Herbert Samuels and you may rest assured that considerable financial pressure was brought on the British government for that work. Historically, and not surprisingly, these events took place just about the time that the international financiers were in the act of instituting the Federal Reserve System, which was created for the sole purpose of instituting a financial monopoly for the Satori in the United States as it had in Europe.[3]

Social conflict is a means to an end for the Satori. No opportunity no matter how small is overlooked as a chance to instill in the population an unqualified dislike for any other group of citizens. Through this conflict, and only through it, are they able to successfully maintain an unbalanced society in need of "controls" and thus introduce their "New World Order." The obvious additional by-product being the masking of their nefarious schemes.

[3]Ibid.

POLITICAL SYSTEMS

In the 20th century there have been numerous political systems, but in the latter half of the century there were only two survivors, Socialism and Capitalism. The reader may dispute this by bringing up the Nazis of Germany, along with the Italian and Spanish Axis powers of the 1930s. The German party was called Die Nazional Sozialistische Partei (NSP). In English, that translates into the National Socialist party. So we have at this time in the Western world, which for all practical purposes controls the world, two opposing political systems. (I have already previously stated that there is no basic difference between socialists and communists. There are, however, some very important factors relating to socialism of which you should be aware. Socialism will not work in a free market economy and, as a consequence it invariably deteriorates into a totalitarian state. Anyone wishing to argue that point is asked to point to one single instance where this was not the result).

It therefore behooves us to remember who the worst despotic governments of this century were: Nazis in Germany, Fascists in Italy, Communists in the USSR and China, each and every one of them a paragon of socialist endeavor. Their leaders Hitler, Mussolini, Stalin and Mao Tse Tung. The outstanding legacy of these individuals is that they each tried to out-do the others in the total number of their own citizens which they murdered. It is a fact that each of these men killed more of their own civilian citizens then they lost in military conflict. The reason for this is inherent to socialism. It promises things that it cannot possibly deliver. When socialist politicians in power come to the realization that it is impossible to deliver on their promises and political unrest develops, they have two options if they plan to stay in power. First, they must locate a scapegoat on whom they can blame their inability to deliver. Any Jew can tell you who that was for the Germans and the Russians. The second is to develop, and rapidly so, a state security apparatus to keep them in office. The SS, the KGB, etc. The basic tenants of socialism are: 1) seduce the populace into accepting the government as the arbitrator of all problems, government from cradle to grave; 2) begin delivering on those services to make the citizens dependent; 3) take away the citizens' guns; 4) increase taxes on all services while destroying any free market alternative services; 5) blame the chosen scapegoat for the inability to meet demand for services; 6) have the centralized national police force round up any dissidents.

Socialism cannot work because the cost of services must be collected in the form of taxes, and this is not a sustainable possibility. The reason is that since government pays for all services, neither the producer nor the consumer cares about the cost, and hence there is an uncontrolled spiral of inflation (today's medical costs are a case in point and healthcare is not yet totally socialized). Furthermore, the government has no funds or assets. It only has the funds it confiscated from its citizens. The total inefficiency of a centralized bureaucracy does not help either. Once citizens are weaned on this cradle-to-grave concept and are no longer self-reliant, they become wards of the state and will not accept any reduction of services. The government subsequently has no option but to reduce services, and as popular resistance develops State repression begins. This is the socialist cycle. It has been found to occur in every socialist state in existence to date.

The current most outrageous examples of this are North Korea and Cuba. These two societies share much in common — both are socialist, both are totalitarian, both have more political prisoners then any nation close to their size, both have non-working universal health care, in both the citizens suffer malnutrition, both have food and fuel rationing. Their leaders and party members, in the meantime, eat caviar and drink champagne.

Socialism can never work in any environment. It violates human nature and logic.

The capitalist economic system differs greatly from its socialist adversary in numerous ways. While the socialist system is a top down centralized arrangement, the capitalist system, which can only exist in a free market economy that recognizes the right of private property, is totally controlled by the market itself. Interestingly, personal freedom, liberty, and the pursuit of happiness can also only thrive in free market economies. Capitalism is a sort of volatile and confusing situation where the capital markets dictate demand, price, and methods of distribution. The reason that the left is so very successful in criticizing capitalism is because it is not regulated and therefore difficult to explain. The reason capitalism works so well is that demand dictates production as well as price thus avoiding market inequities and shortages.

Socialism's principal theorem is centralization of markets under government control. This has never worked and there is not one single instance in world history where centralized governmental market manipulation has been successful. This, however, does not deter the R. Reichs of this world, who continuously make every effort to centralize economic as well as social and political power for themselves and their Satori masters.

George Washington said it best: "Government, like fire, is a good servant, but a fearful master." All capitalist functions are directed at free market concepts. A free market is one that serves society and with little government interference. This concept is unpopular with the Satori because in order to attain more and more power they require centralization of all economic, social, and political functions. Because of their poor performance in the political frame they have altered their modus operandi and are now implementing their schemes through judicial activism. These judicial incursions, which by the way in the United States are in violation of constitutional law, have been sold to the public based on the false misnomer that greedy capitalists don't care about the people, their welfare, safety, or health, but that politicians do. This, without doubt, is a ludicrous statement. The capitalist must perform to market standards. Competition will put him out of business if he provides an inferior product or service. He is furthermore constrained by his customers, stockholders, board of directors, lending institutions, as well as numerous laws, and, if all else fails, product liability statutes. In addition there is a veritable alphabet soup of governmental agencies which oversee his product, conduct with employees, public safety, product safety, environmental compliance, and financial performance. In fact capitalists are over-regulated which causes a considerable burden to be put on the public in the form of increased prices. A noteworthy fact is: *the most egregious acts against the consumer, the environment, and the public in general, have all been made by socialist states.*

On the judicial front, the Mandarins, at the direction of the Satori, have been implementing laws at a rate which is unprecedented in human history. Since the beginning of the Eisenhower administration, more laws have been added to the books than in the previous 200 years. These laws cost each and every citizen of the United States an estimated $4,000 per year, per person, in increased cost of goods. Through it, the Mandarin class, which is interested only in its own self preservation and expansion, is ever increasing in size.

As stated previously, the Satori may well take sides, but in the greater scheme of things, they do not care one iota about which political system is in charge. They control the issues on all sides.

In later chapters I will demonstrate exactly where and how and through whom, the Satori command the political, social, religious, and indeed, every aspect of our lives.

THE GREENS

I call this part of the book the Greens because that's what they like to call themselves. It is an unfortunate fact that in Germany there is a substantial political party called the Greens which has a tangible representation in the Bundestag. I do not oppose the environment. I live in the country partially because I deeply detest the filth, pollution, and decay of the cities. Having been forced into an education which required me to take botany, biology, chemistry, physics, geology, as well as numerous math courses, I truly despise idiots who make unscientific and incorrect statements on issues. This is unfortunately the prevailing circumstance of the entire Green movement. In a frenzied quest for ever increasing donations, to whatever goofy sect of the movement they belong, they will dramatize, expand, bloat, and lie on all issues in order to solicit your, and the government's, donations. The worst of the lot are The Sierra Club, The Audubon Society, and Greenpeace. Relative newcomers like Global Green, and The Green Cross, both run by a former USSR premiere, must not be overlooked. In the instance of Greenpeace, lying and fabrication are only the tip of the iceberg. Their White Paper position on the nuclear electric generating energy industry is a case in point. The paper was issued from their London office, and I reviewed it. This document was so full of errors, mistakes, lies, misinformation, and just plain rubbish, that it could not even pass as acceptable fiction. The document was many pages long and in reading the first four pages I found over 40 mistakes. I wrote them a letter pointing out every mistaken and scientifically false statement. They did not correct the document, nor did they answer my letter. Present society has a real problem due to the poor education of most journalists. This is particularly true in the sciences. Much of what the Greens produce in written and verbal form is simply not challenged by the media because they lack the knowledge to do so. This process strengthens the entire Green movement. This has occurred due to a public education system that prides itself in teaching children to put rubbers on bananas rather then teaching biology. Furthermore, the majority of solutions to environmental problems do more harm to the environment than doing nothing. A curious fact is that environ-mentalist's so-called solutions are seldom subjected to the rigorous scientific evaluation required by the private sector. Just imagine, if you will, environmental solutions being subjected to the rigors of an US FDA (Food & Drug Administration) audit.

This movement, which boasts some of the highest paid executives in the world, has succeeded in getting its own private army to enforce its edicts. An entire alphabet soup of what, in my opinion, are lunatic national and international agencies who enforce the clean air act, the clean water act, wetlands regulations, hell, even the US Army is involved. The Environmental Protection Agency, the Bureau of Land Management, the US Army Corps of Engineers, the list is endless. In 1993 the Clinton administration hired over 2,000 additional federal regulatory personnel. Total newly enacted federal statutes in number of pages for 1993 was 61,166, for 1994 it was 64,914, but that's mild compared to the all time champ. Jimmy Carter, in one single year (1980), holds the world record with 73,258 pages of new laws. That is one hell of a legacy, and I would place a bet that he never read any of it. Understand that the Mandarins wrote these laws so they can control us better. Estimates of the total cost of these regulations is about $500 billion per year. If nothing else, you now know exactly what to tell the next whacko who asks for a donation. To add insult to injury, according to The National Center for Public Policy Research, a think-tank in DC, the Clinton administration has formulated plans to publish another 4,300 laws in the next congressional session.

Just exactly how large is the environmental industry? Well, according to an *Insight* magazine article of Sept. 12, 1993, they collected over one billion dollars in the US alone during 1992.

To this we must add funds provided by government, those by foundations, and tax deductible donations made by business interests. Small wonder that executives of all the larger non-profit environmental organizations draw salaries exceeding $200,000. It is not unreasonable to suspect that the entire environmental industry exceeds $800 billion per annum. That makes it one of the largest single industry segments of the American economy.

Predictions of imminent disaster are routinely touted by various environmental groups. Consider Acid Rain, Global Warming, A New Ice Age, Over Population, World Wide Starvation, The Ozone Hole. Each and every one of these false issues is nothing more than a gimmick for more funding and contributions. The last one mentioned, the Ozone Hole, is particularly popular at the present time. Did you know that it was rediscovered by NASA (National Aeronautics & Space Administration) two weeks prior to the US Senate taking up a bill that would have drastically cut funding to NASA? Another was Acid Rain. Did you know that the largest single contributor to acid rain are swamps (for you wetlands envirofreaks). These swamps naturally produce sulfur and nitrogen, the primary ingredients of acid rain. Environmentalists routinely push for expansion or at minimum, maintenance of swamps. Then they tell us to plant a tree, when swamps are among the greatest destroyers of trees. At the present time the largest destruction of forest in the world is in progress in northern Oregon where these paragons of nature are in the midst of destroying 6 million acres of forest by not allowing insecticide, thinning, or any reasonable forest management practice. This forest is dying. All this can be related to the fact that in 1997 we have more forests on the north American continent then we had the day the Pilgrims landed at Plymouth Rock.

In Europe, the Greens have already forged a coalition with the socialists. It is a fact that worldwide the chameleon of so-

Swamps and wetlands are major producers of "acid rain."

*For trees to give off oxygen, they must take in carbon dioxide.**

*David Schimel, National Center for Atmospheric Research, Associated Press 11/2/97, Study regarding climate phenomenon.

cialism has changed color, as it were, and become green. They are one and the same. Socialists unable to sell their stale can of worms to the public have found a new way. They hide their intentions in a mantle of environmental goodness. The Fabian society was the forerunner of modern socialism, the British Labor Party, and the 20th century American Democrat party. On a stairwell in the Beatrice Webb House in England you can view the coat of arms of the Fabian movement. It is a stained glass window depicting a wolf putting on sheeps clothing.

Global Green, formerly called Green Cross International, and the Gorbachev Foundation are the new leaders at the forefront of this movement.

Government funding of Satori operations as these comes in the form of grants, concessions, direct payments, contracts, and even gifts. For example, let us examine a meeting held at what used to be the Presidio of San Francisco (now a closed US Army base) between September 27 and October 1, 1995. Through it we can demonstrate the duplicitous methods used to finance a Satori operation. We can also get an idea of just how big their plans are. The Presidio was previously a US Army base, so it was government property. For the meeting sponsored by Mikhail Gorbachev's, Gorbachev Foundation, the base was provided free of charge. The meeting was called "The State of The World Forum." (Just you try to get a government facility free of charge!) Five hundred guests were invited at a fee of $5,000 each. When you see the names on the list you will quickly realize that none of these people paid their way for the meeting. Payment in every instance was made by government (taxpayers) or corporations (stockholders). So you paid for the affair — caviar, salmon, Dom Perignon, and who knows what all. In the case of the attendees who worked for think tanks or foundations, it was paid out of their treasury funds which are funded with 98% tax deducted dollars, so you paid for them also.

Gorbachev expounds on worldwide controls to protect the environment. To quote Georgia Anne Geyer, Gorbachev's favorite saying is: "The greater the socialism, the greater the democracy."

Here is a partial list of attendees:

George Bush
Ted Turner
Jane Fonda
Al Gore
George Mitchell
George Shultz
Milton Friedman
David Packard
Maurice Strong
Brian Mulroney
Desmond Tutu
Deepak Chopra
Trich Nhat Hanh
John Nesbitt
Carl Sagan
Hans Dietrich Genscher
Vaclav Havel
Alvin Toffler
Zbig. Brzezinski
Bill Gates
Ted Koppel
Colin Powell
Alan Cranston
Mario Cuomo
John Denver
Shirley McLaine
Theo. Hesburgh
Dwayne Andreas

Also in attendance were high government officials from: Russia, Vietnam, Costa Rica, Turkey, Holland, Japan, Canada, USA, GB, Germany, the Czech republic, as well as from several of the old USSR republics. Most were prime ministers.

During the introduction, Gorbachev (former KGB) introduced the "Counsel of the Wise," George Bush, Ted Turner, Bill Gates, Allan Cranston and Dwayne Andreas. The largest single contributor to the event was none other than Andreas, who through Archer Daniels & Midland (ADM), reputedly contributed the sum of $250,000 toward defraying the costs of the meeting. So, if you are a stockholder of ADM, congratulations, you contributed mightily. Having examined the receipts of Gorbachev's State of the World Forum (500 guests at $5,000 each, plus a $250,000 gift), we can readily see how the Satori finance things at your expense.

How do these elitists hope to increase their power and control over us utilizing the environmental platform? Let us take the simple example of The Endangered Species Act. Environmentalists were successful in having no less than 950 plants and animals coded as either endangered or threatened, and another 4,000 have been earmarked for future inclusion of the listing. For twenty-one years these nutty extremists have wrecked havoc with economic and industrial expansion, property ownership and development worldwide. In total, 28 species have been removed from the endangered list, and of those, 7 were removed because of extinction. The balance of 21 were removed because it was determined that they did not belong on the list and were never endangered or threatened at all. These facts conclusively prove that the legislation not only has done nothing to either restore or protect species, but rather, was written for the purpose of controlling people. It is not unreasonable to state that species will die out, but nature, in the scheme of things, will also create new ones which, in all probability, are more adaptable to changes that occur normally in nature. Is this not what has taken place since the beginning of creation?

Horror stories regarding the enforcement of the Endangered Species Act include a farm seized in California because the farmer ran over a certain sub-species of kangaroo rat. The farm was sold along with all the equipment. In Oregon hundreds of lumber employees were idled because of a sub-species of owl. In southern California over 100 homes were burned down because the whackos refused to allow the construction of fire breaks as they would offend some mice. The underlying purpose of this statute has very little to do with the protection of the environment, plants, or animals, at which it has been a demonstrable failure, and a whole lot to do with controlling people. The exact same supposition can be made of the bulk of most environmental law. Consider the wetlands regulations — they have little value except for the increase of acid rain, but they're very effective in controlling others private property.

If the environmentalists were actually interested in anything other than the control of other people's property, would the following not make more sense? For swamps (if preservation is deemed desirable) offer the property owner a tax incentive of no property tax on land so classified. To protect the habitat of an endangered species, offer the property owner a tax reduction based on possible land utilization. Rather than fining and confiscating land, advise the property owner of methods to use that will minimally impact the environment. Instead of inefficient governmental interference, offer cash pay-out to property owners for each living endangered species preserved on his land.

It is an indisputable fact that all government interference in this sector has been a dismal failure. The exact same statement applies to major industrial safety laws (OSHA in US). If the intent to do good is genuine, then the method of enforcement must be passive, not coercive. Offering an incentive to achieve an intended goal is almost always successful, and considerably less expensive then any forced effort. But we digress. The purpose of all these statutes have nothing to do with the environment and everything to do with the control of the population by the Mandarins for the Satori. The true purpose is consolidation of power. Do not fall into the trap of believing that the environmentalists are the culprits in this as they are but the pawns in the labyrinth controlled from above.

PLAYING THE POPULACE

Without any doubt the most successful single contrivance of the Satori has been their media promoted slogans and phrases. Just think of the cumulative effect of statements like "Cop Killer Bullet," "Assault Weapons," "Homophobe," "Pro-Choice," and their greatest success, "Free Trade." These phrases have been instilled in the citizens, accepted by the media, and may be found in all media sources daily. This issue reminds me of two newspapers, one which can only be characterized as pulp fiction, the *Greek Ethnos*, and its journalistic nemesis, the most accurate newspaper published, *Die Neue Zurcher Zeitung* of Zurich, Switzerland.

We shall examine the last of these pharases, "Free Trade," the concept of which, was and is, promoted by all free market economists from Mills to Mises, as the ideal to which individuals and companies should aspire. Do not be deceived, free markets are not what those today promoting "Free Trade" have in mind. Read Mises, *Human Action*, and you will know what "Free Trade" really is. What is proposed today is not "Free Trade." It is government managed trade, free of import/export tariffs. In economic terms, it would be more accurate to term NAFTA, etc., as State Monopoly Capitalism, the beneficiaries of which are a favored elite.

For a period of over 30 years I was active in international trade. At various times I managed import, export, manufacturing, and distribution businesses. In my last job I was CEO of a manufacturing concern which exported products made in the USA to over 50 different nations as well as all American states. During this time I visited almost 100 nations around the world.

I can tell you that the concept of free trade in not only impossible, but on the face of it, stupid. Only people who are unacquainted with international trade could possible believe that free trade could be a possible circumstance. The idea of free trade has been sold to the public by an eager media which views itself as an intellectual force. It is a fact that journalists are among the greatest egotists in society. They brim with an, "I know what's good for you" mentality.

One of America's greatest industrialists is Roger Milliken. He has over 50 years experience in trade and manufacturing and has been critical of the free trade concept since its political inception. Mr. Milliken is the CEO of Milliken & Co., a $2.5 billion textile manufacturing enterprise located in Spartensburg, South Carolina. He is a very private person who seldom publicly comments on issues. He has, however, spoken out on free trade and its effect on America. Bear in mind that his comments apply to all industrialized nations of the world. In an interview with *Insight* magazine in March of 1996 he stated:

> *"Middle America is being transformed into underclass by trade policies that benefit only Wall Street and ignore the well being of small town America. I reject arguments that free trade can create jobs to offset those lost to overseas competition and dismiss suggestions that if an American turns to protectionism it will provoke retaliatory acts by other nations. No one can retaliate, we have the market in which everyone wants to sell."*

Now, read the above statement over and replace Wall Street with Satori. Mr. Milliken got it exactly right, we have all the marbles, everyone wants to sell in our market, our exports account for but a small portion of our total business. The Mandarins in our International Trade Commission and Department of Commerce are playing poker with a straight flush and lack the courage to play their winning hand. Of course, they will not oppose the mandates placed on them by the Satori. That would mean loss of employment.

It is important for you to understand the underlying reasons why "Free Trade" is a hoax, and why it is an impossible concept. The conceptual slogan, free trade, stems from academia, and, to be precise, comes from socialist theorists in academia who have no grounding whatsoever in reality. Would you, if you had a business, let someone like Laura D'Andria Tyson or Robert Reich or Karl Marx run your business? Not only do these people live in a make believe world, they have absolutely no understanding of the day to day operations of a business. The basis of my position is simple to understand and well known but totally ignored by today's economists. Academia is a closed society which is completely controlled by peer pressure. A dissenting position is not only routinely dismissed as erroneous and inaccurate, but opposition to official dogma is academic suicide.

"Free Trade" is impossible because of the many various economic, political, social, linguistic, financial and other factors that may be attributed to the formula between trading partners. The Satori, knowing this, have thus engaged in the unification of markets through such vehicles as WTO, NAFTA, and EC. By consolidating various nations of differing economic status into conglomerations, the free trade issue becomes moot. The question then becomes: Why? And what is the price? Why is simple: One World Government. The price, on the other hand, for developed economies is staggering. In the United States the cost of this policy has been apparent for over 40 years. Actual per capita income, due to the loss of manufacturing jobs, has declined for the last 40 years. Regardless of what you are told, the reason for this is international trade. "Free Trade" is one of the principal dialectics in the arsenal for the institution of the New World Order as conceived and instituted by the Mandarins under the direction of the Satori.

In order to further your understanding of the absurdity of "Free Trade" as a concept let us take one example, Mexico. NAFTA was an agreement between first the USA and Canada with the subsequent addition of Mexico. The concept of this agreement was to reduce all tariffs between the agreeing partners within 10 years to 0% This took over 2,000 pages when you include explanations and side agreements to describe what I just did in one sentence, hence, it is much more than tariff reduction, it is "Managed Trade." First, understand that we are dealing with two very different economic circumstances. On one side we have Mexico and on the other the US and Canada. The American and Canadian economies are very similar in labor costs, law, and social proviso. Mexico is completely different. Mexico, with a population which is Spanish in origin, rather then English, is 95% Roman Catholic, has differing laws, a completely different social structure, currency that is not only volatile but has had up to 50% swings in value, a government that is corrupt, a nonfunctioning legal system, and is the oldest "Democratic" dictatorship in the world. The PRI has ruled Mexico since the revolution many decades ago. With a population of about 70 million vis a vis the US and Canadian population of 265 million, they represent just under 1/3 the number of people. But that's only part of the story. The Mexican population is on average much younger than that of the US and Canada. On the one side there is the concept of individual liberty and justice, and on the other, authoritarian rule by a special class. I am well versed in Mexico having lived there for some time. I truly love the people who are among the friendliest and most pleasant in the world. Their government stinks. Mexicans are oppressed by some of the most brutal and nastiest politicians this side of the Atlantic. Let's examine the economic differences between the two parties (in dollars per hour):

	Mexico	USA	Canada
Income Blue Collar Manufacturing	$1.14 /hr	$24.00	$20.00
Social cost borne by producer	Nil	$6.00	$8.00
Environmental compliance	Nil	$4.00	$3.50
Pensions/safety standards/etc.	Nil	$2.00	$2.00

Please, anyone, explain to me how such varying economies could pursue a free market between them. Without any doubt the entire manufacturing base of the two higher economies would move their plants south. This is exactly what has been happening. In order to have free trade, the economies of all partners will have to be brought to parity. This will mean an increase of the average income of Mexican manufacturing labor and a corresponding reduction in the other two. For the average North American manufacturing employee it will mean a reduction of income of about 25%. Unfortunately that's only the tip of the problem. Industrial safety codes, (OSHA) Labor laws, (USDL) environmental laws, (EPA) are not even in this equation. Why? — because labor laws, environmental laws, and safety codes where everyone and everything is bribed are nothing more then a farce. To add insult to these facts, Mordita, the practice of kicking back a portion of your wage to the person that hired you, is set in stone and is simply a fact of life in Mexico.

SOCIETAL RELATIONS

To keep your attention focused elsewhere, strife between groups of citizens has long been a Satori initiative. No effort in this direction can be considered without the greatest of them all. When I was a boy of 14 years, coming from the primarily monotone society of Switzerland, to land in New York City, the concept of prejudice was simply not in my vocabulary. Switzerland had not had slaves since Roman times. All citizens were considered equal under the law. The very concept of anyone being better before the law due to race, color, gender, or religion was not even debated. In America unfortunately, equality has taken a strange twist. The concept of the equality of people in relationship, other than the law, is a product of the American public schools. Some people are stronger, some are smarter, some are better looking, and so on. We, as individuals, are not equal, and the effort to create such a false impression is detrimental to all of society. Women in Switzerland did not have the vote in those days, but they were more influential in social and political issues than they are now. I did not learn that there was any difference between races until I came to America and attended US public schools where prejudice has become institutionalized.

Creating hatred is good for the Satori because it takes attention away from the causes and results of their policies and shields them from exposure. About 30 years ago, in the early 1960s, a series of laws were instituted and enforced which resulted in what we now call affirmative action. This gradually took place in other industrialized societies, England included. These laws have, in the USA, been continuously expanded to the detriment of all but the masters. Today, we as a society, are overwhelmed by a plethora of laws and rules relating to our interaction as societal members. The only result of this to date has been the expansion of racial, gender, and other societal friction.

The scope of these laws and their divisive supporters has lead to an ever increasing disharmony between citizens. Racial and gender preference quotas have lead us to prefer diversity over merit. All you have to do is look at Clinton's cabinet to verify that statement. Instead of the best and the brightest, we now have chosen the nominee whose race, gender, or some other ridiculous prejudice meets with the predetermined requirement of social diversity. One of the touted minorities is women. How can a group that represents over 52% of the total population, and controls over 50% of the national asset base be considered a minority? What kind of legitimacy can be attributed to a black man who complains that his antecedents were slaves, when the greatest bulk of whites who came to America were indentured servants? All that has been accomplished by these stupid laws is to stereotype all segments of our population and, in the process, lower expectations for our entire society.

The most ardent supporters of these laws in the past decade have been race baiters and radical feminists. In the case of the feminists they have been overtaken by a group of radical lesbians, who are not only shrill but decidedly obnoxious. National Organization for Women (NOW) is at the forefront of this effort. In 1996 they had their national convention in Washington DC. For a week the airways were bombarded with their bombastic rubbish. The press, ever eager for news, gave them more than ample coverage. Although the total number of participants was under 900, no effort by the media was missed to engrandise the movement in the public eye. Meanwhile, the largest female organization in America is the Concerned Women of America (CWA), whose membership is 50 times the size of NOW. Their convention had 5,000 plus delegates. Their convention was also held in Washington DC — they did not even make the evening news! Why?

Another group whose power is far in excess of its statistical percentage of population is the homosexual lobby. Homosexuals represent 3 to 4 percent of the population. They continuously try to inflate that to over 10% but that is pure bull. This lobby also strongly supports affirmative action because they seek to be classified as a minority through the inclusion of sexual preference. They have been able to muster substantial financial and political support, funneling vast amounts of money to the Democratic National Committee (DNC).

Race preference, remedy for passed generation discrimination, minority set aside, managed racial diversity, and glass ceiling, is all a bunch of crap. The only way that the human race can hope to evolve to a higher plain is through merit advancement. The best and the brightest must be allowed to go ahead of the rest of us. One of the left's main tenants is their unrelenting support of Darwin's theories of evolution, the prominent central theme of which is, "the survival of the fittest." What the Satori have accomplished with affirmative action rubbish is not the advancement of the fittest but control of society.

When I was 16 years old, my friends and I often went to the Apollo theater in Harlem. We usually made an evening of it and went to a restaurant for dinner. Not once during that time were we made uncomfortable, not one bad word was ever uttered to us by any person. If there were racial tensions we certainly were unaware of them. Years later, when I traveled by air, I would get off the train at 125th street in Harlem and take a cab to LaGuardia airport. I stopped doing that in about 1964 after several unpleasant encounters.

A fine example of the workings of affirmative action is Lowell High School in San Francisco, California. This school was a merit school, i.e., an entrance exam was required in order to attain admittance. It is located at the geographic edge of China town — the largest Chinese community in North America. The majority of students were Chinese for two reasons: their intelligence, and their community's close proximity to the school. There was strong community support for the school. Certain members of the black community were unhappy that there was a racial imbalance in the school. (Understand that all that was required to attend was to pass the entrance exam, there was absolutely no prejudice involved). Under pressure from the black community entrance exams were changed so that Orientals required an entrance score of 69, Whites 64, and Blacks 40. Is that not a great way to improve education! SAT (college entrance exams) scoring has also been changed in order to lower expectations of those to be examined. On the gender side it was decided that males were better in math so a handicap was instituted in favor of females. Half of the math questions were made verbal rather than arithmetic in nature. By increasing verbal math, females are provided a preference, and wind up with higher scores. The process is refereed to as "double verbal performance indexing."

Race and gender cards are an important trump in the Satori deck. It pits virtually every member of our society against every other member, and through this allows the Satori to carry out their nefarious schemes in hidden security.

"When the State has granted one privilege, its character as a purveyor of privilege is permanently established, and natural law does not permit it to stop with the creation of one privilege, but forces it to go on creating others . . . which in turn culminates in the decay and disappearance of the society . . . Such is the grim testimony borne by the history of six civilizations now vanished, to the validity of the law that – man tends always to satisfy his needs and desires with the least possible exertion."

— Albert J. Nock, *The Disadvantages of Being Educated*

GAIA, THE NEW GOD

Pantheism, the belief that equates God with the forces of nature, is the new religion of the Satori. Mother Earth is the goddess, and pantheism is the religion. This new cult now has 14 million adherents worldwide. James Lovelock is the high priest. He even wrote a book *Gaia the Practical Science of Planetary Medicine.* None other than the past Secretary General of the UN Butros Butros-Ghali and the Vice President of the United States Al Gore have professed their adoration of gaia on numerous occasions. In fact Al Gore also professed to have written a book *Earth in the Balance,* in which the continuing thread of Gaia may be followed. As previously mentioned, religion is one of the cardinal Satori-identified attack points against the status of our present social structure. Pantheism and the religion of gaia are to replace all monotheistic religions including Christianity, Judaism and Islam. The primary reason for this is that organized religion is not, at present, within the scope of total Satori manipulation. The Christian Protestant sects have been well-infiltrated by such organizations as The World Council of Churches and the American Council of Churches, but a return to planet worship gives the Satori the right to treat people as animals.

In the introduction to his book, Lovelock makes the following statement in a superheating: *I speak as the representative, the shop steward, of the bacteria and the less attractive forms of life who have few others to speak for them. My constituency is all life other then human."* Well folks, there you have it in a nutshell: the complete religious ideology of the Satori. Let us all hasten to build an altar to E-choli. These twits regard bacteria as a more important life-form than human beings. Eons of human improvement and development count for nothing, snail darters are more important. The introduction of his book goes on to elucidate such topics as nuclear winter, greenhouse fever, the demise of our planet, planetary medicine, and then proceeds to inform us that "Established science is ill-suited to cope with global change." I say unequivocally that this entire text consists of mathusian thinking, and unscientific, unsubstantiated rubbish.

Let us examine how scientific consensus is reached and how academia arrives at consensus. The scientific community more than any other societal collection works together to develop a consensus by aligning the opinions of various respected members to the tenant of the discussion. Funding for research, which is not a product of profit orientation, is driven by peer pressure. In other words if you disagree with the majority, or even with the principal theorists who are accepted by their peers, you will be ostracized. This is a truly terrible thing for an academician to contemplate because if you are abandoned by your peers you will obtain no funds, no position, no advancement, and no tenure. You become ostracized from the scientific community. This system creates a mindset in which the majority, if not all members, tout the line of least resistance, and go along to get along.

It is through this form of authoritarian system that rubbish surfaces as accredited rational thought. Consider the "Ozone Hole," a rediscovered and accepted rational scientific disaster. It fits in nicely with religion and environmentalism. It was rediscovered two weeks before funding to NASA was to be drastically reduced. The Ozone Hole has been there since the beginning of time. Or at least since the planet went a few degrees off its axis. Ozone is made in two ways: first, and most commonly, when solar radiation hits the atmosphere and oxygen molecules are converted into ozone (three parts of oxygen stuck together) and second by lightning. As the earth rotates about its axis at a tilt of some 20 plus degrees, only a small amount of sunlight hits the polar region during winter months, presto no generation of ozone, hence a hole in the ozone layer. What a deal! Academia gets money. Environmentalists get an issue. Pantheists get a topic. A complete three-for-one triple. To add insult to injury, the mathusian ludites get us to change our method of refrigeration and method of propelling chemicals because, ac-

The "Ozone Hole" is Not Caused by Freon

"How does CFC rise when it's molecules are four to eight times heavier than air? All experience with freon and related CFCs shows . . . soil bacteria will decompose them."

— Dixie Ray Lee, *Environmental Overkill*

cording to them, they destroy the ozone layer. Never mind that ozone is in the stratosphere because it is one of the lightest gases, and the outlawed chemical is over 50 times heavier and could not, under any circumstance, float to the upper atmosphere. The Satori have fabricated yet another non-issue with which they can exercise their control over us and keep all of us from understanding the real true goal, i.e., our declining standard of living and the centralization of their power.

Karl Marx said, religion is the opiate of the people. The Satori understand the premise very well and unable to control present religion, particularly Roman Catholic, Catholic Orthodox, and

Islamic religions, they have developed a new religion. The major Protestant sects have already succumbed, most of the national and worldwide Protestant organizations having been completely taken over by Satori surrogates. I have been told that the Yale School of Divinity has more homosexuals in attendance then heterosexuals and that Union Theological Seminary is no different. The Jews had their reform movement when the American Jewish Council was taken over by a group with exactly the same agenda as the World Council of Churches (WWC).

Religion has been an unqualified success for the Satori. From gender neutral songbooks issued by the United Church of Christ, to the feminization of the ministry, to homosexual dominance in a substantial portion of all seminaries, to the introduction of gaia worship, all is proceeding in accordance with the master plan. The Satori can ill-afford an organized clergy opposing them. All efforts to eradicate conservative Christians, and to demonize born-again Christians have been accelerated. This is primarily the mission of the media who utilizes the process of linkage and "key words" such as: "Radical Right Wing Christians," "Neo-Nazi Separatist Christians," the linkage of the KKK, as well as other right of center organizations, to smear legitimate Christian churches. The attack against Christians, Hassidic and Orthodox Jews, and Muslims is unrelenting in the media. It is evident in every form of public communication utilized in the Western World. I do not know how many Roman Catholic priests there are in the United States, but I am sure the number is over 100,000, yet the only headline we see about priests is that they molest children even though the percentage is so low that it becomes statistically ridiculous. We have a Protestant bishop living in the town next to mine who ordained a known homosexual as a priest, and as a consequence is being tried for heresy. It was the major religious news of 1996 in the New Hampshire press, all of it in favor of the bishop and against the church. Attacks on Christianity by the establishment are unrelenting, vicious, and without substance. The first major movement against organized religion in the United States was the Church-State issue. The fact that any statement about church and state is not found anywhere in the constitution, seems to be totally irrelevant to the authors of the myth. The only place where the matter of church is brought up in the constitution is in the Bill of Rights. The first amendment, first sentence states "Congress (the only body allowed to make law) shall make no law respecting an establishment of religion, or the free exercise thereof . . ." I would like one of the leftist members of the supreme court (preferably Kennedy) to explain how those words can be interpreted as meaning Separation of Church and State. We know exactly what the forefathers were speaking of: organized, state supported, state sponsored, and state controlled religion as it existed in 16th through 18th century Europe. But our brilliant supreme court has interpreted this sentence to mean: forbid prayer in public places, prohibit religious books in public schools, prohibit the Bible in public schools, remove the ten commandments from public places, forbid the public display of religious symbols or scenes, and even forbid religious meetings in public buildings. America is a nation in which over 85% of the populace belongs to some monotheistic religion while only 4% claim to be atheists. This small group of secular humanists has captured our courts, government, and even the presidency. They have created a society in which ethics, religion, morals, and faith are restricted from the public forum, divorced from our discourse, and removed from our educational processes. The very predictable results of this folly on our society has been nothing short of devastating. Let us examine the situation in Philadelphia:

Population increase 1960 to 1970 .... 13%
Crime increase same period 128%

By 1981 public school crime incidents were:

Police active in schools	67
Assaults in schools	316
Rapes	12
Weapon carriers	244

What a marvelous track record. The Satori can be proud, the Mandarins are performing well. It is a proven fact that over 70% of our graduating high school seniors are unable to reach a rational decision about right and wrong, nor do they have a rational understanding of the types of government, political system, or social issues under which they live. Many are unable to read, and those who can are often unable to comprehend what they read. They are all ready to become worker insects of the Satori in their new socialist insect hive. They are unable to reason or to think, and their attention span is limited to the duration of a rock video.

Stalinists, communists, and socialists have rapidly turned into rampid enviro-freaks. In his new book *The Fate of the Forests,* Alexander Cockburn has switched from socialism to environmentalism. If you think about it, it makes perfect sense, both are pantheist as well as statist. Today's environmental movement is no different from the implacable and messianic Marxism of the 19th century. As they did then, they hold the moral high ground in the mind of the public. In their mantra we find a commonly recurring theme, "some problems like global warming (an unproven theory), acid rain (a product of swamps), the ozone hole (a naturally occurring phenomenon) are so serious as to require global government to solve them." While you read this text, the UN, the American state department, and the EPA are negotiating a plan for a world wide Clean Air Act to be enforced by the UN.

GENDER BENDER

In 1995, the United Nations (UN) sponsored "The International Women's Conference." It took place in 1996 in Beijing, China. What a marvelous place to have this conference! There is absolutely no question but that the Peoples Republic of China has the worst record on the planet when it comes to women's rights. It may be stated that women have no rights at all when it concerns the PRC. They don't even have the right to life, a full 30% of all female children are killed at birth. What is much more remarkable, are the feminists who attempted to control this meeting: Bella Abzug, Hillary Clinton, Jane Fonda, Donna Shalala, and a whole raft of radical liberals controlled not only the platform but the language, structure, and organization. In their foresight, the Satori let this conference, which meets their agenda, take place in the most inaccessible nation in the world. In addition, they had the conference moved to a remote village miles from anywhere. Due to the fact that China is a totalitarian dictatorship, authorities had no problem in containing and controlling the situation and outcome.

What is remarkable is the agenda that the leaders of this symposium attempted to bring to fruition: five genders and the elimination of such words as Mother, Father, Wife, Family, and Marriage from the platform. All this is part and parcel of the Satori-sponsored efforts to destroy the family unit and to drastically alter presently conceived societal norms.

Hawaii is presently at the vanguard of yet another earthquake in their attempt to have homosexual marriage legalized in the 50th state of America. This is a very dangerous proposal because of the requirement in the American constitution that all other states will have to accept this act as legally binding. This would then effect life insurance, health insurance, education, pensions, retirements, social security, not to mention all of societal structure. It would place a behavioral aberration on the same legal status as any legitimate marriage between heterosexuals.

In an article in *Reason* Magazine, attorney David Link states that if the Hawaiian supreme court votes in favor of homosexual marriage, we may expect to see a steady stream of homosexuals traveling to the 50th state to get hitched. In 1993, the court had already heard the case of Baer vs. Lewin and in that case ruled that, "under the equal rights amendment of the state's constitution, the government would be required to demonstrate a compelling interest to justify refusal to recognize same sex marriage." Regardless of how the court goes, the compass has been set and the direction is clearly implicated. If there is one thing we should all be aware of, it is the single-mindedness of the homosexual lobby and their relentless drive to have a chosen behavioral deficiency accepted as normal and mainstream.

A virtual manual for the homosexual lobby is a book written by Kirk & Madsen entitled *After the Ball: How America Will Conquer Its Fear and Hatred of Gays in the 90s.* This manifesto of the homosexual community relates in fluid terms the where, how, and when, of how to neutralize opposition and how to implement their specific agenda. At the cost of being labeled a homophobe (this term is in fact an oxymoron) I state quite clearly that the majority of people do not fear homosexuals but rather feel sorry for their confused state of mind.

We must give credit to the Satori for picking carefully the most decisive problems confronting western civilization, and then capitalizing on our concerns and expanding those very issues far beyond their actual importance and size. For example, the homosexual lobby insists that over 10% of the male population is homosexual when in fact the number is closer to 3.7%. It is interesting to note that all the principal chosen dialectics of the Satori exceed a one issue direction and effect much more than just the issue of engagement. And, that they invent new words to which they give a positive meaning to replace words with negative connotations. Examples are: replacing the word "homosexual" with the word "gay," and the use of "sexual preference" for "sodomy." Nowhere is this more apparent then in the gender issue. For over 2,000 years, western civilization has operated on the principal of family and community. The very foundations of our society, the building blocks if you will, would totally collapse if the feminist and homosexual agendas were allowed to succeed in their endeavor. To date they have had one success upon another. Divorce, once not allowed, subsequently allowed with distaste, is now readily accepted. Years ago, being an unwed mother was just about the worst thing that could happen to a girl. Today it is no worse than a pimple. Among Blacks, over 50% of all children are born out of wedlock and with Caucasians it is rapidly approaching 30%. The primary change in our civilization has been toward what the left calls liberalization. But it is not liberalization. It is the destruction of all moral and ethical societal underpinnings. We all know what happens to a house without a foundation, the same thing happens to a society without one. The Satori, you can be sure, count on that very fact. The confrontation between moral and immoral brings turmoil from which the New World Order is calculated to appear.

What will the new system be like? I don't know, but then neither do the Satori. There is one thing, however, of which I am certain from my studies of history — it will not be an improvement. In fact, as stated previously in this book, these changes will benefit no one except the ruling class.

"There are two methods, or means, and only two, whereby man's needs and desires can be satisfied. One is the production and exchange of wealth; this is the economic means. *The other is the uncompensated appropriation of wealth produced by others; this is the* political means . . ."

— Albert Jay Nock, *Our Enemy, The State*

CHAPTER THREE

POLITICS & CONFLICT

If there is one single issue that can motivate people against one another, it is greed. The greatest players of the greed card are Bill and Hillary Clinton. If I had a dollar for every time a member of the present administration mentioned taxing the rich, corporate greed, the disadvantaged, the challenged, evil profits, and all other such trash topics, I could retire. This issue is universal, it touches all of us, it applies to every living and thinking being in the world. It even effects governments. All of us at one time or another covet something another has. The less intelligent an individual is the more prone he is to greed. The entire Democrat Party in the US as well as the Labor Party in the UK play this greed card on a daily basis — this surely must let you know what these people think of you.

Corporate greed is a much touted epitaph of the political left. There was a very interesting article in the April 1996 issue of *Fortune* magazine on this very topic. First, in a four color graph, corporate profits as a percentage of revenues are shown between 1940 and 1990. What the graph clearly demonstrates is that profits, as a percentage of revenue, have dwindled from a high of 15% in 1940 to a new low of 5% in 1990. Once more, just like worker's income, this has been a slow and gradual decline. Worse yet, projections indicate that it will continue in corporate, as well as in personal income, well into the future. I would remind the reader that without profits there are a number of things that cannot and will not happen. These include: industrial expansion, new products, research and development, pay increases, pensions, profit sharing, returns on investment, new production equipment, and last but not least an improved standard of living for us all. For the fools playing the greed card and the fools who believe them, it would be wise to remember that the implementers could not collect their confiscatory taxes, and the believers would be denied benefits, if it were not for profit.

You have heard it straight from America's socialist Secretary of Labor Robert Reich, "Greedy corporations are screwing their employees, squeezing down wages while increasing profits." This statement from an economic illiterate who has never in his entire life worked for, or in, a business that made a profit. As you might gather, I personally intensely dislike Clinton's minion. He appears to me to be a little man with a Napoleon complex, who, while having no clue about anything to do with economics, presents himself as a great expert. The reason for corporate downsizing, mergers, and staff reductions has a great deal to do with international trade policies, NAFTA, EC, WTO, etc. and very little to do with greed. This is but another example of your attention being misdirected to an issue fabricated for the sole purpose of keeping your eye off the ball. "Free Trade" is the cause of the turmoil in the world business community. It is, if you will, the major tool of the Satori to change our present world. The new world, according to their plan will not have nations, but will be separated into regional trading blocks. Your fealty will then be to a trading entity rather than to a nation state.

Another form taken by the greed line is starvation and food deprivation. It is a proven fact, laid out in over one hundred books, that in today's world starvation is a man-made activity. There is not one single case in which a government or governmental policy cannot be shown to have been the cause of starvation. Socialism and/or communism have been its greatest single cause in this century. An equitable guess would place the total number of humans starved to death by governments at about 170 million in the 20th century. To play the, I-want-to-feel-good card, world relief agencies and religious organizations

Percentage of Total World Trade – 1996

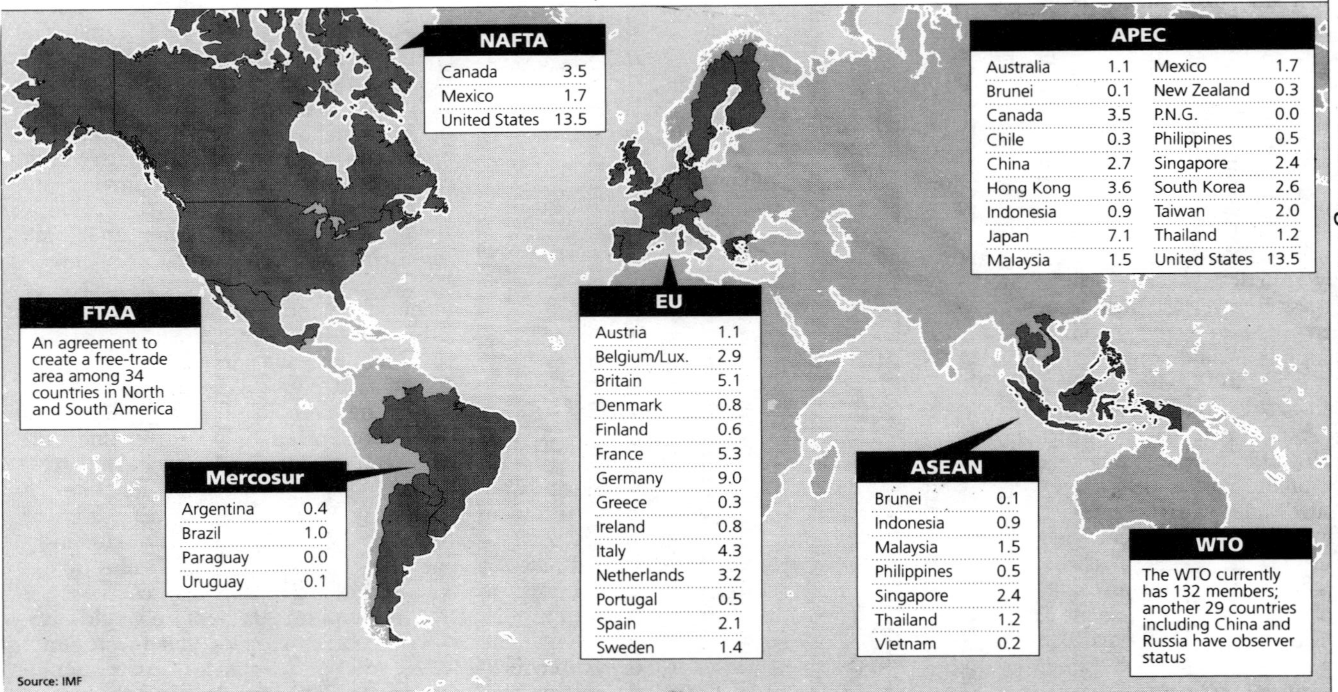

give us the opportunity to feed the needy. UN military incursions, thousands of giveaway subsidies, food banks, and God knows what all, are supposed to solve the problem. The solution is simple: if you really want to do something about starvation, eliminate the operating government, and the famine will soon subside. Why is this kept in continuation? Greed. It allows the Satori to develop the misconception that some people have wealth beyond what they should have, and it must be redistributed to those who have less. What a bunch of ridiculous rubbish. People and nations who have more, have it because they have produced more, and have less oppressive, less intrusive, and more stable governments. It is another proven fact that the wealthiest and most well off societies in world history have been those with the least amount of government, and that the poorest have invariably been those with the most government.

What has been orchestrated by the Satori is the unquestioned expansion of government in every western democracy. There are several reasons for this, the first being that in order to exercise control over the entire world, it is first necessary to bring all economies into closer proximity with one another. The solution to this problem for the Satori has been the international "Free Trade" conspiracy. The second is that the Satori understand there is an inevitable relationship between market freedom and political freedom. The solution to this has been to modify marxism and socialism, which has now been converted into environmentalism. As a top Mandarin said to me 25 years ago, "Marx is out. Keynes is the new radicalism." Always remember the paradigm of Hegel: out of two confronting systems a new and third one will develop.

Any discussion about contrived divisions between the haves and the have-nots must in due course descend to the basics. The immutable tenants of economic fact are almost never factors in the national political discourse on the subject. I actually prefer to call these economic laws. They are as follows:

1.) A reduction of tax rates results in an increase of personal income and more money collected by government.
2.) An increase in tax rates results in lower income, lower employment and less money collected in taxes.
3.) Increased regulation and more laws result in less employment and less individual income.
4.) Reduced regulation and fewer laws result in more and better paying jobs and more tax revenue.
5.) An increase in law and regulations results in lower paying jobs and less tax revenue.

This matter is not up for discussion. The laws given above are absolutes. We have over 2,000 years of recorded history to verify the above laws. Robert Reich, Ted Kennedy, Laura D'Andria Tyson, and Hillary Clinton will all vehemently disagree but will be unable to disprove them. These facts are just plain unacceptable to any socialist, because reduced government gives them less control over the people and business.

The minimum wage was in the news in 1996. Senator Ted Kennedy — a member of the wealthy elite who has never held an actual job in his entire life, whose wealth was all inherited from his father, and who has no conception whatsoever of what a wage even is — said, "Families can't live on a minimum wage, we must increase it by $.90 cents." Teddy, we all know that you can't live on the minimum wage, and a meager $.90 cents over several years is just about as much help as a cold bucket of water. The fact is that minimum wage jobs are entry level jobs. By the time you are the main bread winner for your family, you are supposed to be far beyond entry level jobs. Far more important to Teddy was the union's financing of his elections. Due to the fact that most union contracts are tied to the minimum wage, the unions reaped a huge reward the minute the new minimum was increased. More important is the report from the congressional budget office(CBO) who state that a $.90 cent increase in the minimum wage will result in the loss of 400,000 jobs. The Satori are delighted with this turn of events for it meets their goals equitably: 1) fewer small businesses; 2) a reduction in the standard of living; 3) large corporation expansion; and 4) increased division between citizens.

Could it be that there is one person in America not aware of the class warfare trash emanating from the White House? The present US executive administration is the undisputed leader, the president and his cabinet are the torchbearers. The most outspoken members are Robert Reich and Laura D'Andria Tyson.

Tyson is the current director of the National Economic Council. Previous to her political appointment, she was one of the left wingers at the University of California at Berkley. She was the former chairman of the Council of Economic Advisors, her only qualification was her leftist political leaning, and her many years as an academian. She has never held a job in a working business. She is the most ardent supporter of more, larger, and centralized government in the administration. A major news statement made by her in 1995 exemplifies her philosophy; "Cutting the deficit will expose the macro-economy to considerable downside risk." I simply cannot believe that a supposedly rational member of any government could make such a totally stupid statement and retain their position within the government. In another written statement she said, "In every era, the role of government in helping remedy market failures remains central to the nations well-being." To interpret; first she said that it is economically unhealthy for our nation to retire debt, then she said that if a business is mismanaged the government should bail it out. This is pure Keynesianism. In yet another utterance she said, "There is no relationship between the level of taxation and national economic performance." Well what can I say? It leaves me speechless. This woman states that if you are taxed for 100% of your income it will not effect the national economy. Please bear in mind that she was a professor at Berkley where she taught such rubbish to her students. In 1984, while still a professor at Berkley, she wrote a radiant and complimentary report on the management and central planning of the communist totalitarian regime in Romania. I am confident that dictator Nikolai Ceausescu and his family were well-pleased with her glowing report on his statist administration. Tyson's hero, one of the most brutal, repressive, Stalinist dictators of the 2nd half of this century, was executed by the Romanian people when they were freed from his rule.

Class warfare is one of the oldest and most ingrained political ploys of the century. It is the ultimate greed gambit and is one of the principal Satori Hegelian dialectics. The greatest use to date was during the French Revolution in which an entire class of citizens was liquidated in the name of liberty and fraternity. Class warfare is one of the primary tenants of the British socialist Fabian Society, the forerunner of the British Labor party and the American Democrat party since President Wilson. "New Democrats" are in fact old Fabian socialists.

The Fabian society took its name from Quintus Fabius Maximus, sometimes referred to as Fabius Cunctator. He was the Roman general who won the Punic wars. His claim to fame was that he never directly engaged the enemy, preferring rather to wear them down in a war of attrition. Should we learn something here? The Fabian society's coat of arms is a wolf in sheep's clothing and may be viewed in a stained glass window in the Beatrice Webb House. These two interesting facts, the coat of arms and the namesake of the organization, tell us a great deal about the New Democrats and who really pulls the strings in that party. This part of the Satori scheme was hatched in 1884 when a group of socialists founded the Fabians. The objective of the society was to develop a method by which communism could be brought into western society without bloodshed. Their headquarters, now a museum called the Beatrice Webb House, is located in Surrey, England.

An early member and major benefactor of the Fabian society was Cecil Rhodes, a South African multi-millionaire who was also the founder of the Rhodes Oxford scholarship program, the program which has turned so many young capitalist minds to socialism. Recent converts include George Stephanopoulos, Robert Reich, and Bill Clinton who, incidentally, did not graduate. The class warfare segment of the greed formula of conflict without bloodshed, under the auspices of the Satori, is one of the tenants for one world government.

I am confident that you understand by now that the Mandarins have an almost slavish obedience to the Satori. The reason for this should be obvious. The Satori hold all the marbles in international traffic. Consequently, if you aspire to prominence in politics, finance, or business you had better subscribe to the plan or else forget it.

KULTURKAMPF

Culture war has been a fact of life in western civilization from World War I onward. Unable to legislatively achieve the societal changes they envisioned, the Mandarins, at the direction of the Satori, have instituted a full judicial assault on western civilization, culture, and religion. Beginning with the First World War they have attempted to bring about legislative change in society to make it more amenable to their plans. They met with utter defeat. The reason for this loss is that elected officials, regardless of political affiliation, wish to remain in office. If they wish to serve their masters, the Satori, they cannot propose or enact legislation that is opposed by the majority of the populace. In America, a simple solution was found shortly after the Second World War. It was the Federal judiciary, the majority of whom are appointed for life. They don't have to run for public office, and are not beholden to anyone. They can make unpopular or socially unacceptable decisions and remain in office. Decisions that they have made, hundreds of them, are not based on our constitution or common law but, instead, are based on precedence which they, themselves, instituted. What these judges are really doing is to write law, an act strictly forbidden by the constitution and reserved exclusively for the legislative branch of government.

Without doubt the the most severely impacted people by the acts of the 1960s have been the poor and the black. Sexual liberation was the theme of the mid 60s, and from its beginnings, as a minor societal deviance, it became the mainstay of the political left. Spearheaded by such publications as *Playboy,* the subject virtually became a religion to some. The Satori are not interested in strengthening the family. They are, and always have been, interested in the destruction of the family unit. Family is the nucleus of western civilization, the core without which our entire social culture will disintegrate. One of the dominant effects of welfare policies has been the condemnation of poor blacks into a sojourn of endless illiteracy, welfare dependency, poverty, and crime. After the civil rights legislation in the mid sixties, the then sitting president, Lyndon Johnson (D), came up with the "Great Society." This destructive plan was designed to create a entire class of citizens who were beholden to a political party and who would, generation after generation, be shills for that party. Today American Blacks vote 94% Democrat. This plan, it was said, would bring Blacks up to parity with the rest of society. What was accomplished by the Great Society program were three things. First, it wasted $4 trillion on a program which today, in terms of the percentage of the population, has exactly the same amount of welfare recipients as before the program began. Second, it has created, in many instances, four generations of people completely dependent upon government handouts for their income. Third, it created a Democrat constituency which could be ceaselessly blackmailed into voting for the Democrat party utilizing the stick and carrot principal to curry votes. One must admire Johnson as one of the most effective mandarins in conspiratorial history.

The foremost factors in this culture war, however, have all been judicial. Every one of them was in violation of the precepts of American constitutional law. All were based on casework created for and by the judiciary, based on precedents which they themselves conjured up. Some of these were the Supreme Court decisions of *Engle vs. Vitale* in 1962 and *Roe vs. Wade* in 1973. More than any other decisions made by the court, these changed the entire fabric of American social structure. What these justices did was to divorce sex from any social commitment. Furthermore, they legislated the legal killing of unborn children. They acknowledged acceptance of pornography as a protected right. They laid the groundwork for the acceptance of homosexuality. They undermined the family structure and man's relationship with his creator.

George Washington in his farewell address to Congress stated:

> *"Of all the dispositions and habits which lead to political prosperity, religion and morality are indispensable supports."*

Without the basic tenants of family, morality, and ethics, society will fail. It has happened in every instance of recorded history. This does not change just because we live in a technologically advanced age.

The principal organizational entity responsible for the implementation of Satori cultural policy is the American Civil Liberties Union (ACLU). Their policy of divide and conquer has been very successful. Their modus operandi of utilizing the judiciary to implement their convoluted ideas has resulted in one success after another. They have supported every social aberration from the KKK to the rights of homosexuals to seduce minors of the same sex.

Reflect on one thing, the name of the group, "American Civil Liberties Union." Like all Satori sponsored names it is a lie. The ACLU has no interest in your civil liberties. If they did, their outlook would not be opposed by 90% of the American public. This name is similar to another Satori group. The Federal Reserve System (FRS). The Ú is not federal, it is not a reserve, and lastly it is not a system. It is a Satori monopoly of the American banking system.

The corrosion of religious principals and the destruction of our moral and ethical underpinnings has led us to the brink of disintegration. Today's high school graduate has no moral absolutes, everything being a different shade of gray. His scientific knowledge is minuscule, botany, biology chemistry, physics, and geology having long ago gone the way of the Dodo bird. His political knowledge is non-existent, since most teachers are not even aware that America is a republic. They believe it to be a democracy and moreover do not know the difference between the two. With an electorate like this, no wonder election campaigns are structured on 10-second sound bites. This, by the way, is exactly what the Satori want. In culture and education they have won.

One of America's greatest men, and in all probability the one who should have had a holiday named after him, was a black slave who in freedom, became a giant among men. He did not plagiarize what he wrote in his doctoral thesis, he wasn't even a college graduate. His name was Booker T. Washington. In the 1870s he made the following statement: *"Political activity alone cannot make men free. Back of the ballot box, he must have skill, economy, intelligence, and character."* Is it not interesting that the Satori are doing their utmost to ensure that today's youth will have neither character, skill, nor economy? Washington's writings, particularly his biography, clearly show that the former slave understood that freedom comes with responsibility, as well as privilege, and that a moral and ethical underpinning in a free society is of monumental importance.

The former Roman Catholic prelate of Philadelphia, John Cardinal Krol, said it best when he stated, *"Government has the responsibility of articulating a public morality for the common good of society, and for the happiness and security of it's citizens. If government does not encourage the teaching of virtue and morality, it gives by default free reign to vice."*

The world appears to me to be traveling in a car on a nice sunny day with the radio playing an aria from *Il Travatore* sung by Pavarotti. When all at once we enter a tunnel, our radio turns to static, the air becomes foul. It is dark. We turn on the lights, but it remains dark inside. We open the windows, but foul air rushes in. We stick a tape in the radio, but it's the Zombies. This, it seems to me, is exactly what is happening to our society. We appear hopelessly trapped in a Satori construction lacking both the ability and the will to correct the mishap.

Political Correctness (PC) is now one of the new tentacles of the Satori. We might as well begin with the Queen of PC, Donna Shalala. Shalala is not just another academian but a former administrator of the ultra-left University of Wisconsin where state courts had to intervene on several occasions due to her outrageous anti-male stances. She was brought into the cabinet at the insistence of Hillary Clinton who knew her well. Shalala is presently the head of the largest federal agency of the American government. Health and Human Services (HHS) employs some 120,000 bureaucrats, all of them bent on making life better for all of us through more government, more laws, more regulations, and micro-managing of everything by a bloated army of Mandarins. Like her friends, Janet Reno, Anita Achtenberg, and Tyson, she remains single. She was the unqualified champion of Hillary's failed attempt to socialize America's healthcare industry. She has proposed a value added tax (VAT) on numerous occasions. VAT happens to be the single most expensive tax to collect, both in cost and personnel. No nation that has instituted a VAT collects more the 10% of the total funds of the revenue, and in every single instance, the tax, once instituted, has been continuously increased. By the way, the government spends 70 cents of every dollar of Social Security taxes collected in administration costs. Shalala, along with all her "sisters," have continuously pushed for female combat status in our military as well as homosexual military participation, and she has instituted numerous odious pro-homosexual policies at HHS, which are clearly anti-religion, anti-social, and anti-western. She was the individual behind the successful effort to grant HIV infected Haitians immigration visas. She instituted the "Madison Plan" at the University of Wisconsin that required racial, and gender quotas for all students, faculty, and staff. The plan furthermore required ethnic studies in order to graduate.

Political Correctness (PC), is the insidious method to force our youth into clearly anti-social and anti-western thought patterns and to restructure society to be more amenable to Satori dictates.

FEDERAL FIREARMS LEGISLATION

HEARINGS

BEFORE THE

SUBCOMMITTEE TO INVESTIGATE
JUVENILE DELINQUENCY

OF THE

COMMITTEE ON THE JUDICIARY
UNITED STATES SENATE

NINETIETH CONGRESS

SECOND SESSION

PURSUANT TO

S. Res. 240

NINETIETH CONGRESS

ON

S. 3691

A BILL TO AMEND TITLE 18, UNITED STATES CODE

S. 3604

A BILL TO REQUIRE THE REGISTRATION OF FIREARMS

S. 3634

A BILL TO DISARM LAWLESS PERSONS

S. 3637

A BILL TO PROVIDE FOR THE ESTABLISHMENT OF A
NATIONAL FIREARMS REGISTRY

JUNE 26, 27, 28, AND JULY 8, 9, AND 10, 1968

Printed for the use of the Committee on the Judiciary

U.S. GOVERNMENT PRINTING OFFICE
WASHINGTON : 1968

THE U.S. 1968 GUN LAW IS VIRTUALLY IDENTICAL TO THE NAZI LAW OF 1938

GUN CONTROL

Let's face it, if you were intent upon controlling your fellow man, what would be your worst nightmare? Our forefathers well understood the power of the gun. The second amendment to the American constitution was their first thought after free speech. Why do you suppose this right was so prominent and so early considered by them? The retort to that is really very simple; without the second amendment to the constitution all the other guaranteed freedoms become worthless, as they will be unenforceable by the people.

The first step toward world government was the elimination of the civilian militias. A professional army is easily lead to control its own citizenry. All the great republics of the past had militias of citizens as their army . . . Greece, Rome (before it became a dictatorship), Switzerland, and Israel. Even more in step with control of civilian population is an international army, a multi-national UN force. First, the army is professional, unlike the militia which is made up of private citizens. Second, the force is integrated into a multi-national force without allegiance to any particular population. Third, this force is used in member states to implement the edicts of the rulers (Satori). The constant statement by the left is "it can't happen here!" Ha! Look at Somalia, Panama, Granada, Haiti, Cambodia, Iraq, Bosnia, and the over 50 other nation states where the UN is enforcing Satori control. At the present time there are over 100 conflicts worldwide, and the UN is directly involved in over half of them. How long will it be before it happens here? No reason to wait, the UN has a booklet out naming over two dozen American national parks as being under UN protection.

At the very core of our legal concepts is the right of citizens to own guns to protect themselves and their property. The prospect of even a professional army facing 250 million angry gun-owning citizens protecting their God-given and constitutionally written rights simply scares the hell out of the Mandarins, as well as the UN. For good reason. Consider that Afghanistan and Chechnya both fought the largest land army in the world to a standstill and eventual won.

All presently touted reasons to incorporate more gun laws, by such demagogues as congressman Charlie Schumer (D - NY), are nothing more then smoke screens for proxies of the Satori to deprive the American people of the ability to protect themselves and thus, to enforce their constitutional rights. All the arguments brought by the antigun lobby are specious, none having even a modicum of validity. The entire premise of the anti-gunners is that guns are bad. Guns are inanimate objects, without minds, they are neither bad nor are they good, they are just objects. Guns do not commit crimes, people do. Removal of guns from society does not work. A national statistic by counties of the entire United States brings this clearly to the fore. The statistic compares all counties utilizing two criteria: 1) gun ownership availability and legislation; and 2) crime. In every single instance, and in every single county in the United States, crime is lower where gun ownership laws are less restrictive. Counties in America with the most draconian gun laws have unilaterally the highest crime rates — I give you LA, Washington DC, and NYC. When I had a carry permit in NY I actually had to get a judge to sign my license, but I could purchase a gun on the street in front of my apartment house. No bill of sale, no waiting period, no sales tax, no BATF forms, no hassle, and at a price considerably lower than in the local gun store.

In 1920, Hitler was contemplating his "New World Order" when he came upon a little snag. Germany, during the 20s, had the highest per capita gun ownership in Europe. Austria, to be annexed in the Anschluss, was third. How was he going to implement his plans which would be opposed by many who owned guns and, knew how to use them? Hitler put to work the greatest minds of the NSP (National Socialist Party) and they jointly came up with a solution. The *Reichsgesetzblatt*, the

Nazi equivalent of the American Federal Register, published *Das Waffengesetz* on March 18, 1938. It was the new German law on the ownership of guns.

265

Reichsgesetzblatt

Teil I

1938	Ausgegeben zu Berlin, den 21. März 1938	Nr. 31

Tag	Inhalt	Seite
18. 3. 38	**Waffengesetz**	265
19. 3. 38	Verordnung zur Durchführung des Waffengesetzes	270
21. 3. 38	Ausführungsbestimmungen zu § 9 Abs. 2 Satz 2 und § 11 Satz 2 der Verordnung zur Durchführung des Waffengesetzes	276

Waffengesetz.

Vom 18. März 1938.

Die Reichsregierung hat das folgende Gesetz beschlossen, das hiermit verkündet wird:

Abschnitt I

Allgemeines

§ 1

(1) Schußwaffen im Sinne dieses Gesetzes sind Waffen, bei denen ein fester Körper durch Gas oder Luftdruck durch einen Lauf getrieben werden kann.

(2) Als Munition im Sinne dieses Gesetzes gilt fertige Munition zu Schußwaffen sowie Schießpulver jeder Art.

(3) Fertige oder vorgearbeitete wesentliche Teile von Schußwaffen oder Munition stehen fertigen Schußwaffen oder fertiger Munition gleich.

§ 2

Hieb- oder Stoßwaffen im Sinne dieses Gesetzes sind Waffen, die ihrer Natur nach dazu bestimmt sind, durch Hieb, Stoß oder Stich Verletzungen beizubringen.

Abschnitt II

Herstellung von Schußwaffen und Munition

§ 3

(1) Wer gewerbsmäßig Schußwaffen oder Munition herstellen, bearbeiten oder instand setzen will, bedarf dazu der Erlaubnis. Als Herstellen von Munition gilt auch das Wiederladen von Patronenhülsen.

(2) Die Erlaubnis darf nur erteilt werden, wenn der Antragsteller die deutsche Staatsangehörigkeit besitzt und im Reichsgebiet einen festen Wohnsitz hat.

(3) Der Reichsminister des Innern kann im Einvernehmen mit den beteiligten Reichsministern Ausnahmen von den Vorschriften des Abs. 2 zulassen.

(4) Die Erlaubnis darf ferner nur erteilt werden, wenn der Antragsteller und die für die kaufmännische oder für die technische Leitung seines Betriebes in Aussicht genommenen Personen die für den Betrieb des Gewerbes erforderliche persönliche Zuverlässigkeit und wenn der Antragsteller oder die für die technische Leitung seines Betriebes in Aussicht genommene Person die für den Betrieb des Gewerbes erforderliche fachliche Eignung besitzen.

(5) Die Erlaubnis darf nicht erteilt werden, wenn der Antragsteller und die für die kaufmännische oder für die technische Leitung seines Betriebes in Aussicht genommenen Personen oder einer von ihnen Jude ist.

§ 4

(1) Bei der Erteilung der Erlaubnis kann eine Frist bis zur Dauer eines Jahres bestimmt werden, innerhalb deren das Gewerbe begonnen werden muß, widrigenfalls die Erlaubnis erlischt. Ist eine Frist nicht bestimmt, so erlischt die Erlaubnis, wenn das Gewerbe nicht innerhalb eines Jahres nach Erteilung der Erlaubnis begonnen wird. Die Fristen können verlängert werden, wenn ein wichtiger Grund vorliegt.

(2) Die Erlaubnis erlischt ferner, wenn der Gewerbetreibende das Gewerbe seit einem Jahr nicht mehr ausgeübt hat, ohne daß ihm darüber hinaus eine Frist gewährt worden ist, innerhalb deren das Gewerbe wieder aufgenommen werden muß. Diese Frist beträgt höchstens ein Jahr; sie kann verlängert werden, wenn ein wichtiger Grund vorliegt.

(3) Der Gewerbetreibende hat binnen einer Woche schriftlich anzuzeigen, daß er das Gewerbe begonnen hat oder nicht mehr ausübt.

Reichsgesetzbl. 1938 I 72

In 1995, I read a book that absolutely astounded me, *Gun Control: Gateway to Tyranny* by Jay Simikin and Aaron Zelman, which was published by Jews for the Preservation Of Firearms of Milwaukee, Wisconsin. This text clearly demonstrates the relationship between the 1938 German law and the 1968 American law. In fact, it shows that the American law is virtually a verbatim copy of the Nazi gun law. On July 19, 1968, in a letter signed by Lewis C. Coffin, Law Librarian at the Library of Congress, to then Senator Thomas I. Dodd, (father of Senator Christopher Dodd [D - CT]), Coffin confirmed that Dr. William Solyom-Fekete had translated the Nazi gun law of 1938 for him, of which a copy was enclosed. *(See Appendix A)*

The book has the original German text in Gothic German, which I read well. The American translation is accurate and everything in the US 1968 law is identical to the Nazi law. What senator Dodd did was to have the Library of Congress translate the Nazi law, and then within just a few weeks offer the entire text for adoption by the US Senate as the Gun Control Act of 1968. I have no idea how you feel about this, but as for me, I'm dumfounded. *(See Appendices B, C, D)*

To prove the existence of a multi-national and multi-generational conspiracy such as I am discussing, at least two factors must be present:

1.) For multi-national, I must show acts by varying entities having differing national jurisdictions.
2.) For multi-generational, I must prove generational linkage.

Both of these requirements are amply met by the aforementioned situation.

In the takeover of any government by a would-be dictator, the first to suffer are invariably the minorities in that culture. Just ask a Jew, a Black, or a Gypsy. In America, virtually everyone has been identified by the legal system, or by the Mandarins, as some form of a minority. One substantial minority are

Blacks. Slave masters understood what power emanated from the gun, and slaves were not allowed to own guns. Even touching a gun could get a slave whipped. In the 1850s, then chief justice of the supreme court, Roger Brooke Taney, told Dred Scott that American free blacks could not, legally speaking, be free citizens, because if they were, they could carry guns wherever they went. Today, in most states, it is still ten times harder for a black to obtain a gun carry permit then it is for a white. Even after the Civil War, most states continued to make it very difficult for blacks to own or carry guns.

The Satori, understanding the relationship between master and slave very well, have an unrelenting fear of an armed citizenry. It is a predictable fact that our government will, within the next ten years, institute laws making gun ownership illegal. Once citizens are unarmed the Mandarins will, with the use of foreign surrogate troops under the UN banner, build up the courage to show their hand.

> *"Firearms stand next in importance to the Constitution itself. They are the American people's liberty teeth and keystone under independence . . . From the hour the Pilgrims landed, to the present day, events, occurrences and tendencies prove that to ensure peace, security and happiness, the rifle and the pistol are equally indispensable . . . The very atmosphere of firearms anywhere and everywhere restrains evil interference — they deserve a place of honor with all that's good . . ."*
>
> — George Washington

In 1928, in an effort to curb gang activity (fights between Nazi and Communist party thugs), all gun owners were registered. When the Nazis took power in 1933, they used the registration lists to seize guns from persons deemed "not reliable." The 1938 law enhanced the prior law and added handguns. Later that year another law restricted firearm ownership to Nazi Party members and other reliable people. Jews were forbidden to own any type of gun. The above picture should remind us of the grim results of gun registration.

How Did This Happen?

Masked gunmen who legally kill American men, women and children (Waco, Ruby Ridge, etc.), and a legal system in which a person is guilty until proven innocent (Rico Laws), is not our America, the "Land of the Free and Home of the Brave."

As in Germany's welfare state, it began with the "war against crime." What created the crime wave? New laws. Laws that made hiring help for miscellaneous jobs too expensive. Laws that destroyed family life. Laws that penalize honest work. And, laws that made drugs used by Americans for over 300 years, illegal, resulting in huge profits for those who promote and sell them. How do we rid ourselves of the masked gunmen? We get rid of welfare state collectivism and return to Americanism — individual freedom and responsibility.

THE NEW YORK TIMES, WEDNESDAY, MAY 20, 1936.

TEACHERS IN DRIVE ON LOYALTY OATH

Union Mass Meeting Pledged to a Renewed Fight Against 'Tyranny' in Schools.

RED INQUIRY BILL SCORED

Hundreds of Please to Lehman to Veto McNaboe Proposal Will Be Mailed Today.

A mass meeting held last night under the auspices of the Teachers Union at Washington Irving High School, Irvin Place and Sixteenth Street, launched a campaign for repeal of the Ives loyalty oath law.

The resolution appealed to labor, civic and progressive organizations to join with the teachers to combat "reactionary" legislation affecting teachers.

Charles J. Hundley, president of the Teachers Union; Professor George S. Counts of Teachers College, Columbia University, and Dr, Kirtley F. Mather of Harvard University spoke in bitter condemnation of loyalty oaths for teachers and students. Such measures, they said, were expressions of Fascist tendencies which might lead to a rule of "barbarism" here.

David Horowitz, noted author and scholar, whose parents belonged to the New York City Teachers Union, and were active members in the Communist Party, writes regarding his father's trip to Russia in 1932 as follows:

> "The trip was arranged by the New York Teachers Union, an organization the Party controlled . . ."[1]

Need we comment further regarding the radical changes made in the curriculum taught our children?

[1]*Radical Son, A Generational Odyssey,* David Horowitz

EDUCATION

Under the heading of education you should be informed that the National Education Association (NEA), which is the largest labor union in the world, spent more money on political lobbying efforts than did the National Rifle Association (NRA), US Chamber of Commerce, and Libertarian political party combined. Every cent was spent illegally. It is a violation of US statute to spend collected union dues for political purposes. Union dues are exclusively to be used for collective bargaining and pension expenditure. It is an indisputable fact that the NEA is the culprit behind the decline of American education. It is a fact that we can directly trace students' dropping aptitude scores to NEA unionization by county. The NEA's plebeian efforts to restructure and modernize our educational system remind one of a musical farce. All this is in keeping with the "New World Order." The Satori want unthinking, obedient dolts, and that is unquestionably what our educators are striving to produce in our public schools.

In a list of failed new programs, the latest and most precocious effort has now been introduced under the title of Goals 2000. This is really nothing more than an attempt to bring Outcome Based Education (OBE), into our school systems. OBE was first introduced in the Chicago school system some years ago, and within three years the average student aptitude score had fallen by 15%. In fact, in every country, state, county, and district where OBE was implemented it resulted in lower student output.

The two entities most directly involved in bringing OBE to fruition are the NEA and the United States Department of Education (USDE). Understanding outcome based education, or logic for that matter, is a simple matter. The most exhaustive book on the topic is *America 2000/Goals 2000 – Moving the Nation Educationally to the New World Order*. It is a voluminous 824 pages in 8½ x 11 format.

One thing is evident — the people who produced this odious and failed concept love slogans. The entire OBE diatribe as outlined in *Goals 2000* is riddled with sound-bite slogans such as: "all students can learn," "success breeds success," "all children will enter school ready to learn," and "first in the world in math and science." Not one of these stupid slogans addresses education or the process of teaching anyone anything. They are do-good, feel-good garbage, meaningless drivel to divert attention away from the real issues, and an attempt to blame parents for the failure of the edu-crats. Teachers cannot teach and students cannot learn in the absence of reasonable discipline and order. Our schools lack not only discipline, but they contain no understanding of morals, ethics, religion, or politics, which will make the product a poor one for a free society. In this total vacuum of the socially redeeming factors most important for a free society, our schools become nothing more than prisons to keep unruly children off the streets.

To have outcome determine the method and product of a process, to sit around in a circle, to have students work in groups, to make students feel good about themselves rather then to be correct, these are the foundations of OBE. Instead of teaching personal achievement and personal excellence or the process of logically thinking out a problem, students are taught to feel good about themselves, to be happy and well adjusted. What utter crap. When you reflect on the Satori's desired outcome, all this begins to make sense. Always remember the game plan. The Satori want:

1.) Obedient workers,
2.) Unquestioning organizational loyalty,
3.) A hedonistic self indulgent populace,
4.) Slavish materialism,
5.) No organized opposition.

These are the actual goals of OBE and its parent *Goals 2000*. The entire plan is for everyone to be employed either by government or a large multi-national corporation in perpetual servitude to a ruling elite. Our present educational system is designed to meet those ends. In education there should be but one objective: the maximum teacher effort toward the students' achieving personal excellence, everything else is a total waste of time and effort. Many teachers, students, and parents place more importance on sports and fluff than on the education of the young. I admonish you to keep an eye on the target. Place yourself in the position of the Satori, and then ask yourself, what do I, as a Satori, want?

It may be reasonably argued that the fathers of American socialism, the architects of the 20th century "New World Order" were none other than Woodrow Wilson and Franklin D. Roosevelt. Unbeknownst to most Americans, Roosevelt had no more to do with the end of the depression than the Civil War did with the instituting of the emancipation of slavery. The great depression was not caused by tariffs, but by the Federal Reserve,[2] and was brought to an end by the Second World War. What I recall about FDR were his many speeches and fireside chats broadcast over the radio (there was no TV at that time). What comes to mind now was one of those speeches in which he outlined what he referred to as his "Economic Bill of Rights." Among these rights FDR said "we have the right to an education, to healthcare, to a decent standard of living," etc., etc. These are all admirable and desirable things in a free society. However, they are not rights. Think about the American Constitution and the Bill of Rights — those men got it right. Every single item in the Bill of Rights does not cost you, or me, or the government one centime. These were God-given rights. FDR's "rights" are not free, they cost money, and someone other than the recipient must pay for them. Hence they are not rights, but

[2]*Free to Choose*, Milton and Rose Friedman

wants. At the basis of our modern education is the misconception that society owes its citizenry an education. This concept is pure socialism — a socialist educational system teaches socialist principals to its students. The very concept that I owe your children an education makes my blood boil. It is wrong, I don't owe your children anything. The basis of my argument is the concept of personal responsibility. We are, or should be, responsible for ourselves and our families. We are also responsible to society not to cause others dissimilitude. If I choose to have 6 children, then it is my responsibility to take care of them and to see to their education. That responsibility does not belong to my 60-year-old neighbor, who has already paid for his children. America has had tax funded education for about 100 years. What has the expenditure of billions of tax dollars achieved? Would not that amount of money have achieved much, much more in a competitive, free market eduational system? The right to learn is in the constitution, the 9th amendment allows us, at our own expense, to seek education. Think again about the Satori goal and why they want compulsory state-controlled, i.e., Satori-controlled, education. They want and need a uniform product to fit into their new world order (the subtitle of *America 2000/Goals 2000*).

WHO ARE THE MANDARINS?

It is the incredulous actions of the Mandarins who, through their acts of accommodation with the Satori, are at the forefront of destroying our constitutional republic. Unlike the mandarins of old China, these are not solely state employees. They are, in a roundabout way, workers for the Satori. As in 4th generation war, they are among us, particularly if you live in the northeastern USA, in London, Tokyo, or Brussels as the headquarters for numerous organizations are in those locations.

To understand the devious workings of the conspiracy you must first realize that the majority of the Mandarins are not aware that they are saddled with an ulterior occupation. They are ignorant of the conspiracy. This suits the top conspirators well, as it allows publicly believable deniability. The Satori, through control of finance, media, and foundations, are able to reward their Mandarins with promotions, stipends, grants, and financial remuneration at will. They are also the world's greatest dispensers of power. This powerful force of money and influence is the method by which Mandarins are rewarded. Take, for example, the meteoric rise of Dwight D. Eisenhower and Alexander Haig in the American military, or the catapulting of Henry Kissinger — even the resettlement of Mikhail Gorbachov to San Francisco. They have served well and been well rewarded.

The Satori control the Mandarins through numerous surrogate organizations around the globe. Some, like the Council On Foreign Relations (CFR) are national; some, like the Trilateral Commission are international; and some, like the Bilderbergers or Bones are secret. Through leadership of those organizations, they control governments, foundations, labor unions, and centers of finance in the G7 nations. There are approximately 5,000 Mandarins worldwide. The payroll of the Mandarins comes from your taxes (about 75%) and the balance from foundations and union dues.

AMERICANA

What will the Satori call their capitol? If historic memory serves me well, I would guess that Karakorum has the proper historic ring to it. The already implemented NAFTA plan is in full swing as I write this chapter, not withstanding current congressional efforts to rewrite this disastrous treaty. America, Canada, and Mexico are in an economic union which will automatically consummate in the year 2005. Meanwhile our Secretary of State under the first Clinton administration returned in the fall of 1996 from a trip to Asuncion, Buenos Aires, and San Paulo where, in February, he most decisively informed the assembled leaders of Chile, Argentina, and Brazil of our government's plan for an American continent under NAFTA. One must assume that a $5.4 billion trade surplus with Mexico, now a $16.7 billion deficit since the inception of NAFTA, must be a good thing for the citizens of the USA. The new Satori-inspired and American-introduced organization is to be called Free Trade Area of the Americas (FTAA). Bingo! An American EC. The only amazing thing about this is that it was not reported in one single American newspaper, and where it was reported not one person noticed the parallel with the European Common Market (EC).

As you can see, the Satori are far ahead of all of us. In order to keep up with their antics we must read the press of a dozen different nations. How could anyone seriously claim that he cannot see a connection between what has been instituted in the old world and what is being brought to fruition in the new? The plans are basically identical. Just as in Europe the less affluent southern nations will have their standard of living increased at the expense of their northern neighbors. Who can deny that the standard of living in North America and Northern Europe are not declining even as you read these lines? And furthermore, who can deny that the southern regions of these trade accords are not better off since their inception?

In order for the Satori to implement this plan of world control they must first align the economies to a parallel and equal status. North America and Europe are not alone in this; the exact same thing is transpiring in Japan vs. Korea, Taiwan, and the other economies of the Pacific Rim. All the great economic successes of the later part of the 20th century are the primary targets of the Satori. The Satori long ago became internationalists whose holdings are not tied to any single economy. They

NAFTA is Scheduled to Become FTAA

Free Trade Area of the America's*, with the inclusion of Chile, Argentina, Brazil and other Central and South American nations. FTAA's Secretariat controlling all trade, is to be located in Texas.*

control all the money markets, and as a wise man upon founding the Federal Reserve System (FRS) once said, "Give me control of the money, and everything else will follow" (US Senator Aldridge).

Consolidation of the North and South American economies would be nothing short of a disaster for those of us living in North America. In order to achieve economic parity, our standard of living will have to be reduced by more than half.

This will be attained through the gradual de-industrialization of the northern regions, while industrializing the southern ones. This, make no mistake about it, is happening as you read. It is indisputable. The UN's own statistics, as well as those from the World Bank, verify it. Already, since the inception of NAFTA, Mexican industrial production has increased by 18.9%, while in the neighboring north (the U.S.A.) over 3 million manufacturing jobs have been lost. This is not unlike what is happening in Europe. With the exception of the Germans and the French who are resisting the Satori, we Americans are being led to the slaughter like sheep. The Europeans have a longer tradition and are nationally more monolithic in culture as well as in trade, but they are succumbing just as we are.

Always remember that the Satori have no national, social, or religious allegiance to anything, except each other, and thus their loyalty is to money and power, whereas yours is to family, community, country, and, I hope, to God. They do not carry this additional weight and thus act differently from the rest of us. I have known and met many people who are intimate with this power structure and who curry favor with the Satori. They are people who will go to any lengths to seek favor with the masters, people who want to appear sophisticated, worldly, as insiders. They will tell you that love of country is jingoistic, that religion is the opium of the masses, and that character does not matter. What a sad world they envision: a place where you can trust no one, a place where people believe in nothing, a place without honor, character, ethics, or morals.

THE MANTLE OF CHARLEMAGNE

The world's most visible international consolidation is the EC. Remember that the Satori are of the old world in character and makeup. In order to understand the European Union and the reason for the pressure to create and expand the EC you must have an understanding of past European unification and consolidation efforts. When Julius Caesar conquered the Gauls, the Helvitians, and the Germanic tribes of central Europe he created the first European union. When the emperor Hadrian subsequently unified the British isles south of the Hadrian wall, a new union of Europe spanned the continent from the rivers Rhine and Fino in the north to substantial parts of the middle east in the south. After the collapse of the Roman Empire, Europe would again be united under the reign of Charlemagne. This was the first Christian empire. Karl Der Grosse had unified Europe as heir of the Roman empire. He called himself the Holy Roman Emperor, and placed his capitol at Aachen, Germany. European visionaries have long been enthralled with the prospect of covering themselves with the mantle of Charlemagne. Napoleon, Mussolini, and Hitler are examples of this.

Throughout the decades, European aspirations for a new Christian empire has remained, and our clever friends the Satori, have seized the opportunity, taking advantage of these desires in order to bring about unification under their control. Present day Europe is not all that different from that of the past. Consider the monetary alliance present and past between the low counties and Germany. Consider the French with their Grand Nation political aspirations, or the British who have always remained outsiders and who are much more tied to America than Europe. England was never Euro-centric. This phenomenon is wholly continental in nature. The basic idea of a Euro-centric Christian national entity has been a significant historic fact for centuries. Once we understand that this is a continental concept we will be able, under closer scrutiny, to see a group of alliances that are the primary protagonists in this unification process. The monetary alliance is Germany's Die Deutche Bundesbank and their Dutch and Belgian allies. They represent the financial power in the EC. France, with arguably the finest diplomatic corps and the most developed bureaucracy (even the word is French), has the best diplomats in the world and therefore controls the intellectual and social development. The British remain, as always, the outsiders but not without influence. The rest remain basically impotent due to one of the following factors:

1.) Relative size compared to the rest,

2.) Political instability,

3.) Economic weakness compared to Germany, France, and Britain.

This then, tells us that the Satori are active in controlling the economies and structure of France, England, Germany, and the Low countries where they use their superb organizational skills in the expansion and control of the EC. The principal Mandarin organization responsible for this are the Bilderbergers. They are the European Mandarins in the service of the Satori.

The primary problem with European unification is not social or political in nature, but is instead monetary. Monetary unification has been the greatest obstacle to the unification process, it is also, to the Satori, the most important. The obstacle to monetary unification is that in order for European monetary union to become a reality, five factors, as outlined in the treaty of Maastricht, must be met by all partners:

1.) Inflation may not exceed 1.5% above the average of the 3 lowest states.

2.) The average prime interest rate may not exceed 2% over the lowest 3 states.

3.) The actual deficit of any applying state without the inclusion of unemployment compensation and social security payments may not be more than 3% of the GNP.

4.) The total state debt may not exceed 60% of the GNP.
5.) Exchange rates with the primary EC member states must not have had any major problems within 2 years prior to application.

Only two nations in Europe can meet these criterion, Germany and Luxembourg, but with the rising unemployment in Germany they will not qualify by the end of 1997. Other nations in the EC have deficits as high as 9% and debt up to 139% of GNP.[3]

These treaty obligations were no haphazard arrangement. They were dictated by the Bundesbank, who did not want to see their hard-earned Mark devalued by some international debacle, nor watch their currency debased, but who have since waived the economic requirements to allow the Satori plan for monetary unification to proceed.

The remnants of the two major European political systems discussed in this book demonstrate an interesting fact: namely, the two opposing systems have a great deal more in common with one another than either will admit. Where the Russians have their Apparatchiks, the Europeans have Eurocrats. Brussels is awash with a mind-boggling array of bureaucrats that can easily rival Moscow. Their respective ideologies do not differ greatly. Both are enamored with the idea of doing away with the nation state. Both believe that their particular system will lead the world to some imaginary Nirvana. Both speak of a utopian classless society.

Now consider NAFTA and the American movement in the same direction, with the same goals — thanks to Satori active involvement Europe is already pre-federalized. America is next! Structurally, all the necessary arrangement for a single centralized authority is already in place, both in Europe and America.

[3]*Schweizerische Demokraten*, Jan./Feb. 1996, Europaeische Waerungsunion-eine groteke.

Why did you think that the NAFTA treaty exceeds 900 pages?

In the NAFTA nations, a secretariat with much the same structure and purpose as the European structure in Belgium, is to be set up in Texas. Implementation and legislative passage of all trade treaties in the US as well as in Europe — NAFTA, GAT, WTO, and Maastricht also share one commonality — not a single one of them was read by the legislators who voted for them, because they were not published until after ratification. As you can see, the Mandarins write a treaty binding numerous nations into a pact, do not publish it, but get the elected officials of the signatory states to vote for ratification without even knowing what they have voted for, or even what it is all about. So much for constitutional representation.

Let us again reflect on the Satori plan — world domination. Let us consider how one would accomplish such an endeavor. Obviously it would be impossible to control over 200 different nation states, and the millions of businesses contained therein. Just as a plain fact, Rockefeller controls the Chase Manhattan Bank with only 9% of the outstanding stock. You see, total control of everything is not a requirement. If you just control the G7 industrialized nations plus certain raw material deposits in Russia and South Africa, you can effortlessly rule by intimidation. To ease that control burden the G7 block has been separated into three different entities managed by varying groups of Mandarins: the Bilderbergers do Europe, the Council on Foreign Relations does North America, and the Trilateral Commission does the Pacific Rim.

Do not think that these three organizations represent the totality of Satori-Mandarin structure — there are, in fact, many others.

JAPAN

Japan is without a doubt the most advanced nation on the Pacific Rim. It therefore stands to reason that they would, along with other G7 nations, be involved in the global plan. This is particularly the case because of the structure of Japan's economy. Japan, unlike the rest of the industrial nations, has closed markets and consists basically of less than ten production enterprises. This small number of businesses controls the entire economy of the country. With just over 100 members in the TC-Mandarin organization representing one third of that membership, Japan is strongly involved. Japan's industrial makeup would be called feudal if such a thing actually existed. With less than ten firms controlling over 70% of industrial output and the balance working full time for them, a classic feudal system is in operation. This is exactly what the Satori want in the rest of the world as such systems are easily controlled by a very small group.

Due to this structure in which even labor unions tote the line, it is easy to manipulate the entire society. The fact that Japan came out of a feudal society less than 100 years ago, has made the transition from hereditary warlords to industrial lords effortless. The current structure that exists in Japan is the model for the EC and FTAA nations. This plan includes the structure of a small number of very large multi-national corporations managed by a corps of professional business managers, Mandarins.

The acceleration of international corporate mergers in the last decade is unprecedented. The total number of operating large corporations keeps getting smaller, while the size of these firms continues to grow. Centers of control for political construction will be Brussels for the EC, Texas[4] for FTAA (North & South America), and Tokyo for the Pacific Rim.

[4]Ibid.

This then brings us to the rest of the Pacific Rim nations, and why they have not been included so far. The largest problem remains the PRC. China's economy is growing at a rate of about 10% per year, and has done so for the last ten years. At the present rate of growth, China will overtake America as the largest economy in the world around the turn of the century. China is not an international team player, and who can fault them for that. China's external relationships in the past have consistently proven disastrous for them. China remains the only major player which has no known association with the conspiracy.

The balance of the Pacific Rim nations have numerous treaties and working arrangements among themselves and with outside influences. Japan has found it difficult to assert political authority over the region due to Second World War treatment of many of these nations by Japan.

Operative agreements and treaties for the gradual consolidation of Pacific Rim nations into an EC type of arrangement are proceeding as you read. Planned participation at present include Japan, Australia, New Zealand, The Philippines, Indonesia, Singapore, Thailand, and Korea (South). What will happen to North Korea and Taiwan is still impossible to ascertain. A guess would be Korean unification and the unification of Taiwan with China.

Once all this is in place there will be three major related trading blocks in the world: EC, FTAA, and Pacific Rim. In essence this will then create a situation in which China will be an outsider. Russia will eventually join the EC or become a free agent, and the economic war for control of economic resources located in the Middle East, Siberia, and Africa will be waged.

WILD CARDS

Islam

As they say, the best laid plans of man or beast . . . In all the nefarious Satori plans, they appear to have simply ignored some very big players in the global environment. By far, the most important of these with worldwide consequence is Islam. Satori influence in the Islamic nations is superficial at best. In Muslim nations where they do have a presence, it is restricted to small minorities of the ruling elite whose rule is based on fear and bribery, and thus is weak. The fundamentalist tide that is emanating from Iran's Shiite sect has already infected most Shiite communities. Furthermore, the Sunni sect is not without its fundamentalist factions. It is the author's opinion, who has traveled widely in the Middle East, that it is only a matter of time before someone effects some sort of a unified Islamic Jihad. Individuals not familiar with Islam tend to underrate the situation. One should never lessen the potential of any religious group, who in their opinion has God on their side. They are particularly exemplary in 4th generation warfare.

The linchpin in Middle Eastern politics is Egypt, where the secular government is in serious trouble. The present circumstances in Egypt rotate around a government which is presently unable to trust its own state agencies and must send troops from Cairo to other parts of the nation to effect their edicts. If I were a gambling man, I would place my bets on an Islamic fundamentalist state in Egypt within the next few years. As the most populated state in the region, and one of the intellectual centers of Islam, this is a factor that cannot be overlooked. Turkey has, for the first time since their revolution that westernized the country, elected a fundamentalist as head of state. Turkey is in NATO, and is the long-standing buffer between Western Europe and the Middle East. Most Western analysts do not clearly understand Islamic social and religious thought, and for this reason considerable errors of judgment are evident in that orbit. Western Europe's and, in particular, America's one-sided support of Israel will come to haunt us all.

Unlike present Western political thought, in Islam there is a direct and historic relationship between state and religion which is similar to 16th century Europe. This has been the situation from the beginning when Mohammed crafted his group of followers into a theocracy. The relationship between the governed and the rulers has historically been one of a head of state who is at the same time leader of religious life and rules under Islamic law in the name of Islam. This is the principal reason for the remarkable staying power of Islamic heads of state. Note that this is not the case in secular Islamic nations where assassination is the most common way in which governments change. Islam is the fastest growing religion in the world and presently has well over one billion adherents. There are many admirable traits associated with Islam, and that, plus aggressive recruiting, makes them very successful. Unfortunately, the fundamentalists tend to go to excess and are often not in alignment with the Prophet. The Koran, for example, strictly forbids the taking of hostages, and nowhere does it propose or promote terrorism as a tool of the church. Even in holy Jihad there are very strict rules of engagement which, by the way, are substantially more civilized than the way Islam has been treated by its opponents over the centuries.

All this has a decidedly chilling effect when you consider that the two largest Islamic nations in the Middle East have related political problems. To this we can add the Kurds, Muslims who live in Turkey, Iran, and Iraq, and we have what may be called a boiling cauldron. Turkey is in NATO and guards the Dardanelles, the historic point of invasion of Europe and vice versa throughout history.

There is no doubt that were Turkey and Egypt to become Islamic Fundamentalist states, the world would become a very different place. Remember that the adherents to Islam are one billion plus strong and are considerably more animated in their convictions then we are. It is also wise to remember that the most populated Islamic state is not in the Middle East but on the Pacific Rim. For a reason known only to God, Islamic nations control the bulk of all the world's oil, a commodity the rest of us cannot forego.

Minerals

The second factor of almost comparable import is the world distribution of minerals. Any equation for power must seriously consider this. The largest mineral deposits in the world are unevenly distributed in a very few geographic locations. The largest deposits, and those most easily mined, are located in southern Africa. The second cache is in Siberia, and the balance is in North America. In order to maintain their grip on the southern half of Africa, the Satori have destabilized that part of the world for many decades. Siberia is only now, with the aid of Western technology, beginning to be a viable producer. The climate and political system, however, make this a very hard place for the production of anything. Russia has long been under the influence of the Satori. Since its recent collapse, however, their political system has, until now, kept them inactive in international affairs.

China

China, with over one billion citizens and good natural resources, appears to have been completely overlooked by the Satori. This fact really perplexed me until I realized that China has been a closed society for most of the 20th century. Satori influence and interference has been minimal in China. It is, in all probability, the only large resource of any kind of which that statement may be made. The growth of the PRC economy, which is projected to overtake America's in 2002, makes China a big player in global matters. In 1997, China took control of Hong Kong, without a doubt the prize economy of the East. It gives China access to markets which they were previously unable to reach. It provides 6 million free market-trained people. It will accelerate Chinese industry, production, and distribution to levels heretofore unthought of. Speculatively, if all goes well with Hong Kong, it is not unreasonable to expect that Taiwan will be reunited with the mainland. This would give China another dramatic spurt in growth. China could be the superpower of the 21st century if they stay on track.

In summation, regarding these Wild Cards, the Satori plan has several large holes in it. I am not privy to any manner they may have devised to cope with these matters. It would, however, not be unreasonable to assume that the Satori feel they can control, or at least influence, the Wild Cards.

FOURTH GENERATION WAR

Just as in the Napoleonic period of history, warfare, at the beginning of the 21st century, is in a state of immense change. Unfortunately, the established military cadre of the world have not accepted this as reality. As demonstrated so well in Johan Await's diary of the 1770s, a completely new concept of warfare was developed. The Prussians produced what they called the Jaeger concept. This strategy had never before been used and was brought on by the firearm. Jaeger, in German, simply means hunter and in Germany forests are still kept by foresters who are also the gamekeepers. What the Prussians did was to organize Jaegers into small combat companies which were loosely organized to fight independently rather than in skirmish lines, as was the practice at the time. This was a very radical concept and it was frowned upon by all military leaders. But not by Napoleon, who quickly noticed that these Jaeger units were not only more successful than regular military configurations, they delivered staggering losses upon all whom they engaged. Some of these units wound up in the American revolutionary war in 1775-78 where they proved equally effective against the colonials. American units, after several severe defeats to this new fighting method, adopted it themselves. American Indians were not the originators of this concept as is often thought. The Indians used similar methods but without a command or control structure. So we see that in a very short time this concept, which came to be called the Jaeger idea, turned 18th century war strategy on its head. After this period in history, the Jaeger concept was forgotten until the Germans again employed it in their very successful Blitzkrieg of the Second World War. All militaries had to rapidly adjust to this new strategy or, as happened with the French, be swept away in defeat. That was third generation warfare. In the latter part of the 20th century the gradual development of 4th generation warfare began to emerge, primarily in German occupied territory and most pronouncedly in the Balkans.

Fourth generation warfare is as radically different from the third as the third generation is from knights in armor. In fact, the difference is far greater then the previous change from 2nd to 3rd It has become painfully obvious that present military structure is wholly unable and unwilling to grapple with this new warfare method. The concepts of 4th generation warfare are that the war is not necessarily between national entities. Just this first point drives the established military right up the wall. The first rule of all previous wars was that the enemy represented an established military and national entity. This will not be the case for future wars. Another factor is that previous armies wore a recognizable uniform identifiable by the enemy. This is no longer the case. In previous wars definable and established lines of battle allowed commanders to peruse rigid plans of attack and defense. This is no longer the case. Modern warfare establishes no lines of battle. Present military conflicts around the world number just over 100. Almost none of these involve any established national entity, all are based on religious, ethnic, tribal, or racial grounds. They are transitional. Another concept is that the enemy is not identifiable. In fact, the enemy may be within your own national entity. The enemy does not wear uniforms or any other identifiable markings and is usually mixed in with the civilian population. There is no capital to attack, there is no recognizable command and control center to capture, there are no identifiable enemy concentrations. The enemy, thus can be, and is, everywhere and anywhere. Modern military organizations simply are not designed to cope with such a situation. 4th generation war is much more suited to police (i.e., detective and military) infiltration units.

Consider Hamas, Bader Meinhof, Islamic Jihad, or any of the hundreds of terrorist groups running around the world. England, America, France, Spain, India, Russia, China — in fact almost every nation in the world has experienced terrorist 4th generation war during the latter half of the 20th century. Where previous war had generally been static, 4th generation is dynamic. In late 3rd generation war, defense lines were constructed parallel to the enemy aggressor. In 4th there are no lines because there is no definable enemy position. I am confident the reader will understand the extreme difficulty that this places on our military.

Unlike our government, the Satori, who have financed just about every war in the last 100 years, not only understand the concept but use it to their advantage. They use it to create social change. It is a fact that when given the option of safety or freedom, most people choose safety. If you create enough civil fear through bombings, kidnappings, mass murder, and then have the media bombard the public about gun owner nuts you create an atmosphere where the population will accept the state's confiscation of firearms for their safety. Consider that in our present crime-wracked society the media and our elected officials do not offer anti-crime performance but instead give us gun control. In fact, the loss of individual rights in the last 20 years has accelerated into a blur of speed. Much of this was brought about by 4th generation war which facilitated the legislative oppressive acts. In Western culture led by Germany, England, and America, the growth of legal statute during the last half of the 20th century has been nothing short of astounding. Every single law enacted in some small way reduces the amount of personal freedom all of us enjoy. Consider that in America, since Eisenhower's term, more laws have been enacted than in the previous 200 years of American history. Everyone must realize that this cannot be allowed to continue.

Our current military is process oriented, i.e. the existing command and control systems are dictated through established process. This is with regards to all field operations. Such a command and control system based on military dogma of past combative strategy cannot hope to respond to the new paradigm without severe losses, both civilian and military. Any attempt at forceful reaction upon the civilian population where the 4th generation unit is hiding will prove counterproductive. It will lead to frustration by the military and the command structure with deterioration into Martial Law and eventually into totalitarian government. All this will happen while alienating the very citizens the system is designed to protect.

The Satori, ever mindful of opportunity, see this as a watershed for their plans. Thus they finance through surreptitious means most of the paramilitary terrorist groups around the world.

The most successful opposition to 4th generation war has been the militia-type of citizen military. For terrorism to succeed, any base of national citizen soldiers must be neutralized. Examples of successful counter-4th generation war can presently be seen only in Israel.

It is my impression that terrorism, which is really what 4th generation warfare is, cannot be fought by the military structure as it is currently organized. The only way to successfully combat this plague is through an organized, locally instituted militia. The militia members must come from the same community and have known each other for a considerable time. In this way they are impossible to infiltrate. Furthermore, they are already in position to handle the situation. They will have an automatic surveillance system in place, and thus will be immediately able to identify an outsider.

In the last decade the Satori have viciously and relentlessly attacked, through their media surrogates, any and all militias. Today most citizens feel that the militias are a bunch of Nazi racist nuts. The second important reason the Satori want to obliterate the militias is that they are difficult, if not impossible, to control, a fact that was appreciated by the Founding Fathers when they instituted a national militia rather than a professionally paid army. The third reason is that any militia will, by nature, resist any foreign (non-national) influence and will not obey orders which are contrary to their community interests. Last but not least it would prove burdensome to attempt international (UN) takeover of militias. All this makes militias very untenable for the Satori. They present a powerful force in opposition to Satori plans. Thus the general direction in which we are being led is the formation of a UN-based international army whose allegiance will be to the UN power structure. By heavily integrating various national entities it has proven possible to utilize these forces in opposition to the national character of any national entity. Haiti, Somalia, and Macedonia are examples of this.

In 1996, at numerous American military installations, servicemen were given a questionnaire to fill out. Some of the questions are more than revealing of the nature of the general plan.

Q. Would you accept orders from a non-American officer?

Q. Would you serve in a UN army ?

Q. Would you, if ordered, shoot at American citizens?

This questionnaire, containing numerous other offensive questions, could be viewed as a test; a test most servicemen,

based on their responses, have failed. Where does this get us? Well, we currently have foreign troops of battalion strength training in the United States. Just some of the nations training here are: Germany (including a full airforce wing), France, Russia, Pakistan, Italy, Spain, Saudi Arabia, and England.

Two great books on the subject, both entitled *The Art of War,* are certainly worth reading. Each book points out the social, political, and civil consequences of war which appear to be missing from current thought. Both Machiavelli's and Sun Tzu's books clearly show the overbearing need for intelligence prior to and during any military engagement. The concentrated, and certainly successful, effort of the Satori to destroy Western military, as well as civilian, intelligence is an historic fact. Through various means — exposure of spies, demoralization of agencies (i.e., the CIA), and the ludicrous effort to replace human agents with spy satellites — Western intelligence agencies have been neutered. In the US, the CIA, for instance, has been run by a Satori surrogate for the last five presidential administrations, and is today, a mere shadow of what it should be. The Satori, which operate the world's largest and most complex spy system, are undoubtedly anxious about any potential competitor.

Who are these military organizations that represent 4th generation war? The Irish Republican Army (IRA), Spain's Basque separatists (ETA), Hamas (the Iranian client group), Sekigun (the Japanese red army), Fatah (the Palestinian group), RAF (red army faction), RAB (red army brigade in Italy), Black June and Black September (both Middle East), and M19 (Columbia). This is really only the tip of the iceberg, but it does prove my point. All of these groups have a number of things in common. They are basically all cowards, they attack only targets unable to defend themselves. They champion the cause of the people, the very individuals whom they hurt. Their espoused goals represent utopian stupidity. They are financed from outside (during the Evil Empire many were KGB funded). They desire social change which they invariably attain, in the form of suppressive government. All this, of course, plays into the hands of the Satori: most of the control lost by citizens is transferred to the Satori-controlled centralized structure.

The serious action in 4th generation warfare is not in the small terrorist acts that may kill a few hundred people, but in the large theater operations like Bosnia, Macedonia, and Chechnya. The Russians, with the largest land army in the world, have already lost in Afghanistan and Chechnya. NATO, after the UN loss in Bosnia, is in a quagmire — a situation that will revert to war the instant the UN's NATO troops are withdrawn.[4]

[4]NATO is affiliated with the United Nations, as is SEATO, under whose auspices we fought in Korea and Vietnam.

Today's militaries are unable to win this type of warfare (think of Vietnam) simply because the rules of the game have been changed. The militaries are not trained for this. They are not commanded for this. The concept of pacified enclaves within a hostile controlled geographic region as tried in Vietnam and Afghanistan is nonsensical. There is only one way to succeed in a terrorist war. To win, you must, 1) get the citizens to support your position; 2) develop a citizen militia made of regionally local people; 3) train and supply them. Such a system will eradicate the problem in short order. A confrontational military solution is not in the stars.

The Satori understand these principles all too well, and thus are active in academia, religion, and politics, who then, through their media control, build public consensus in support of their position. In this way opposing force loses by default. The populace becomes so fed up with terrorism, fractionalization, racial and religious strife, and class envy, that they will accept any draconian laws or rules imposed upon them which promise to create safety and security.

To be able to impact this form of war in any way you must clearly understand that the terrorists have in their mind a specific goal. Furthermore, we must understand that they are simply a tool of the people financing them, who in all probability have an entirely different outcome in mind.

Oklahoma Bombing

Consider the terrorist act of the bombing in Oklahoma City of a federal office building. The circumstances of it are so peculiar as to leave one confused. Without going into that, what was the outcome of the bombing? An insane attempt by the executive to institute the "Anti-Terrorism" bill in Congress and a call for stricter gun control. Media attempted linkage to a militia. One can only call the circumstances bizarre.

THE NEW WORLD ARMY

For the last 15 years the consorted effort to develop a multinational UN army has been escalating as one of the primary Satori activities. It is interesting to speculate that with the possible exception of Korea, every single UN military sponsored action was a total flop. In fact the only UN military action that did not result in a total loss was Korea. A "conflict" in which the UN policy was stalemate, not victory. The present American Executive, whose military experience may be measured in minutes, is at the forefront of turning US armed forces over to the UN.

As a former soldier who has had plenty of exposure to the militaries of Germany, France, Italy and Holland, as well as several others, the recurring problems are simple for me to explain. It is, as I am quite certain, well understood by our military, that the following factors differ between armies:

Training
Command and Control
Equipment
Armaments
Insignia
Structure
Language

Every one of these differs sufficiently so as to make militaries, even within alliances like NATO, incompatible. There is also, of course, unit cohesion which is not possible in a multi-national outfit. The Germans knew this well during the Second World War. Units allied to the German Heer where kept in contact with their own officers and non-coms. The Wermacht consisted only of Germans, but they had Dutch, French, Croat, Russian, Polish, Czech, and Rumanian troops under their command. Historically, others did the same thing: Egyptians, Romans, Greeks, Macedonians (Charlemagne), and French (Napoleon). But Butros Butros-Ghali, a Coptic Egyptian bureaucrat, knew better.

The growth of the American contingent at the UN, according to USA Major Joseph F. Napoli, Chief of the UN Department of Peacekeeping, has been nothing if not exponential since Clinton came to the White House. A staff of 23 with 6 officers ballooned into one of 315 with 160 officers by the fall of 1995. Napoli should know he is the military advisor to the Secretary General of the UN. By treaty, the commander of all UN forces is a Russian. During the formation of the UN in San Francisco one of our traitors, Alger Hiss, saw to that. We still adhere to it, just like the ABM treaty, even though the evil empire is long gone.

Our State Department, which is responsible for treaties and agreements, is staffed by an unimaginable troop of ludite ideologues who don't work for "We The People" but for the Satori. A prime example of this is John Naisgitt, the author of *Global Paradox*. In this work he states:

> *The good news is that human-rights violations are being exposed wherever they occur, and in the international community, not a single country is assuming the role of enforcer and peace-keeper (the UN is).*

It would be wonderful if Mr. Naisgitt could travel to, say, China, Tibet, Mongolia, Iran, Liberia, Nigera, Cuba, or North Korea and give all their citizens his fine message.

To understand the plan we must examine current history. In 1992, the UN had 11,496 military personnel deployed worldwide in peacekeeping operations. This number increased to 73,469 by 1994, (not counting Bosnia) with troops located in 17 different nations. The operating costs were US $3.6 billion, of which the US assessment was $1.6 billion. The net result of those 17 incursions was 17 Losses. Interestingly, the American Government Accounting Office (GAO), disputes UN numbers claiming instead, that as early as 1992 peace-keeping costs at the UN exceeded US $10 billion for that year, in US assessment alone.

Naisgitt, shill for the Satori, goes on in his book to suggest that "UN military operations should be drastically expanded

One Day – The Victim Could Be You!

UN Peacekeepers, Claude Baert and Kurt Coelus, Belgian paratroopers, punish a Somali they accused of stealing. No trial, no jury.

so that world government would have an army to enforce its edicts." He goes on with "Such military should rival even that of the United States" and "Such troops could even be deployed in the United States." Now we're at the crux of the matter. Indigenous military of any country would hesitate enforcing foreign UN initiatives and laws on its own people. This is the one, and the only, reason for a continuously expanding UN army. If a military force is composed primarily of third world initiates it would not hesitate to enforce with prejudice any UN orders upon the citizens of the host nation.

On January 31, 1992 Butros Butros-Ghali made the following proclamation on behalf of the UN:

> *"Under article 42 of the UN charter, the Security Council has authority to take military action to maintain or restore international peace and security . . . This will require bringing into being, through negotiation, the special agreement foreseen in article 43 of the charter, whereby member states undertake to make armed forces assistance and facilities available to the security counsel for the purpose stated in article 42, not only on an ad hoc basis but on a permanent one."*

The Satori regard the UN military as their private little army. The Clinton administration has done everything possible to facilitate that occurrence. The previous Bush administration did exactly the same thing. I quote:

> *"My vision of a New World Order foresees a United Nations with a revitalized peacekeeping function. It is the sacred principals enshrined in the U.N. Charter to which we henceforth pledge our allegiance."*
>
> — George Bush, February 1, 1992

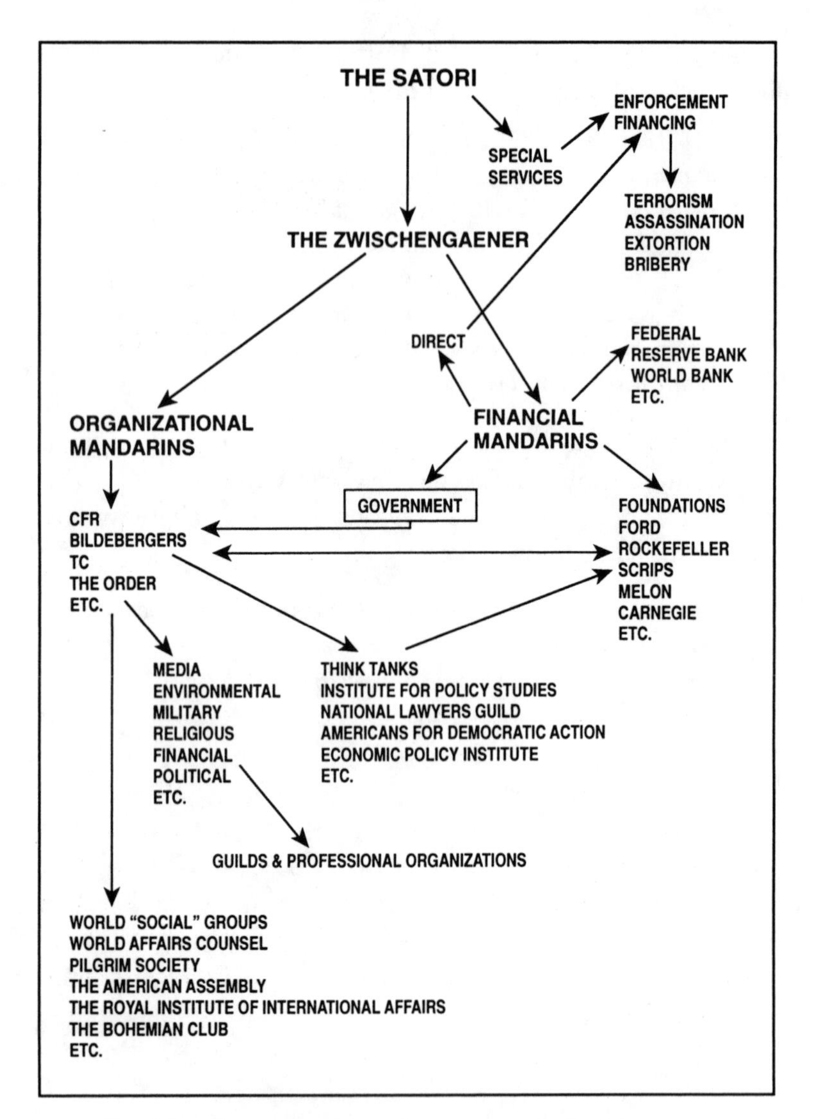

The above diagram is a basic illustration of the Satori organizational structure. Space does not allow the listing of all groups, nor their interlocking activities.

CHAPTER FOUR

THE MACHINE

SATORI ORGANIZATIONAL STRUCTURE

It is difficult to understand that the Satori control so much in the spheres of media, politics, and finance. In addition, they also control almost all foundations as well as the political bureaucracy. In order to understand how this is accomplished you must comprehend that it is not necessary, or even desirable, to control all the rank and file of the entity under command. Indeed, if one controls the dialogue and the management, one then dominates the organization. In fact if we were to speak of desirability, we would conclude that it is preferable for the general membership to be unaware of the master plan. This will ensure deniability and this is particularly important if many of your members do not agree with your goals. For example, Greenpeace does not want their members to know that their ultimate goal is a 40% reduction in world population, the elimination of fossil fuels, the elimination of nuclear fuels and research, the turning over to the UN of all American national parks, the elimination of meat from the human diet, etc. If people knew this, how would they be able to con well intending citizens into funding their operation? How would they raise enough money to pay their lead executives in excess of $200,000 per year? Thus the general membership remains unaware of the outcome plan and feel good about contributing to a worthy cause.

All establishments have a structure and a corporate organizational chart. Secret groups however, if they desire to main-

Newt Gingrich, "conservative" Republican leader, is a CFR member and promoter of NAFTA, GATT, WTO, and in short, the agenda of what his fellow CFR member George Bush terms, The New World Order.

tain their clandestine leadership, must institute a structure that differs markedly from the corporate or the governmental norm. The Satori organizational structure is a draconian convoluted plan designed specifically to protect the leadership from exposure. Satori are terrified of exposing themselves or their plans, and for good reason. In my opinion if the majority of the people in the free world came to understand Satori plans and membership, they would rise up against it. Remember that this structure has evolved over a 200 year time frame and that the originators were a group of Machiavellians. They have been able to hide information about themselves for 200 years and have kept their secret well.

The advent of the computer, home publishing, and the Internet (the information age if you prefer) has put an end to this conspiracy of silence. Up until the development of the aforementioned they were able to monopolize virtually all mainstream publishing. Things are different now. Consider the relevant fact. How many times have you read in a newspaper or heard on the radio or TV the name CFR or Council on Foreign Relations? Every executive cabinet member, the Joint Chiefs of Staff, and many members of congress are members. With 4,000 nationwide members out of a population of almost 250 million doesn't this strike you as remarkable? These are the Mandarins. When we consider them to number, worldwide, less than 5,000 out of a total population of over 4 billion with memberships in a G7 nation, is it not strange that you hear almost nothing about them? In the last six American presidential cabinets 96% were CFR members. Almost all present and past Joint Chiefs of Staff, are or have been members.

Past/Present Members of Joint Chiefs of Staff who are Members of Manadarin Organizations:

Name	Organization	Position
Allen, Lou Jr.	CFR	c of s usaf
Boorda, Jeremy M.	CFR	chief naval ops
Crowe, William J. Jr.	CFR,Tri	chair JCS
Dugan, Michael J.	CFR	c of s usaf
Fogleman, Ronald R.	CFR	c of s usaf
Gabriel, Charles A.	CFR	c of s usaf
Jones, David Charles	CFR	chair
JCS Kelley, Paul X	CFR	com marine
McPeak, Merrill A.	CFR	c of s usaf
Merritt, Jack Neil	CFR	director JCS
Mundy, Carl E. Jr.	CFR	com marine
Powell, Colin	CFR	chair JCS
Shalikashvili, John	CFR	chair JCS
Sullivan, Gordon R.	CFR	c of s army
Vessey, John W. Jr.	CFR	chair JCS
Vogt, John W.	Bil	director JCS
Wickham, John A. Jr.	CFR	c of s army

An excellent example of Satori power may be demonstrated in the 1996 American presidential election. All third party candidates Brown (L), Bucannan (C/R), and Perot (I), were successfully sidelined. The contest between consummate insider of 35 years, Dole (R), and TC member and insider, Clinton (D), was a sham. Although the two men speak a different game, when we examine their voting records the differences evaporate. The Satori win in either case.

At the peak of the structural pyramid are the Satori. A relatively small group of probably less than 30 people. On the side and directly controlled by them is the Special Services section (SS). SS caries out direct mandates by the Satori which cannot be entrusted to normal channels. Enforcement and 4th generation war, special financial transactions, pay-offs, bribery, and extortion are the services the SS provides. None of the SS people know who they work for, who pays them, or that the Satori even exist. Payment is carried out in cash or via wire transfers to clandestine bank accounts in Europe and Asia. Please understand that direct orders for acts of violence are rarely, if ever, given by the Satori. They simply provide funds to a crew that will provide the desired outcome in keeping with their plans. By seeing to the funding of certain groups of miscreants they insure the desired outcome. These acts are accomplished on a colossal scale: Bosnia, Kurdistan, as well as terrorist acts in America and Britain are on the menu. These groups ensure continued turmoil and thus a continuous stream of legislation in national and international bodies. Through this, freedoms are stifled, and Satori power is increased. It facilitates increased centralization, federalization, UN world government, and ultimate control of everything by the Satori surrogates — the Mandarins. The Mandarins are unaware of the SS who function completely independently of all other Satori organizations. The proof of the existence of the SS is not possible. It is based on a general knowledge of organizational structures. The following lead me to reach this conclusion:

1.) It makes common sense that enforcement and extortion groups exist.
2.) The overall structure and modus operandi of the Satori requires it.
3.) Any conspiracy must have a means of enforcement.
4.) A method for keeping dissenters in line requires it.
5.) There are numerous examples of Mandarins changing their position 180° in a few days.
6.) Although reward is the chosen method of ensuring fealty, it is not always effective.

President Reagan's funding of the World Bank with billions, after clearly stating he would not do so, took place only days after a Bilderberger meeting held in Montebello, Québec, Canada. A subsequent meeting on Long Island with two Reagan officials the day before the reverse, is a typical example.

The next group I refer to as the Zwischengaener. This German word means go-betweens, but more than that it implies a clandestine agent who conveys information. This is the exact purpose of the Zwischengaener, they provide a buffer between the Satori and the Mandarins. The reason for this is:

1.) To prevent the rank and file Mandarins from realizing the Satori existence.
2.) To ensure secrecy.
3.) To shield Satori members from public scrutiny.
4.) To allow Mandarins and Zwischengaener the ability to deny existence of conspiracy.

A large portion of the Zwischengaener are members of multiple mandarin organizations or are at least in the leadership of one of the Mandarin groups.

Please understand that the Satori command and control structure, unlike conventional ones, functions in a completely different manner. In a normal structure, instruction travels down the management pyramid from the CEO and board all the way down to the party that is to carry out the function of intent. This, by necessity, leaves a paper trail which can be followed.

The Satori structure leaves no such evidence. This is the principal reason that it is so difficult to prove the existence of this conspiracy. The desired outcome is attained without leaving any tracks.

Let us examine an example of a Satori planned outcome. The British Prime Minister, in disagreement with Satori plans, opposed the EC activities for monetary convergence between all EC members. The Satori, through an intermediary, explained to the Prime Minister that they want a single European currency and that they are not pleased with her position. At the very next Bilderberger meeting, the Satori Zwischengaener, who control the meeting, bring into discussion the English Prime Minister's opposition to a Bilderberger directive. A vote is taken and the unanimous Satori position is secured. The Prime Minister is given an ultimatum: "change your position or you will be removed from office." This took place. The Prime Minister was Baroness Margaret Thatcher, and she was removed from office exactly six months after the Bilderberger meeting.

Do you think that the election, debate, or argument were the operative acts here? No, they were not. Orders were given and the "process" carried throughout. A large number of Mandarins are employed in public service, education, think tanks, and foundations. Individuals employed in these sectors are to an extraordinary degree influenced by peer pressure and funding. Thus, there are four distinct ways in which Mandarins are controlled:

1.) Peer pressure.
2.) Pay — in the form of grants, travel perks, honoraria, publishing advantage.
3.) Profitable employment and investment opportunity.
4.) Extraordinary pension benefits.

Due to this management method, particularly the pensions, it is very easy for the Satori to control outcome, and for mandarins to deny the existence of an overlord power structure. Remember that most Mandarins are not acquainted with the elite.

Thus any Mandarin always uses the same tactic of ridiculing anyone who speaks of historical conspiracy. Active ridicule is ceaseless and unrelenting. A prime example of this is the John Birch Society which is ceaselessly maligned and mocked without any cause but to make their message appear false. It is a fact that certain special insider publications have attempted to paint them with the brush of racism, lunacy, and even equated them to the KKK. Nothing could be further from the truth. They are simply a patriotic organization who has figured out what's going on.

Foundations provide about 25% of the funds for the operation of the Satori. The rest comes from the government via your taxes. Any Satori contribution to the pot is so structured as to cost them nothing. Monies are distributed in ingenious ways. An example would be the Ford Foundation (which retains no connection whatsoever with any member of the Ford family) making a contribution to the Institute for Foreign Policy Studies, which in turn funds and supports the National Lawyers Guild, which has long been called the legal arm of the American Communist Party.

The Mandarin groups are positioned in such a way as to exert control over special segments of the body politic. Their command classifications may be separated into:

Political	Education
Environmental	Military
Financial	Religion
Media	

The back of the great seal of the United State contains the motto of the Satori, Novus Ordo Secolorum — "New Order Of The Ages," or as used today, "New World Order." Its pyramid design depicts the structure of the organization. The all-seeing eye represents what I term, the Satori. The seal was designed by Adam Weishaupt, a founder of the Illuminati (forerunner of the Satori), and submitted to the secretary of the Continental

Congress, Charles Thompson, who chose to place it on the back of the great seal.

I wonder if you are familiar with Weishaupt's theorem? His theorem, or more correctly, his formula, was postulated in 1782, the same year that Novus Ordo Secorum was placed on the great seal. The basic formula can be found repeated in the *Manifest Der Kommunistischer Parti,* published in London, England but written in German by Karl Marx in 1848. It was dedicated to *Proletariat aller Laender vereinigt euch* (Workers of the World Unite). It appears that Marx, among other things, was also a plagiarist. In any event Weishaupt's theorem is short and to the point:

1.) Abolish all monarchies and all ordered government.
2.) Abolish private property and the right of inheritance.
3.) Abolish patriotism and nationalism.
4.) Abolish the family unit, marriage, and the establishment of communal education.
5.) Abolish organized religion.

It appears, to me at least, that the Satori have up to this point in time met with considerable success in implementing Weishaupt's plans.

1.) Monarchies are but a remnant of the 18th century. Those still in existence are purely ceremonial. Ordered governments are, as you read, being converted into regional trade blocks, examples being EC and NAFTA. Organized governments are falling to 4th generation warfare.
2.) Private property ownership is under very serious attack by environmentalists. Inheritance taxes are so high in most western nations as to make inheritance a mere shadow of what it once was.
3.) Through media and academia, patriotism and nationalism have been defined as myopic and stupid, a remnant of the 19th century.
4.) The family unit is under attack from every angle. Tax structures in America discriminate against the family

through higher taxes. Hillary Clinton, in her ghost written book *It Takes a Village*, informs us that families don't bring up children but that communities do. Homosexual marriage is under consideration in Hawaii. We are continuously bombarded with the misnomer that a family can be anything from single sex onward. Communal education is a fact of life since it was brought over from Germany.

5.) The assault against Christians in this decade on a worldwide basis can only be compared to Nazi propaganda against the Jews in 1935 Germany. Gaia appears to be taking over as the pantheistic female goddess in replacement of Judeo-Christian philosophy and belief in the one true God. Orthodox Jews and born-again Christians are maligned by the media at every opportunity. Christian values are ridiculed .

Is it not interesting that all aspects of Weishaupt's hypothesis (communism/socialism) have been the most extraordinary failures of this century? All of eastern Europe, Sweden, England; every nation which has tried it went to financial ruin. In the academic community, which is isolated from reality, socialism/environmentalism is now the avant-garde of academic political thought. You would really think that they would learn from experience and know better. Socialism represents a statist concept which allows top down management and is substantially simpler to control then a free market economy. Not the highest paid professor at Yale can argue that point. All the great pushes for the theories of Marx, Engels, Weishaupt, and Keynes have come from academia with financial support from the Satori. Those in academia who teach free market economics (the Austrian School of economics) have to fight to keep their jobs as they are not politically correct. The very fact that the leftist economists cannot point to a single success in socialism anyplace in the world seems not to deter them. Like the Clintons and the

Reichs of this world, they think that their particular brand of rubbish will work because they are so well meaning, such great thinkers, and better administrators. The Satori have all their organizational pins in line. All the seeds for the "New World Order" have been planted. The Mandarins are positioned to control society in accordance with their rules of engagement, which are:

The Five Cardinal Obligatory Rules
For Totalitarian Control

1.) Banking
  a) Investment b) trade c) production

2.) Communication
  a) media b) schools c) academia

3.) Judiciary
  a) courts b) police

4.) Religion

5.) Military

There can be no serious doubt that the above listed are not either under Satori control or influence. Let us take an example of the media. Below are some questions which were presented to media people in news, radio, TV, and newspapers. The percentages represent conclusive proof of control.

Question		
Q. Do you support WTO	Yes	99%
Q. Do you support NAFTA	Yes	87%
Q. Are you in Favor of free trade	Yes	96%
Q. Do you support the UN	Yes	98%
Q. Did you vote for Bush or Clinton	89%	Clinton
Q. Do you consider yourself liberal or conservative	91%	Liberal
Q. Are you a (D), (R), or other	96%	Democrat
Q. Do you think that the contract with America was serious	Yes	4%

Every single position is one preferred by the Satori!

The Satori are no more than a group of families and business interests which are tied to one another. Each of these groups or families has what I call an "Elector." This is the individual person who becomes the Satori candidate representing that group. It is my estimate that there are between 30 and 40 electors. The membership is very stable but not static. New groups may be added if and when that group attains the correct mix of wealth and power.

To sum up and clarify this chapter I believe that the words of a consummate Mandarin should be used. Strobe Talbott is the Deputy Secretary of State. He was also Bill Clinton's roommate at Oxford. In 1992, Mr. Talbott made some remarkable statements in an interview with *Time* magazine.

> "I'll bet that within a hundred years Nationhood as we know it will be obsolete, all states will recognize one global authority." He further wrote, "All countries are basically social arrangements, accommodations to changing circumstances," and "No matter how permanent and sacred they may seem at any one time, in fact they are all artificial and temporary." Then comes the clincher, ". . . The cold war forced independent nations to give up, to surrender bits and pieces of their sovereignty to international institutions . . . The free world formed multilateral financial institutions that depended on member states' willingness to give up a degree of their sovereignty."

Read that last sentence again with care as it lets the cat out of the bag: "Multilateral Financial Institutions" . . . "States Willing to Give Up Their Sovereignity." That says it all!

The Federal Reserve Building, Washington, D.C.

"This Act establishes the most gigantic trust on earth. When the President signs the Act, the invisible government by the money power, proven to exist by the Money Trust Investigation, will be legalized. The new law will create inflation whenever the trusts want inflation. From now on depressions will be scientifically created."

— Charles A. Lindberg, Sr., *at the time of the passage of the Federal Reserve Act in 1913*

FINANCIAL MONOPOLY

In 1958, the noted economist Hans Sennholtz wrote:

> "... adherents of liberty and capitalism cannot rest until the Federal Reserve System has been abolished ... 110 years ago, Karl Marx enumerated in his *Communist Manifesto,* ten prerequisites for the conversion of any nation to a socialist State. Point 5 reads: 'Centralization of credit in the hands of the State, by means of a national bank with State capital as an exclusive monopoly.' Since the abolition of the gold standard in 1933 this point has been realized in America. The Federal Reserve System constitutes its realization."

Of course, President Wilson's signing of the Federal Reserve Act on December 23, 1913, while congress was on its Christmas break, was not the first attempt to get a monopoly on our money. However, it was, and is, the most all-encompassing. The FRS has total control of all our money and credit — and it is privately owned.

The Federal Reserve System is owned by its 12 participating banks, the percentage of ownership is as follows:

New York City	27.2%
San Francisco	13.9%
Chicago	11.3%
Atlanta	9.3%
Richmond	8.3%
Dallas	6.8%
Cleveland	6.8%
Philadelphia	4.1%
Kansas City	3.7%
Minneapolis	2.7%
St. Louis	2.3%

These banks are, in turn, owned by the stockholders of for-profit corporations. For example, the stockholders of the largest bank in the system, the New York City bank, are:

CitiBank N.A.	20.51%
Chase M.B.N.A.	16.70%
Chemical Bank	15.56%
Morgan G.T. Co.	8.87%
Bankers Trust	4.86%
Republic National	4.60%
Bank of New York	4.46%
Marine Midland	4.15%
Nat. Westminster	2.94%
MidAtlantic	2.76%
United Jersey	.58%
Key Bank	.08%
Other banks	13.83%

In addition to controlling our money and credit, the Federal Reserve is the major stockholder in The Depository Trust Company, 55 Water Street, NYC. The other major stockholder (35.1%) is the New York Stock Exchange, which is 100% owned by its members.

THE DEPOSITORY TRUST COMPANY is the largest securities depository in the world with more than $10 trillion of securities in custody. In 1995 they processed $41 trillion of securities through their book-entry system. US statute requires that all securities traded in the United States pass through DTC books. They are the national clearinghouse for the settlement of trade in corporate and municipal securities. They perform all securities and custodial services required in such financial transactions, and they take a percentage of every single trade, be it sell or buy. In fact, they always get you twice, the first time when you purchase a security and the second when you sell it.

In a news release dated Sept. 97, DTC announced the launching of a new joint venture to be called "The International Depository & Clearing Inc." On we march into the Brave New World. It is envisioned in the news release that the new firm will carry out on an international scale, what DTC has been doing in America, taking a percentage on trades internationally. Furthermore, they will log and file all securities purchased by Americans on foreign markets, or domestically purchased foreign stocks or bonds. The new corporation is a partnership between DTC and National Securities Clearing Corporation (NSCC). Conveniently, the CEO of DTC and NSCC have appointed each other to their respective board of directors.

The newly appointed president and CEO of IDC also announced that plans were in the process of being implemented to set up a Global Clearing Network (GCN) which would link all trades internationally.

FOLLOWING THE MONEY

At the close of the Second World War, in July 1944, at a meeting in Bretton Woods in northern NH, a group of 750 international financiers met to decide on the outcome of a devastated world. Two men were pivotal in that meeting, Harry Dexter White and John Maynard Keynes. At that time there were only five nations which were economically sound; USA, Canada Great Britain, France and Switzerland. Gold supplies, which have always been the underlying structure of fiat money, were concentrated in only three of those: USA, Switzerland and Canada. These three, therefore, called the shots when it came to policy. Keynes wanted to untie all monetary valuation from gold, but the Swiss refused to go along with that plan. Thus the dollar would become the international medium of exchange and in value tied to gold at $35.00 per ounce. One dollar being 1/35th of the value of one troy ounce of gold. All other currencies would be tied to the dollar.

THE BANK OF INTERNATIONAL SETTLEMENTS was created to be the world central bank. It was the bank that banks went to if required to borrow money. It was organized similarly to the American Federal Reserve System in that the BIS, which would be located in Basel, Switzerland, would be controlled by the "Basel Committee." This Committee would be made up of ministers sent from each of the G7 (now G10) nations. It has been traditional for the Chairman of the "Basel Committee" to have the same persona as the chairman of the Federal Reserve in New York. The Bank's main responsibility is the settlement of transactions among the various central banks of participating nations. In addition, it prescribes the standards by which a bank's capitalization is set, and coordinates the orderly distribution of currency as well as ensuring sufficient supplies of currency.

THE WORLD BANK is a commercial bank and was formed to be a lender primarily to governments for the rebuilding of infrastructure. Ultimately as a loaner to reconstruct the devastated economies of the nations ravaged by the Second World War. Depositors and borrowers from the World Bank are not individuals but governments. The fund created as a means of transaction is called the **International Monetary Fund** (IMF). Like the BIS, the governing structure is comprised of ministers from the G10 nations. These are: USA, Canada, Great Britain, France, Switzerland, Germany, Belgium, Holland, Italy, and Luxembourg.

We can now clearly see that the providers of credit, money, and transactions are in the hands of a very small group of Mandarins. With this we come very close to the Satori whom, we may be assured, are at the head of this pyramid.

By the beginning of 1960, the world refinance scheme had succeeded beyond the best hopes of the Satori, so much so that a serious problem occurred. The supply of dollars based against a finite supply of gold held by the US government was of insufficient size to continue to be the world's international monetary medium. The solution came in the form of forfeit finance: this is a method by which international transactions are secured through a guarantee (aval) which is a form of guarantee under (Code Napoleon) and is issued by major banks in the form of a document. All this would subsequently be codified by the **International Chamber of Commerce** in Paris France (ICC). This use of documents rather than currency provided a relief for required dollars and thus enabled the system to continue without violation of the binding treaty negotiated at Bretton Woods.

Naturally all such instruments carried a fee, which is happily collected by the Satori on every single international transaction. Not only was a crisis in the form of a shortage of currency averted, but banks reaped substantial additional benefits:

1.) Reduced reserve requirements on all international transactions.
2.) Support of all international transactions by central banks, The World Bank and BIS.
3.) Off-balance sheet accounting of the transaction.
4.) Instruments legally ranked the same as deposit funds (Para Passu).
5.) The ability to leverage depositor funds with central banks, and use same as collateral instruments to borrow.
6.) The ability to hold such documents for several days prior to transfer to the beneficiary and thereby increase interest earnings.
7.) The ability to consolidate multiple transfer documents and thereby borrow from BIS, amounts in excess of $100 million at lower interest rates.

Things proceeded very well indeed until during the Nixon administration — the United Kingdom issued a demand to the American UK ambassador Connolly demanding gold for dollars. His response was "I will answer you tomorrow." What Nixon did was to untie the dollar from a fixed gold valuation which immediately let gold seek its adjusted and corrected value, and thus increased the US Federal gold supply value on the world market by ten fold (gold value immediately climbing to about $350). Britain, as well as all the other participants of the agreement, had no option but to accept America's decision to go off the gold standard. They had neither the will nor the military muscle to enforce the agreement. (The reader should clearly understand that market interference such as price or wage fixing has never worked, and never will. The only equitable way is to let markets set price). Through their surrogates, Nixon and Kennedy, the Satori now had in place an international currency which they controlled. The IMF and the BIS ensured that the US dollar would hold its value in all markets, and could simply salvage dollars from nations with a positive balance to nations with a negative balance. The illusion of a dollar backed by hard assets was not only gone, currency from here foreword would not be worth the paper it was printed on. The official statement is "Backed by the Faith and Support of the US government" (read "Taxpayer").

The fact that these international bankers share directors, and have what one might call a more than cozy relationship with one another does give one cause to reflect. This, particularly in view of the pressure to internationalize all monetary transactions under single custody. Mergers and acquisitions in the banking sector have accelerated in the last eight years far beyond any reasonable level — in the United States alone over 800 banks have closed their doors. The original plan of the Satori, as instituted on Jekyll Island upon setting up the Federal Reserve System, unrealized for decades, is now close to fulfillment.

> *"Does it not seem strange to you that these men just happened to be CFR and just happened to be on the Board of Governors of the Federal Reserve, that absolutely controls the money and interest rates of this great country without the benefit of Congress? A privately owned organization, the Federal Reserve, has absolutely nothing to do with the United States of America."*
>
> — Senator Barry Goldwater, *With No Apologies*

CHAPTER FIVE

FOUNDATIONS

Way back in the 1950s someone came to the conclusion that there was something wrong with foundations and the way they distributed their services and funds. The accepted conclusion at that time was that there seemed to be an ulterior motive in the way funds were allocated and distributed. Editorial after editorial stated that foundations were employing their tax advantage for the sole purpose of changing society. The facts are that by the late 1920s, most of the larger foundations were under Satori control, today they all are. By the 1950s they seemed to be marching in lock step with a uniform agenda. American patriots were troubled by this, and thus the Reece committee was instituted by Congress. Congressman Brazillia Carroll Reece was in charge of the committee. The mandate of the committee was to investigate all tax exempt foundations. A previous committee had attempted the same mandate. It was the Cox committee. They were stonewalled to the point that they gave up to defeat. This was no small assignment and it took considerable courage for an elected official to stand up to a structure that controlled many billions of dollars with names like Rockefeller, Melon, Ford, and Carnegie.

From day one the liberal media, which at that time consisted of *The New York Times, The Washington Post*, and *The NY Herald Tribune* presented formidable opposition to the Reece commission. Editorials abounded demeaning the issue as well as Congressman Reece. This should have been expected since the same had occurred to Cox. And as the editorial boards of those papers were known to be CFR members, their opposition was a foregone conclusion.

The principal question to be answered by the Reece commission was: To what extent the foundations were influencing America's social and political structure, and what they were doing to change it.

> On December 21, 1954, John Odonnell in a column in the NY Daily News explained the problem to readers of the paper. He wrote, "The Reece committee had the impossible task of informing the American public of the incredible fact that the huge fortunes piled up by America's industrial giants John D. Rockefeller, Andrew Carnegie, and Henry Ford were being used to systematically discredit and destroy the very free enterprise system that had allowed them to make their fortunes."

The foundations had been taken over by a group of radical social and political engineers (Mandarins) whose goals were the socialization of America. So we can prove that by 1950, the Satori were in control of the financial gold mine of foundations.

On August 1, 1951 congressman Cox of the 82nd congress made the following remarks in the congressional record (p.A5046):

> *There are disquieting evidences that at least a few of the foundations have permitted themselves to be infiltrated by men and women who are disloyal to our American way of life. They should be investigated and exposed to the pitiless light of publicity, and appropriate legislation should be framed to correct the present situation.*

I regret to inform you that absolutely nothing happened as a result of the Cox findings. Not until the 83rd congress was the matter even brought up for a vote. Because Cox had criticized a black man, Langston Hughes, a communist poet, who authored *Good-bye China,* he was accused of being a racist. Later he was critical of the Rosewald Fund for making grants to communists and was branded an anti-Semite. Nothing has ever changed through history: if liberals don't like the message, they immediately slander the messenger. The Cox committee ultimately named many foundations which were engaged in various shenanigans, among them were The Rockefeller Foundation, The Guggenheim Foundation, The Carnegie Foundation, The Rosewald Fund, and the Ford Foundation. As a result the funding for the Cox committee was suspended on May 8, 1952 by a vote of 247 ayes to 99 noes. In conclusion, the Cox committee stated:

> *There can be no reasonable doubt concerning the efforts of the communist party both to infiltrate the foundations and to make use, so far as is possible, of foundation grants to finance communist causes and communist sympathizers.*

Now in light of what you know so far, just change the word communist to Satori, and remember the Hegelian dialectic.

The Reece Committee issued a lengthy report upon completion of long and arduous investigations. This report is of considerable interest because it was the last time in American history that politicians mustered the courage and independence to investigate foundations. In the four decades since then, no other dissenting voice has appeared. The summation of the report is as follows (Federal Register):

1.) Foundations were not founded with any philanthropic goal, but rather as a vehicle of tax planning. There is a substantial possibility that a large part of American industry will eventually come into the hands of the foundations. Because they are tax except they will continue to outpace the growth of all other sectors of the economy. This will perpetuate the control of a substantial portion of America's economy in the hands of a very small group of individuals. There are at the present time so many foundations that the Internal Revenue Service is inadequately staffed to over-view them.

2.) Foundations are desirable when operating in the natural sciences by making direct donations to religious, educational, scientific, and other such recipients. There is, however, a clear danger of social engineering to which the public must remain alert.
3.) The power of individual foundations is enormous. They can exercise various forms of patronage which carry with them the elements of thought control. They exert immense influence in education and upon academia. They extend invisible pressure for their agenda through the power of the purse. They materially predetermine the development of social and political courses of action by the process of granting or withholding grants, and through this implement their designing and direction upon society.
4.) This power is amplified enormously when they act in concert. They operate in part through certain intermediary organizations supported by foundations. They consist basically of a group of major foundations, representing a gigantic aggregate of the American economy.
5.) Foundation funds are public funds and trustees must act in the highest fiduciary responsibility. Unfortunately the trustees in all cases have long ago relinquished their responsibility, turning over to professional administrators their responsibility over intermediary organizations.
6.) A professional class of administrators of foundation funds has emerged, intent upon self engrandisment. This has created a bureaucracy within a bureaucracy (i.e., the Mandarin class).
7.) The power of these administrators has become so great as to influence the media, and government to a very substantial degree. This has reached the level where any criticism of foundations' actions becomes ridiculed, slanted, distorted, or discredited in the media.

8.) Research in social sciences plays a key part in societal evolution, and this is now the sole domicile of foundations. Even the huge amount of funds utilized in this government has come into control of this group.
9.) This group has thus produced a real mass of empirical research, as contrasted with theoretic research. Associated with this empirical method, the concentration of power has been used to promote "Moral Relativism" to the detriment of society as a whole. This societal engineering can be directly linked to our present social problems.
10.) Accompanying these directions in research grants, the concentration has shown a distinct tendency to favor the political opinion of the left.
11.) The impact on education has been very substantial, and has been used to centralize, promote uniformity, and induce educators to become instruments of social change to the left. Text books and other material considerations confirm this.
12.) In the international field, foundations and their interlocking organizations have effected strong influence upon American foreign policy, education, and society as a whole. This has been accomplished through propaganda, advisors, consultants, all directing society to a inevitable internationalism.
13.) Some foundations have directly, as well as indirectly, supported subversion of American principles.

The above 13 condensed findings are not mine, but those of the Reece Congressional Committee. Its function was to investigate a financial sector of our economy which currently holds assets over $200 billion dollars. It demonstrates clear proof of conspiracy.

There are about 38,600 foundations in America with combined assets of just over $200 billion. They make donations of approximately $11 billion per year. Now let's make some sense out of that information. First we find that the foundations are still amassing more assets, because their accumulated income is certainly greater then the amount they give away in grants. A further investigation reveals the inevitable rule of business, that 20% account for 80% of the assets, is not the case. The fact of foundations is that just over 14% account for 87% of the assets. This then means that the very small number of about 2,400 foundations control over $178 billion in assets. These, as we have seen from the Reece and Cox committee reports, act in unison to the same political agenda. Although the monies are small when compared to the entire marketplace, we must remember that all of the contributed funds, $11 billion per year, are utilized for social and political engineering. Due to this, it is the largest amount of money spent on such issues, and its impact on society as a whole is enormous.

Foundation direct grants are but a small portion of Satori funds directed at social and political infrastructure manipulation. Consider governmental funds as these distributed by HHS (Donna Shalala, CFR). This is the largest of all federal agencies. Shalala controls the giving away of 250,000 grants annually. The total funds involved exceeds annual grants by foundations 10 fold. And this is only one out of hundreds of agencies of the American federal government. It is an absolute fact that Mandarins, working on behalf of the Satori, with single purpose and concert among each other, distribute billions of dollars of your tax money to the sole advantage of the Satori.

An interesting new program instituted by Bill Clinton (AmeriCorps) stands out in this charade. The correct name is The Corporation For National Service. It has little to do with service, but a great deal with social engineering and political patronage. The program was started in 1993 and its budget had swollen to $480 million by 1994. The freshmen in congress not yet accustomed to the workings of the Satori succeeded in forcing an audit of the program. GAO, after nine months of inten-

CHAPTER SIX

THE MANDARINS

A Special Note To The Reader

Every possible effort has been made to portray the organizations and individuals listed with the greatest possible accuracy. Because many of the groups are either secret or disdain publicity, information in some instances was difficult to obtain and even harder to verify. Almost all information contained has been cross-checked through multiple sources. All information is factual. It is unfortunate that much information had to be discarded due to my inability to verify sources and facts. Conclusions drawn are those reached by the author after over two years of exhaustive research.

INTRODUCTION TO MANDARINS

It should not come as a surprise to you that politically powerful and wealthy people, who after all have much in common, plan and act in concert. They represent a community of sorts, and as such, have similar interests and act accordingly. It is unfortunate that there are numerous books and texts on this subject which, in my view, offer no facts and represent nothing more than personal opinion. In retrospect, it is highly possible that the Satori are responsible for such authorship as another way of ridiculing any possible exposure. Planning by elitists is surely nothing new.

Throughout recorded history there have been plots, plans, and conspiracies. Why should our age be any different? The growth of the conspiracy by the Satori has accelerated markedly in the last 50 years. The greatest growth has been after the Second World War, from seeds carefully planted at the turn of the century. The largest Mandarin group to be created in this century, is the Council on Foreign Relations (CFR). Founded in the 1920s (along with a sister organization in England), it has grown, prospered, and in doing so has even produced several children. There are older organizations in the conspiracy such as The Order. But in sheer size and number the CFR overshadows all the rest.

It is a fact that all these groups shape the policy-making process of the nations of the world and thereby influence and control the political dialogue as well as the ultimate outcome. Controlling the media of many nations also helps. When these groups are exposed for what they really are, they invariably will retort in their defense: "Look, this is all BS. We represent varied political and ideological thought. We are in no way alike. Your 'theory' is bunk." In response, I say it is not a theory. Furthermore, in a grouping of almost 5,000 individuals, members could not possibly be of one mind or political persuasion This, however, in no way means that they could not all share the same goal. In fact, they do exactly that, they all share the same goals, even though they may have differing opinions on how to reach those goals.

With this in mind let us examine the principal groups in Satori service. What is "The New World Order?"

In the early 1990s, Willy Brandt (deceased), former socialist chancellor of West Germany, chairman of the Fifth-Socialist International, and long time Soviet spy, chaired the Brandt commission. Important members were Robert McNamara, former U.S. World Bank president; Pete Peterson, former U.S. Secretary of Commerce, and big CFR functionary, print mogul Katharine Graham, *Washington Post*, *Newsweek* etc. All are members of the secret Bilderberger group. The commission was accommodating enough to tell us exactly what the New World Order is:

> *. . . a world that has supranational authority to regulate world commerce and industry; an international organization that will*

> *control the production and consumption of oil; an international currency that will replace the dollar; a world development fund that will make funds available to free and communist nations alike (World Bank); and an international police force (UN) to enforce the edicts of the order.*[1]

If I'm not mistaken, I thought that was exactly what the USSR was all about. Lest you think that I exaggerate about Mandarin infiltration of the American government, as of May 1996, the following individuals in our government held or hold memberships in either the CFR, TC, Bilderbergers, or others.

US Presidents

Clinton . . . Bild., CFR, TC
Bush . . . Bones, CFR
Carter . . . CFR, TC
Ford . . . Bild., CFR

US House of Representatives

30 plus staff

US Senate

27 plus staff

US Supreme Court

3 out of 9

Government Departments & Committees

Arms Control	15	HUD	2
Agriculture	3	NRC	1
Pres. Advis.	4	Justice	3
Commerce	9	OMB	5
US Trade Rep.	5	State Dep.	131
Defense	60	Foreign affairs	9
CIA	19	UN Assigned by US	18
HHS	3	Miscellanies	31
Export Control	2		

[1]In and out of office.

Council On Foreign Relations

Principal Address:
The Harold Pratt House
58 E. 68th St.
New York, NY 10021
Tel. 212-734-0400
Fax. 212-861-1789
Web page, yes

Washington Address:
2400 N. St. N.W.
Washington, D.C. 20037
Tel. 202-826-7780
Fax. 202-862-7787

CFR Membership

Corporate Memberships	188
Personal Memberships*	3206 +or-
Staff	151
Directors	32
Officers	12
Honorary Directors	10

**See Appendix E for complete list of personal memberships.*

IMPORTANT CFR PERSONALITIES

OFFICERS:
Peter G. Peterson, CEO
Maurice R. Greenberg, Vice Chair.
Leslie H. Gelb, Pres.
Alton Frye, Sr. Vp. & Nat. Director
Larry L. Fabian, Sr. Vp. and COO
Kenneth H. Keller, Sr. Vp. for Programs
John A. Millington, Vp. Planning and Development
Karen M. Sughrue, Vp. Meetings
Janice L. Murray, Treasurer
Ana Fihueras, Assist. Treasurer
Judith Gustafson, Secretary

Else Carson Lewis,
Assist. Secretary

DIRECTORS: ***Term Exp. 1996***
Paul A. Allaire
Mario L. Baeza
Thomas R. Donahue
Helen L. Kaplan
Peter G. Peterson
Frank G. Zarb
Robert B. Zoellick

DIRECTORS: ***Term Exp. 1997***
John E. Bryson
Kenneth W. Dam
Rita E Hauser
James R. Houghton
Charalayne Hunter-Gault
Frank Savage

DIRECTORS: ***Term Exp. 1998***
Robert E. Allen
Peggy Dulany
Robert F. Erburu
Karen Elliot House

Cyrus R. Vance
Glen E. Watts

Joshua Lederberg
Garrick Utley

DIRECTORS: ***Term Exp. 1999***
Clara A. Hills
Robert D. Hormats
William J. McDonough
Theodore C. Sorenson
George Soros
Paul A. Volcker

DIRECTORS: ***Term Exp. 2000***
William S. Cohen
Jessica P. Einhorn
Lewis V. Gerstner, Jr.
Maurice R. Greenberg
George J. Mitchell
Leslie H. Gelb, ex officio

HONORARY OFFICERS & DIRECTORS
Douglas Dillon
George S. Franklin
Caryl P. Haskins
Grayson A. Kirk
Charles McC. Mathias, Jr.
Lames A. Perkins
David Rockefeller
Robert A. Scalapino

SOME PAST DIRECTORS:
Archibald Cary Coolidge
Paul M. Warburg
Allen W. Dulles
Hamilton Fish Armstrong
Walter Lippman
David Rockefeller
W. Averil Harriman
Adlai E. Stevenson
Bill Moyers
Cyrus R. Vance
W William Blumenthal
Zbigniew Brzezinski
Paul A. Volcker
Lane Kirkland

SOME PAST DIRECTORS (Cont'd.):

Winston Lord
William D. Ruckelhaus
George P. Schultz
Warren Christopher
Allan Greenspan
Brent Scowcroft
Jean Kirkpatrick
Richard B. Cheney
Strobe Talbott
Donna Shalala
George Soros

PROMINENT CFR PARTICTPANTS:

Tom Brokaw
Walter F. Mondale
Alton Frye
Hasib J. Sabbagh
Stephen Robert
Graham T. Allison
Leslie H. Gelb
Roy M. Goodman
Rudolph Giuliani
John Kornblum
Jean Kirkpatrick
Michael Kramer
Richard Allery
Barbara C. Samuels II
W. Anthony Lake
Sidney R. Jones
Michael Clough
James J. Shinn
Kenneth H. Keller
Caio Kock-Weser
W. Michael Blumenthal
James J. Shinn
Richard C. Macke
Peter Tarnoff
Dale A. Jenkins
Alice H. Henkin
Virginia A. Kamsky
Richard Mallery
William H. Luers
Arthur Schlesinger, Jr.
Robert S. McNamara
Hanan Mikhail-Ashrawi
Geraldine Ferraro
Zbigniew Brzezinski
Marshall I. Goldman
Butros Butros-Ghali
Edward P. Djerejian
Carlos Saul Memem
Alexander Haig
Les Aspin
Madeline K. Albright
Robert C. Waggoner
Dan Rather
Abraham Ribicoff
William F. Buckley, Jr.
Arnaud de Borchgrave
Marvin Kalb
Harold E. Stassen

See Exhibit E for complete list of Personal Memberships

CFR STUDY GROUPS

Study groups located in New York City, Boston, Chicago, Washington D.C., and San Francisco, examine topics chosen by the leadership for investigation, and make non-binding reports on them to the leadership. An annual brochure lists the topics currently under investigation.

According to the CFR annual report, dated 30 June 1995, the Council is a non-partisan and non-profit membership organization. The Council's principal activities are conducted in New York City and in Washington DC. *Foreign Affairs* is the flagship publication of the organization and has been published since 1922, the second year of the CFR's existence. Membership is restricted to US citizens. The CFR states that it is financed through membership dues, publications, subscriptions, corporate endowments, foundation grants, and voluntary gifts. No relationship with the US government of any type is claimed. In light of the facts, this statement is somewhat comical, when you consider that over 80% of all executive branch cabinet members since FDR have held membership, and the State Department has been a CFR satellite operation for well over 50 years. This organization holds a very low profile and believes in massive understatement. In an effort to influence young minds, we learn that they offer fellowships annually. They are for the term of one year and generally require writing a book, naturally in line with CFR dogma. They claim to be non-partisan, but this very much reminds me of the French saying " Pas d'ennemi a la gauche." Certainly it does not universally represent any particular political or economic philosophy, but it most assuredly represents one single uniform direction — that being one world government under Satori rule. CFR universally supports the

UN, NATO, NAFTA, WTO, GATT, and the EC, as well as expansion of all of them. As a consequence they are very partisan. They unwaveringly follow the direction of one world government, the ultimate Satori goal. Rarely, if ever, is the CFR or one of its sister groups mentioned in the press. When members speak, they always tout the same ultimate goal whether coming from the political left, right or center.

They have an objective — look at your dollar bill again. I'm not talking about "In God We Trust" either. The New World Order, with the Satori in charge is the name of the game. The CFR is the largest Mandarin group in service to the Satori.

An overview of the CFR establishes a similar makeup in membership as in all the other Mandarin groups. Of the total membership we find about six hundred in very influential positions, another six hundred are employed in important centers of influence. The balance are active in academia, the media, business, law, finance, the military, or government. The overwhelming membership, regardless of political affiliation, is to the political left. The actual number of conservatives or Americanists is small enough to be considered a rouse.

The exact beginning of the CFR is not well documented. The year 1921 has been mentioned in some texts, but suffice it to say that the CFR's dominance of US foreign and domestic policy did not begin until the election of FDR. The formative years of the Council were those following the First World War. The first attempt at globalization was under President Wilson through the Geneva, Switzerland based League of Nations. The basis of the League, referred to as the Covenant, was part of the Treaty of Versailles, which stripped Germany of her colonies, while Britain, America, Belgium and France expanded theirs. Thus Germany was economically at a severe disadvantage in the world market of raw materials. In order for Germany to engage in world trade, or to purchase raw materials, they had to borrow funds from the Satori in the United States and England to finance their transactions. The Satori profited on every transaction that crossed the German border. Hitler saw this as a serious problem and used it to gain power in Germany. Once in power, Hitler decided to circumvent the Satori banking operations through the institution of a barter system. This represented a serious threat to Satori international banking profits and set a dangerous precedent others may follow. As a result, the Satori in England and America began to demand of their governments an intervention on their behalf. Thus it was that a boycott of German-made products became national policy in England and America. Enraged, an egomaniacal Hitler spread his gospel of hate which eventually culminated in WW II and the holocaust.[2]

During the period prior to WW II, the CFR suffered many setbacks, the plebiscite in the Saar basin was 9 to 1 in favor of unification with Germany rather than France. The failure of the US Senate to radify the League of Nations despite their strong support. The subsequent withdrawal of Germany, Italy, and Japan from the League. The failed attempt to stop Japanese aggression into Manchuria in 1931; Italy's conquest of Ethiopia in 1935 and 36; and the German *Anschluss* of 1938 spelled the end for the League, which collapsed in the first weeks of World War II, and was subsequently dissolved in 1946.

Events in the first two years of WW II were chaotic and fast paced. The German Wermacht — utilizing the Jaeger concept and Blitzkrieg — threw their joint opponents into confusion. By 1939 the CFR was in disarray, but began long-term planning to deal with the ultimate problems that would be faced by the US in the coming war. Within weeks of the outbreak of war on 12 September 1939, a meeting was called in Washington which was attended by Hamilton Fish, editor of *Foreign Affairs*, congressman Walter Mallory, executive director of the CFR, and

[2]Douglas: *Gestapo Chief Heinrich Mueller* (1948 interrogation)

Assistant Sec. of State George Messersmith (CFR). They set the groundwork for what was to become the total domination of the American State Department and Executive branches of government by the CFR. This domination is still in effect today. Events were established to develop several working groups of CFR members to focus on long- and short-term problems faced by the United States in the probable coming conflict. The developed recommendations would be made available to FDR and kept from pubic scrutiny.[3] By December 1939, all details were completed and the planning for virtual take-over of the American government by the CFR. The central steering committee consisted of Norman Davis (CFR) ambassador at large and CFR Chairman, Armstrong Mallory, Shepardson, Baldwin, Bowman, Viner, and Allen Dulles. Each man was a member in good standing of the CFR. Each man headed a study group dealing with one or two specific topics. For example, Hansen, a Harvard economics professor, together with Viner, a university of Chicago economics professor, led an economics and financial group. The groups consisted of, on average, ten members. A total of over 100 people were devoted in the total arrangement. Funding was provided by The Rockefeller Foundation who supplied the required working capital with a contribution of $300,000. In today's equivalent that would be about $2 million. This was spread over a six-year time frame from 1939 to 1945.[4]

During this time the CFR started a new group christened the "Century Group" after the name of an upper class social club in New York where they met. The Century Group was formed to influence, by any means available, whoever needed to be influenced according to CFR agenda. It was this group who was responsible for development of the strategy to provide England with fifty naval destroyers in exchange for bases in the western

[3]Messersmith memorabilia Sept. 12, 1939 Dec. File 811.43 CFR
[4]Harvey Notter, Post-war Foreign Policy Preparations 1939-45

hemisphere held by the British or their interests. This plan was presented to Roosevelt on 1 August 1940 and culminated in a treaty with England in September of that year. It can be said that this treaty ended America's neutrality towards Germany. By 1940, the CFR was in full charge of the war effort: they controlled not only the State Department, and most presidential advisors, but much more importantly, they were the sole dispensers of foreign policy and governmental dialogue. They were in charge of everything outside of the military. FDR had for all purposes relinquished his presidency to the CFR. The only change that has taken place since then is that the American military has also succumbed to the CFR, of which well over 100 senior officers are members. In the last 10 years virtually all government departments have become aggressively politicized, a new phenomenon in the USA.

There is little doubt when CFR planning and implementation became a major factor in world politics. In 1940, the German Wermacht circumvented the French and Belgian defense lines and defeated those nations with a force of less than one third the number of troops at the disposal of France. This single occurrence was a considerable blow to the CFR, which had assumed that the Germans would be stopped by the French static defense lines. At that time, the entire world did not understand that a new method of warfare was being implemented by the Germans. Third Generation War was not then an accepted concept in the world's armed forces except for in Germany

The first precept of any plan must be self-survival. Thus, the first CFR consideration in early 1940 was whether the United States could survive in a world without access to Europe. Self-sufficiency in raw materials and manufacturing technology were also considered. In the summer of 1940, a large study group of the CFR tackled these questions. Part of this was a survey of world trade which included virtually all commodities. In October 1940, that report was submitted to the government as E-

B19. All subsequent war and foreign policy considerations were thereafter based on that report. We can clearly see that early on, the considerations of our government were converted from national self-interest to the mercantile banking interests of the Satori. The E-B19 study did not deal primarily with American self-interest but rather with the interest of certain internationalists plans.

The next problem confronting CFR planners was Japan. Japan refused to be subordinate to the United States and moreover displayed considerable expansionist tendencies. Realizing that the E-B19 report had to consider that the United States would be cut off from the Far Eastern suppliers, additions to the report were necessitated These factors then caused E-B26 to be written. This report entitled *American Far East Policy* was issued in January 1941. This report and the implementation of its recommendations is what actually caused the war between Japan and America. The report recommended the isolation of Japan and the financial and military support of any forces opposing Japan. The first large-scale action by the US was to support China with weapons, advisors, finances, munitions, and even the "Flying Tigers" to be used against Japan. Japan required raw materials for national as well as defense interests and the US did its best to interrupt the flow of those resources to Japan.

Later in 1941, a new report was issued, E-B34 entitled *The Grand Area.* The Grand Area encompassed all the territory not under axis control. This report is what set the stage for the present CFR position and strategy: one worldwide economy with American "planners" domination of it all. Consider now the planned successor for the EC, NAFTA, and FTAA. It has taken a total of fifty-five years for the actual plan to surface. The Grand Area consists of North and South America, soon to be unified (plans call for 2006) according to the American Secretary of state in speeches made in Argentina, Chile, and Brazil in February of 1996 (FTAA).

An interesting quote from E-B34 is:

> *"In the event of an American-British victory, much would have to be done toward reshaping the world, particularly European Grand Area organization should prove useful. During an interim period of readjustment and reconstruction, the Grand Area might be an important stabilizing factor in the world's economy. Very likely the instructions developed for the integration of the Grand Area would yield useful experience in meeting European problems, and perhaps it would be possible to interweave the economies of European countries . . ."*

There you have it. Circa 1941, beginning of US involvement in WW II the EC was already formulated in the USA by the CFR.

This clearly shows that the Satori plan has been the same for decades. It shows that the EC was planned in 1941. It clearly shows the Satori plan to create trade blocks, managed by them, to optimize trade and banking profits. Wars are profitable. However, a world economy controlled by a single group is substantially more profitable.

America was not in the war in June of 1941 when the Germans attacked Russia. By August of that year the United States began an undeclared war against Germany in the North Atlantic. Subsequently in December 1941, unable to continue to accept US resource blockade in Japan's sphere of influence, Japan attacked the US fleet at Pearl Harbor. These results, as listed herein, were the direct results of CFR action. The CFR needed a world war in order to bring about changes they viewed as necessary to establish their New World Order. In Europe that was accomplished through the WW I peace treaty, and in the Far East by interfering with Japan's ability to obtain oil and raw materials.

To understand the Japan of 1941, you must grasp that, like the United States, Japan also had survival instincts. Japan felt that in order to continue its national ability to produce, it required a geographic region which had the ability to supply sufficient raw materials to keep its industry operational. Japan envisioned what it called "The Greater Asia Co-Prosperity Sphere." This region would consist of the Dutch East Indies, China, Indochina, Thailand, Burma, Malaya, the Philippines, and certain pacific islands for naval security in the pacific. Almost the entire region of planned Japanese expansion was the colonial empire of Europe. The major players were the Dutch, French, and British. Roosevelt agreed with Churchill and the CFR that the flow of raw material supplies from the Far East to Europe and America should not be interrupted. Thus the course to isolate Japan, forcing that nation into an association with the European axis powers.

The three Great European powers that controlled Southeast Asia were Holland, France, and England. Since England, Holland and France were weakened by the European conflict, Japan saw this as a prime opportunity to obtain much of this mineral-rich real-estate from the Europeans. What the Japanese had not counted on in the beginning of this venture, was the involvement of the United States of America. FDR, who was completely controlled by his advisors in the CFR, froze all Japanese assets, issued a total economic embargo, and blocked oil delivery to Japan. Naturally France, Britain, and the Netherlands immediately followed suit either directly or though governments in exile. The inflexibility of the American (i. e. CFR) position on Manchuria was the reason that Japan attacked Pearl Harbor. Japan needed oil and raw materials, and the United States blocked all Japanese efforts to obtain them unless Japan agreed to give up all its conquered territory in Manchuria. This was not tenable as Manchuria was Japan's primary source of most raw materials. In November 1941, the United States, in final negotiations and under CFR tutelage, gave Japan a twenty-six point ultimatum. It stated that in order for relations to be normalized, Japan would have to relinquish all conquered territory and return all borders to their position prior to 1931 . The

CFR knew full well that there was no way Japan could comply with that demand. They also knew that Japan's oil reserves were at the point of depletion, and therefore Japan had no option but to go to war.

This is how and why the Satori, through their surrogates, were the primary reason for the war in the pacific. They arranged matters in such a way as to ensure a conflict on both sides of the continent. The most important reason for forcing the Japanese to attack the US was that it would have been impossible, even for FDR, to convince the American public to go to war against Japan in order to save European colonial interests.

Between 1941 and 1944, the CFR planning committees were, in effect, turned over to the State Department and became part of it. It is imperative to understand that the interests of the CFR in no way coincided with those of America as a nation, or the American public. The CFR represents an ideology that is in conflict with all that the United States stands for. It is the concept of unbridled internationalism, elitism, and political as well as social control of all of society. These are the elites, which I call the Satori.

In early 1943, a new group was formed by the CFR which FDR called his Advisory Committee. It consisted entirely of CFR members: Bowman, Davis, Hull, Pasvolosky, Taylor, and Wells. These same men eventually became involved in the founding of, and the drafting of, the UN charter. This group, from then forward, ran the US government by guiding all advisory groups within the State Department.[5]

The objective in the 1940s was to assert, on a world wide basis, the old Roman concept of Pax Americana.[6] This was the beginning of actual conceptualization of the concepts of "Free Trade" and the geo-political concepts of regionalization over national existence

[5]Minutes S-3, 6 May 1942 Notter file
[6]Ibid.

It became obvious to the Satori that a system of financing this entire operation must be found. Funding on a scale this vast was an historic first. Bear in mind that this was no small undertaking. Entire new concepts were to be put in place: the International Monetary Fund (IMF); the International Bank for Reconstruction and Development, later called the World Bank; and all the myriad of wealth redistribution schemes that were to follow. And remember, the Satori reap a profit on every single international transaction of any kind, both private and governmental, while the citizens of the world foot the bill. In fact, a proposal for the implementation of the aforementioned was made as proposal P-B23 in 1941. The recommendation clearly stated the need for "currency stabilization" and "financial institutions capable of carrying out the planned objectives."[7] It is through this information that we again see the hand of the Satori in creating a method through which transfers the wealth of one nation to another, while making a profit for themselves. It is an undeniable fact that if we take just those funds from the United States that were redistributed in various plans and combine them (i.e. free trade, World Bank, health aid, UN, foreign aid, etc.) that the US would have no deficit, a fully-funded social security system, the largest gold reserve on the planet, and the highest standard of living. What the Satori have done to this nation would result in immediate war were they a nation state. Unfortunately they are, like Fourth Generation War, among us, and unidentifiable by the citizenry.

By autumn 1941, the CFR no longer bothered to transmit information and directions through the state bureaucracy; it sent its directives directly to FDR and the State Department. Harry Dexter White, not a CFR member, is credited with authorship of the plan for the IMF and World Bank. Secretary of the Trea-

[7]Ibid.

sury Morganthau took White's recommendations directly to FDR who had it brought up at the cabinet meeting on 25 May 1942. The rest you know.

In 1942, the Satori realized that the world was becoming more nationalized, and this was contrary to their plans. If their plan for trade, markets, and banking managed by them were to succeed, they needed a vehicle to implement their political plans. Financial considerations having already been settled with the World Bank and IMF. A principle problem lay in the fact that 19th century political system of colonialism was strongly out of favor. The Satori did not want to be labeled new colonialists. The answer was found by resurrecting the old League of Nations, as the United Nations. Through the very clever voting arrangements of the UN, Satori surrogates are always in a position to veto any act they disapprove of. The charter of the UN underwent numerous change, but it is accepted history that the actual foundation of the structure as well as the planning for the UN came from the US State Department, which was run by the CFR. Indeed it was at a meeting called the Dunbarton Oaks Conference, which ended in July 1944, that the actual work of the UN Charter was completed. Charles Evans Hughes, John W. Davis, and Nathen N. Miller presented the final draft to FDR who affirmed it on 15 June 1944, and shortly thereafter issued a communication about it to the American people.

The UN was the last and the most pronounced act of the decade of the 40s. It is also without doubt the largest undertaking of the Satori in their history. The UN was conceived, enacted, and financed by the CFR. David Rockefeller, who was at that time chairman of the CFR, donated the land on which the UN stands on Manhattan Island. A donation on which he made a handsome profit because the land was of little value, being a slum, and by giving away half of it to the UN, the rest increased in value 100-fold.

Planning for the UN was accomplished through a secret planning committee headed by Secretary Hull in January 1943. Later members of the committee were, Bowman, Davis, Pasvolosky, and Taylor. Wells was also a member, but he left government service in August 1943. All others except Hull were CFR members.[8]

Fifty years ago society asserted national interests as paramount in the foreign policy of all nation states. This has drastically changed over the years, and it would be fair to say that national self-interest counts for nothing in Satori plans having been replaced by regionalization and globalism. With the changing ownership of most hard assets to multi-national business concerns, the corporate entity has replaced national interest. This fact was further impacted by the fact that, through this occurrence, personal loyalty has also shifted from national to corporate or ethnic, or religious allegiance. The current fractionalization and polarization of society can be directly linked to Satori inspired plans that now are paramount in our culture.

The Satori in this equation represent the wealthiest members of the world. The Mandarins are the opportunist class of society, who realize that by pleasing their masters they will achieve personal wealth and advancement. This does not necessarily mean that individual Mandarins are, in all instances, aware of who masters them. That is, after all, not obligatory. A bureaucracy of such enormous size, encompassing many organizations within its structure, and almost 5,000 members, creates its own hierarchy for advancement. Furthermore because the Satori never deal directly with any of the mandarin groups, but always through an intermediary, only the leaders of the various Mandarin groups know of them.

It should come as no surprise, then, to learn that the CFR, more recently, has been actively enlisting for the expansion of NATO and, of course, subsequent trade block enlargement as an outcome of that act.

[8]Notter, 1949 pp. 169

Partners for Peace (PFP) was their concept to bring new member prospects into NATO. The concept revolves around political and social stability of former Soviet client states. The first PFP member was Rumania. In April 1996, National Empowerment Television (NET) featured an interesting program with three ambassadors of former USSR client states. Having a fair amount of experience with ambassadors, I can tell you that it is unusual to have three on the same program at the same time. But having all of them agree, was down-right eerie. Present were Slovak ambassador Lichaardus, Hungarian ambassador Ambaniaki, and Rumanian ambassador Gezana. All of them were not only anxious to join NATO they were positively animated. Do they know something that we don't? Is it perhaps that they understand clearly what is taking place geopolitically, and who is running things? If we look ahead a few years we can see the western world separated into huge trading blocks. Now understanding that NATO membership is a first step to becoming an EC member, and that PFP is the first step to becoming a NATO member — you get the point. These ambassadors and the nations that they represent are rational and intelligent; they want a piece of the pie. In this way we see how the Satori are able to influence politics and national agendas in nations in which they do not even have a presence. PFP was an initiative developed by the CFR, as was NATO, EC, WTO, NAFTA, and so on. Once an organization attains a certain size, like a rolling avalanche, it gains momentum and increases in size. The ambassadors mentioned share many facets of their interest in the EC: commonality of interest, similarity in politics, mutual security, and a desire in some way through NATO and then EC to be linked to a large trade block. All of the ambassadors clearly and repeatedly stated the CFR slogan: Europe was unable to act as a power broker without American participation. All mentioned the unique American (CFR) foreign policy which allowed "free and stable markets." This is the core of the Satori mandate: *Con-*

trolled Markets and Trade Between Them. We must remember that the Satori may be bankers, but that in essence they are mercantilists of the first order. All functions, all acts, are designed with but one prime objective; make it easier to control trade and more stable to guarantee payment.

The last dark age was brought about by a feudal society of which the only object of perpetuation of the system was based on the privilege of birth. The coming dark age will be based on a society of which the only appeal of perpetuation will be material wealth and the control of it. The fact that over half of the Mandarins do not understand the outcome should not surprise you, and will not have any effect on it.

THE ORDER

The oldest currently operating Mandarin organization in the United States is The Order. They have been in business, as you might say, since the mid 1850s. This is not the same crowd as The Group in England, which operates under a similar name. Also be aware that The Order functions under several different names: Skull & Bones, Bones, and in the 1860s as The Order of Death. It came to America by way of Germany, in all probability from one of the popular German dueling societies, which were very prevalent in and around Heidelberg at that time. One may also speculate that, in the 17th century, The Illuminati were active and that their ritual was strongly influenced by the York Masonic Rite from which the founder of the Illuminati had been expelled. The Order is referred to as Chapter 322 which leads one to speculate that the charter of the organization originated in Heidelberg, where all the fraternities had numbers. The Order was incorporated in 1856 as the Russell Trust in the state of Connecticut. The American Charter was instituted in 1833 at Yale University by General William Huntington Russell, and Alphonso Taft who in later years (1876) became Secretary of War. Alphonso Taft was the father of William Howard Taft, the only American ever to be both president and Chief Justice of the Supreme Court.

The meeting place of Bones, since 1856, is the "tomb." It is a two story building without windows, whose walls are covered with vines. On Sept. 29, 1876 an organization which called themselves "The Order of File and Claw" broke into the "tomb" and reported on what they found: Large room all walls covered in black velvet . . . Room 324. Upstairs they found Room 322. All walls in 322 were covered in red velvet. On the west wall was a large pentagram. In the halls were pictures of many past members. Below the pentagram, an old engraving representing an open burial vault, in which on a stone slab, rest four human skulls, grouped about a fools cap and bells, an open book, and several mathematical instruments, a beggar's scrip, and a royal crown. The following poem on the wall:

Wer War der Thor?
Wer Weiser
Wer Besser odrer
Kaiser?

Translation from German:

Who was Thor ?
Who wiser
Who better or the
Kaiser?

Also: "Ob Arm, Ob Reich, im Tode Gleich!" Translation from German: "If poor, if rich; in death the same!" Accompanying the picture is a card: From the German Chapter. Presented by D.G. Gillman 1850. Gillman was one of the original incorporates of the Russell Trust (the later established host for Skull and Bones) in New Haven, CT in 1856. Three men originally went to Germany to study at the university of Berlin in 1850: Gillman, Timothy Dwight, 49, and Andrew Dikinsen, 53. They were already Bonesmen when they went to Germany. The order's power was structured and consolidated during the 14 ensuing years by Gillman as treasurer and Russell as president.

Gillman was made chief librarian of Yale in 1858. He was then able to obtain funding to start Yale's science department, The Sheffield Scientific School. Next, he was able to get Abraham Lincoln to establish the Public Land Grant Act (Pres. Buchanan had refused). He then maneuvered Yale into grabbing all the land grants in the state of Connecticut for itself. This bill is now called the Land Grant College Act, needless to say, since Yale got 100% of it for Yale, no one else benefited from the legislation in CT. For these services Gillman was promoted to full Professor of Geography.

A very substantial number of the members of The Order are also members of either one or all of the other Mandarin organizations: the CFR, the TC, or the Bilderbergers. The Order also has two associate fraternities at Yale, these are Scroll & Key and Wolfshead. They appear to function the same way, and are also secret. They are called Senior Societies and exist solely at Yale University. A Senior Society invites only seniors at Yale to join. Petitioning for membership is not possible, Senior Societies are available only on invitation. The most obvious fact about these fraternities is that membership over the years has always been from the same families. Membership is absolutely related to family affiliation. Females cannot become members, but if a member's daughter has a male child he will, in all probability, be asked to join. The Order inducts fifteen new members every year. Just under 600 members are alive at this time, but only about half are active as Mandarins, or Satori. The Patriarchs (full members) of the Order meet annually on Deer Island in the St. Lawrence River in New York State.

The power of this relatively small group of individuals must not be underestimated. Its tie to the Satori is the strongest, many Satori are members, and almost all Zwischengaener are members. The Order is completely secret, all members being sworn to secrecy on the day of initiation. They have strict rules and lengthy initiation rituals. They do not answer mail from non-members (called Vandals), they will not admit that they exist, and individual members almost always deny participation in The Order. Federal office holders, in violation of federal statutes, in every known instance have neglected to enter the fact of membership on national security checks by the FBI. The Order has its own calendar: the date of the year is arrived at by adding the number 322 to the year . . . thus 1997 becomes 2319. This characteristic stems from the Jewish and Masonic calendars which similarly add a quantity to the year. Since the founder of the Illuminati was an outcast Freemason he would have remembered this practice from that fraternity. Upon entering the Order, an initiate (called a Neophyte) has his name changed, i.e. is given a special name within the Order of Knight so-and-so. Established members are thereafter referred to as Patriarchs and non-members as Vandals or Gentiles. As of this time it seems that The Order has evolved into a core of about 50 families. Names which are prominent are: Whitney, Phelps, Lord, Wadsworth, Allen, Bundy, Adams, Harriman, Rockefeller, Payne, and Davison. In the past 100 years, only two articles on The Order have been published: one on 13 October 1873 in the *Iconoclast* and the other in 1977 in *Esquire* by Ron Rosenbaum. Yale University, it can be said, is run for and by The Order to meet its, and not the University's, goals.

To support my claim that The Order is family-directed, I give the following examples: Eight Whitney family members and nine Harriman family members have been associated with the Order. Brown Brothers Harriman & Co. is a substantial banking business. The following is a list of the firm's principal partners along with the dates of initiation to the Order:

W. Averell Harriman 1913
Prescott Sheldon Bush 1917
Edward R.N. Harriman 1917
Knight Wooley 1917
Robert A. Lovett.. 1918
Stephen Young Lord.................................. 1921
Granger Kent Costikyan 1929
John B. Madden 1941
Walter H. Brown 1945

Brown Harriman & Co., which is the largest and oldest private banking house in the Americas, lists their assets, as of December 1995, as being $1,682,137,041.00.

It is an interesting fact that the British equivalent of the American Order, The Group, is also centered in academia, namely Oxford University and All Souls College (both based in Oxford). The British organization referred to as "The Group" is sometimes also known as Milner's Round Table (after Lord Milner).

All this is surely related to Cecil Rhodes, the South African multimillionaire, and his strange wills and bequests, some of which were, and still are, kept secret. Rhodes was very much involved with the socialists at the turn of the last century. He was certainly involved with the Fabian Society, the forerunner of the English Labor party, and the modern American Democrat party. Around 1930, Beatrice Webb, in what is now called the Webb house, was the hub of the largest socialist organization in the world at that time. It is not difficult to speculate that there are certain connections between The Order and The Group.

There is an additional communality between these two groups; both have a basic family core membership outside of which few new members are accepted. If new members from new families are taken in it is because of extraordinary ability or incredible wealth.

One way that The Order controls outcome is through foundations. The Ford Foundation is an interesting case in point. Members of The Order infiltrated the management of the foundation until they had a plurality in management and on the board. They then began to fund structures which were political and social with which the members of the Ford family objected. This funding continued even over the strenuous objections of the Ford family which in effect was rendered impotent by the plurality of Order members. The situation became so strained that the remaining two members of the Ford family resigned from the directorship of the foundation. The Order accomplished the exact same thing in the Carnegie Foundation, which it now controls as well. No members of the Ford or Carnegie families were ever members of The Order.

Professor Quigley (CFR) came to the same conclusion I did; namely that in most secret societies not all members are aware of the organizational motives. There is, in my opinion, a cadre of people who unquestionably not only understand the purpose but also its function and direction, and carry them out to the letter. There is also likewise a portion of the membership who knows or at least suspects. These people in most instances enjoy their lifestyle and their income and thus go along to get along. Finally, there is a group who do not understand what the outcome is, and who through peer pressure and a desire to get ahead simply follow instructions.

It is my opinion that due to the age of The Order, the fact that members are recruited at a very young age, and that they, in a preponderance of cases, come from Mandarin families, they are the Mandarin group with the largest Satori membership. It is almost certainly a fact that most Zwishengaener are of The Order. In a hierarchical assessment, The Order would be placed higher than the CFR, the TC or the Bilderbergers. Please understand that it is not necessary to micro-manage governments or any other institution for that matter. To control any desired outcome, in any organization, all that is necessary is to control the dialogue, and the input. Through these, one controls the language and policy and thus determines the output. It is the people who control the dialogue in the opinion-molding process and the media who determine societal direction. Along this line, The Order has fastidiously infiltrated all major opinion-molding and educational institutions of America, while The Group has done the same in England and the EC.

Many institutions and associations were in fact infiltrated or started by The Order for the sole purpose of controlling the debate or for expanding their base of operations. Harvard, Cornell, and Johns Hopkins in academia, as well as the American History Association, the American Economic Association, the American Chemical Association, and the American Psychological Association are cases in point.

Religion has been compromised through Yale Divinity School and Union Theological Seminary. Both institutions are thoroughly under Satori control via people like Henry Sloan Coffin.

Likewise, law, media, and politics all have been infiltrated. All have been compromised. Let us take some examples. The media: Here we have Henry Luce, member of Bones and former chairman of Time-Life; Editor William F. Buckley, Jr. (CFR, TC, Bilderbergers, Bones); and Archibald McLeach, member of Bones and the first director of the coveted journalistic award, The Nieman Fellowship. How about that for controlling the outcome? The ability to choose the winner of one of the most desirable journalistic awards.[9]

As you will recall, I pointed out earlier that the Satori represent varied political as well as social ideology. This was for me the most difficult concept to grasp. Most of us tend to think in rather absolute terms: good and evil, hot and cold, free and enslaved, black and white, right and wrong. It is hard for us to realize that the Satori have no such concepts. They are indifferent to political and social ideology. Although they do favor statist, centrally controlled political systems of the type that have top-down management because such systems are easier to control.

The Bundy family has long been affiliated with The Order. The Bundys have also been on the left end of the political spectrum for a considerable length of time. During the Senator Joseph McCarthy hearings, McCarthy wanted William Bundy to testify in senate hearings. The Bones arrayed against any forced testimony by Bundy, even though Bundy had contributed $4,000 to convicted communist spy Alger Hiss' defense fund. A brief investigation into Bundy's employment record produces the following:

[9]Because the Bones and Bilderbergers are totally secret organizations, membership cannot be proven, even though strong evidence for membership exists. Membership in the CFR and TC can be proven as their members are not sworn to secrecy.

1947 – 51	Law firm of Covington & Burling (Washington DC)
1951 – 61	CIA
1960	Staff Director Presidential Commission on National Goals
1961 – 63	Deputy Secretary of Defense for Internal Security
1964 – 69	Assistant Secretary of State East Asia (Vietnam)
1969 – 71	Professor MIT
1972	Editor Foreign Affairs CFR

With that kind of employment and background why would you be the major contributor to the defense fund of a major spy? Many of his other associates are also interesting, if not downright colorful people. John Douglas, the son of Senator Paul H. Douglas, was the premier left-wing radical nut of the 1940s. Michael Boudin, son of partner Leonard Boudin and brother of Kathy Boudin, made the FBI's most wanted list. Leonard was the communist front man for the National Lawyers Guild. Kathy was a founder of the Students for Democratic Society (SDS), a bomb-manufacturing antisocial enterprise that got her arrested.

For many years there has been speculation that the CIA has been involved in left-wing terrorist groups trying to change the direction of society. Internal strife, bombings, and crime all contribute to a climate that allows government to increase regulation and law at the loss of freedom and liberty. This is the exact direction the Satori wish to go. Another example of CIA involvement of this sort is (according to several newsletters), when Bill Clinton was at Oxford, he worked as a snitch for the CIA. It is said that the entire time he was organizing demonstrations in London and Oslo, he was passing the names of his friends on to the CIA. When blood relatives belong to the same organizations, their families have high ranking members in the CIA, and all of them are involved in stirring up social conflict, you just have to reach conclusions.

However unrelated, the recent American bombing of the Oklahoma City Federal building has certainly brought similar suspicions to the forefront. Consider the sloppy handling by the FBI, the BATF agents all being out of the building, General Partin's assessment, the peculiar circumstance of the McVeigh arrest, the fact that the FBI lab fabricated evidence, and the already prepared anti-terrorist legislation ready for immediate release.

Do you remember the Hegelian dielectic? Bundy's 1960 commission made the following statements: "A role of government is to stimulate change." Find that in the US constitution!

The pro-active government is what causes most of our national and international problems. Governments, i.e. Mandarins, do not create jobs, expand economies, improve the standard of living, or increase national GNP. These come only from the private sector.

Satori-directed Mandarins utilize the Hegelian dialectic process to bring about a society in which the Satori's power will be absolute. Mandarins refer to war as "managed conflict." Does this not mean that the war is being manipulated to meet Satori desired ends, for either profit or power? It is through the continuous application of all these principles of philosophy that their "Novus Ordo Secolorum" is to be instituted.

As in most other Satori-sponsored organizations, The Order is resolutely absorbed in education. The Order, as previously demonstrated, was responsible for the foundation of numerous universities and colleges. Daniel Coit Gilman (Order) was president of Johns Hopkins University when he influenced that institution to import the German Wundt psychological structure, which was subsequently merged into the American public educational processes. Wundt had developed the first psychological laboratories in Leipzig and then subsequently at the University of Berlin. We should all be aware of the catastrophic effect this has had on American public schools. The present malaise in our school systems can be directly linked to these developments. At that time, there were two schools of Hegelian thought: on the right was the Prussian model of Karl Ritter, Otto V. Bismarck, and others including advisors to the British crown;

on the other side were Karl Marx, Fredrich Engels, and the author Heinrich Heine, Max Steiner and Moses Hess.

What has all this to do with education? A great deal, and is what I refer to as the Janus effect. Janus was a Roman god with two heads each on the opposite side of a single door; always looking in as well as out. Think of the Hegelian process, the division of forces, the act of creating two actions, with a previously determined outcome. Is it not interesting that both aforementioned products resulted in a larger and more centralized power? In fact the two differing philosophies resulted in Nazism, a form of socialism, and communism, both totalitarian systems. The bringing of these concepts to America can be credited to Gillman, one of the founders of The Order, and subsequent president of the University of California. As we can see by this, the foundation on which modern American education rests is not American, not republican, not based on the great principles of our constitution, but instead on a state-centralized totalitarian German model. The foundation of any system of education is of great importance because it is the foundation upon which the entire structure sits. With a foundation based in Nazism, socialism, and communism, it is a small wonder that our educational system has gone to pot. The underlying cause of all American educational problems rests with The Order, which the Satori directed to introduce undemocratic social, psychological, and political thought to the previously republican educational system. Again the reason is simple, centralization of power, and the dumbing-down of the population to simplify top-down control.

Prominent Family Surnames in the History of The Order (Bones)

Bundy	McLeash
Bush	Percy
Buckley	Pratt
Coffin	Phelps
Cooper	Pillsbury
Emerson	Payne
Gallaudet	Sage
Gillman	Rockefeller
Griswold	Taft
Hall	Thompson
Harriman	Walker
Kellogg	White
Kingsley	Whitney
Lewis	Weyerhauser
Lord	Wadsworth

The above list of surnames has grown over the years as daughters of members marry and their grandsons, if outstanding students at Yale, are recruited to become members of The Order (Bones).

Prominent Americans who were, or are, Members of Bones include:

Bingham, Sen. Jonathan	Heinz, Sen. John
Boren, Sen. David	Holden, Reuber
Bradford, Armory H.	Jay, Pierre
Buckley, James	Kerry, Sen. John
Buckley, William F. Jr.	Lilley, John
Bundy, McGeorge	Lord, C.E.
Bush, Pres. George Walker	Lord, Winston
Bush, Sen. Prescott Sheldon	Luce, Henry
Chaffe, Sen. John	More, Richard A.

Cochran, Thomas
Coffin, Henry George
Coffin, Sloane
Cowles, Alfred
Cunningham, Hugh
Daniels, John Thomas
Davenport, Russell W.
Davidson, F. Trubee
Davidson, Henry P.
Dine, V. Van
Drapper, William III
French, Robert D.
Galbrath, Evan G.
Gates, Artemus
Gow, Richard
Harriman, William Averell
McBundy, George
McBundy, William
McLeash, Archibald
Pinchot, Gilliord
Rockefeller, Percy
Roosevelt, Pres. Theodore
Stanley, Morgan
Stewart, Potter
Taft, Pres. William Howard
Walker, Charles
Walker, George Herbert Jr.
Weyerhauser, Fredsrick
Whitney, Harry P.
Wilson, Hugh
Witter, Dean Jr.

The purpose of the above list is to impart an historic perspective of Bones, Chapter 322, that people may realize the important role individual members have played, and do play, in American life.

"The Trilateral Commission is international and is intended to be the vehicle for multi-national consolidation of the commercial and banking interests by seizing control of the political government of the United States. The Trilateral Commission represents a skillful, coordinated effort to seize control and consolidate the four centers of power — political, monetary, intellectual and ecclesiastical."

— Senator Barry Goldwater

THE TRILATERAL COMMISSION

The Trilateral Commission (TC) was founded at a meeting on the Rockefeller estate in upper Westchester county, New York, on the 23rd and 24th of July, 1972. The name relates to the fact that membership is primarily from the United States, Europe, and Japan, thus Tri-. In 1972, David Rockefeller was chairman of the CFR. The eight individuals who attended that meeting at the Rockefeller estate were all CFR members. Thus, the TC may be looked upon as a child of the CFR.[10] A portion of the founding statement of the CFR is very similar to the founding statement of the Bilderbergers: "Close Trilateral cooperation in keeping with peace, in managing the world economy, in fostering economic redevelopment, and alleviating world poverty will improve the chances of a smooth and peaceful evolution of the Global System."[11] This enlightening statement informs us that the TC plans to keep the peace (UN military), manage the world economy (control trade and banking), and effect economic redistribution (socialist redistribution of wealth). Also note that this is to be done on a global scale. The only way this can be effectively accomplished is with a world government that they control. That is, of course, the very plan. Retired Senator Barry Goldwater, whose presidential bid was deep-sixed by the Satori, got it exactly right in his book *With No Apologies* when he stated: "What the TC truly intends is the creation of a worldwide economic power, superior to the political government of the states involved. As manager and creator of the system they will rule the world."

[10]Robert W. Lee, "Confirming the Liberal Establishment," *American Opinion* 1981
[11]Barry Goldwater, *With No Apologies*

One TC creation, which gives the false appearance of having failed, is former president Jimmy Carter. Carter was fastidiously tutored by none other than Zbigniew Brzezinski, a TC founder, along with Professor Richard N. Gardner of Columbia University.[12] From this we can reach only three possible conclusions: (a) Carter was too stupid to understand what he was being instructed in; (b) the teachers were inept; (c) the message was too early, in that the public had not yet been properly indoctrinated by the media. In retrospect it is easy to see the incredible damage done both to this republic and to the world by the Carter administration. This must be the major TC and Satori victory of that decade, judging from the results achieved by the elite. In that realm, Carter stands head and shoulders above all others, before or since.

David Rockefeller's power and influence must not be underestimated. As early as 1973, he met with a total of twenty-seven heads of state, including those of the USSR and the PRC. Considering that he has never in his life held any public office, nor even been appointed to any governmental organization, this is truly remarkable. Perhaps many leaders are very much aware of who really runs things. In 1964, he visited the Kremlin where he had a two-hour plus meeting with then General Secretary of the USSR, Nikita Khruschev. Within less then six months after that meeting Khrushchev was relegated to the dustbin of history.

The idea for the foundation of the TC came from Brzezinski, who sold it to Rockefeller, the man with the necessary finances and connections to be able to bring the entire plan to fruition. Brzezinski realized that CFR plans could not be instituted on a global scale without worldwide participation. Certainly the CFR needed an organization which linked the economies of Japan and Europe with that of America. Brzezinski is well published,

[12]*NY Times*, 23 May 1976

and we can glean much from his writings of the plans of the Satori. He is without doubt the current intellectual force behind the New World Order. His writings tell us a great deal of the plans of the Satori. He writes;

> *"I should like to address myself to the problem of political change. I think we accept the idea of vast expansion in social regulation. It may take such forms as legislation for the number of children, perhaps even legislation determining the sex of children once we have a choice, the regulation of weather, the regulation of leisure, and so on and so forth."*

Well there you have it, George Orwell's *1984*, the Satori plan for the world. Orwell, by the way, was a frequent visitor to the Webb house and a confirmed Fabian socialist. The entire cabal is laid out in Zigi's book *Between Two Ages*. I have no idea how you feel about this plan, but frankly it scares the hell out of me. On page 300 of that tome, he introduces two concepts which are central to the philosophy of the New World Order. One, the introduction of a new and universal monetary system to replace the dollar along with the elimination of cash, and two, the reduction of the standard of living in the industrialized west. He states;

> *"In the economic-technological field some international cooperation has already been achieved, but further progress will require greater American sacrifice."*

In other words the present national decline of America's standard of living is not yet rapid enough to meet with Satori timetables. They want to speed up the process of making us poorer. Again he writes;

> *"More intensive effort to shape a new world monetary structure will have to be undertaken, with some consequent risk to the present relatively favorable American position."*

We as a nation who have worked hard, been industrious, and inventive for generations, are now to be ordered to give up our hard-gotten gains so that the Satori can rule us and profit by the sweat of our brows, to rule us as they see fit.

Zigi is also a resolute and unapologetic supporter of Marxist dogma. The following are quotes about Marx in the aforementioned book by Zigi; "Marxism represents a further vital and creative stage in the maturing of man's universal vision," and "Marxism is simultaneously a victory of the external man over the inner, passive man, and a victory of reason over belief." I do wonder what all the poor souls from the old USSR think about that, and why Zigi ,who came from a communist nation, is living here if things are so much better and fairer over there. Another statement is, "Marxism disseminates on the popular level in the form of communism, and represents a major advance in man's ability to conceptualize his relationship to the world." The text goes on ad infinitum extolling in great detail just how wonderful communism is. Well, Zigi, if it's so wonderful, would you mind just naming one nation, state, town, or community where it has been successful, and if communism is so good, why are you living in a capitalist nation, other than to help destroy it?

His writings are, without doubt, the master plan of the Satori. It is, moreover, a sort of outline for the whole cabal. Nuclear themes are centralization and authoritarian rule. This is generally represented as if only two choices, namely, Satori dictatorship or anarchy, existed. With societal consensus not being in tune with the plan, it calls for imminent mass media domination by the Satori of the dissemination of all information, the gradual appearance of a more controlled society, and the movement toward larger groups (EC, NAFTA) and communities of nations.

The fact that these SOB's have succeeded to such an extent should give us all pause to contemplate how our children will like being enslaved to a bunch of megalomaniacs bent on controlling everyone from cradle to grave.

We are told that movement in this direction will require several broad overlapping phases which can take place simultaneously: the merging of major corporations into larger, and in all cases, multi-national conglomerates; the affiliation of trade blocks which will, for the benefit of the corporations, maintain trade and monetary market control; and the creation of a multinational, multi-cultural military for enforcement. Anyone can see that this is exactly what is presently taking place.

A big problem for the Satori, who you will recall make most of their income from trade, is the instability of currencies. This problem is also covered in Zigi's book with the prediction: "We would anticipate some major monetary change around the turn of the century." The EC is planning to have their new currency, the EUC, online by 1999. A real gem is to be found on page 304, "might also lead to the possibility of something along the line of a global taxation system." If you have been reading the newspapers you will be acutely aware of the attempts by the UN to have global taxes imposed on international air travel and international currency transactions. Let's remember what it takes to have a conspiracy: numerous separate organizations acting in concert. Seems to me they are doing exactly that.

Just a few pages further on we learn that "Though the objective of shaping a community of the developed nations is less ambitious than the goal of world government, it is more attainable." In other words, the industrialized west must first be subjugated into a trade block, and then, when that has been accomplished, it can be converted into a one world government.

Now I defy anyone to disprove that this is a plan for world domination by a select group of planners (i.e., the Satori) and that they employ others (i.e., the Mandarins) to carry out their scheme.

It is an interesting fact that opposition to these plans by the population of the many various nations is universal. Resistance to the Satori-inspired plan is at just about the 89% level in all

Western states. The problem is with business, and more specifically with professional managers of corporations. Many of these are Mandarins, and even if they are not, they have to play ball according to the rules of the Satori or else find themselves unemployed and without prospect of a future job. It is my assumption that all government workers in management capacity are either Mandarins or are controlled by them.

Without a doubt it is a hard sell to convince people to give up their family, religion, national entity, and community, replacing them with allegiance to a Satori-run, multi-national corporation. The Satori have fashioned an unholy allegiance between big money, politics, and the Mandarin class. A demonstrable example of this is the round of bank failures which occurred in the 1980s in the USA, Europe, and Japan. The failures were orchestrated through government manipulation and the taxpayer wound up on the hook for the money lost. In each case, central banks became stronger, competition was reduced, and not one Satori-controlled bank failed. These well-managed and taxpayer financed bank failures were designed to consolidate the entire banking industry into the hands of a very small group of individuals. In the United States alone they were successful in eliminating over 600 competitive banks and through consolidation and mergers eliminated another hundred. The Satori plan calls for no more than ten to fifteen international banks to control all the world's finances.

On 10 April 1996, in an article in the *Wall Street Journal*, a planned merger between CS Holding and The Union Bank of Switzerland was announced. The merger failed, but if successful would have created a monolith with assets of over SFr. 800 billion, that's US $670 billion. What you must understand is, these are the size of amounts of money that the Satori control. When you have that type of capital strength you do not ask governments or people, you tell them.

How the Trilateral Commission (TC) is financed follows the pattern set by the CFR. Financing comes from government and foundations. The largest single supporters of the TC are the Rockefeller and Ford foundations, with Ford historically being the larger of the two. Foundations represent, without any doubt, the single cleverest act of the founders of the Federal Reserve System (FRS). Foundations have a very special advantage over any other entity in existence; to wit, their tax exempt status. This allows them continuous growth at the expense of society as a whole. As has been shown, this is not used for the benefit of mankind but instead as an instrument of subjugation. The men at Jekyll Island first set up the Federal Reserve System (FRS) and then went to work on a way by which they, and only they, could circumvent the confiscatory tax structure to be imposed on the rest of us. They set up a foundation tax structure and then used it to fund their pet projects out of untaxed income. Now they had it all their way! First they pay no tax. Then with their corporation's before-tax profits they fund tax-exempt projects. Then the foundation funds the CFR. The CFR funds any number of organizations that are in accordance with their plans. Everything is paid for with before-tax dollars. This meets all their goals, expansion of power, influencing society, and expanded centralization.

Commentary about the TC is in no way restricted to the United States. The English publication *Weekly Review* stated, "International communism of the Moscow order has many features in common with the TC — such as the undermining of the national sovereignty of the United States."

John Foster Dulles, a founder of the TC as well as of the CFR, wrote, ". . . Establishment of a common money might be vested in a body created by, and responsible to, the principal trading and investing people." Well, we do know who the "principal trading and investing people" are, don't we — the Satori.

In 1972, a southern politician went on a TV program called *What's My Line*. He stumped everyone; not one person on the panel, not one in the audience knew who he was. His name was Jimmy Carter, and a short two and a half years later he was elected President of the United States. He was a protege of David Rockefeller and a new member of the recently founded TC. Tutored by Zigi along with an entire troop of academians, financed by Rockefeller and sold by the media, he could not fail. This man, who proved to be a godsend to the Satori, was a full blown catastrophe for America. It will take this nation decades to undo what President Carter managed in four short years. He single-handedly destroyed our capacity to reprocess nuclear fuel, he brought down the most pro-American government in the Middle East (Iran), he instituted more new law than the previous five presidents combined, he actively supported the South African Communist Party (SACP) against the legitimate government in power, he gave away the Panama Canal to a Marxist drug dealer, he betrayed the Somosa government of Nicaragua, and allowed the communist Sandanistas to rape the country and its population. The list is endless.

Carter's betrayal of the Shah of Iran was the worst act ever committed by a head of state in this century with the possible exception of Clinton's communist Chinese policy. The reason for the betrayal is vested in the fact that the Shah was quite expressive about the distribution of profits from Iran's natural resource, oil. The Shah was in a partnership with the Satori. The Shah often lamented in court and public that the multinational oil companies were, via the American government, subverting his authority and rule. This, he claimed, was because he wanted a larger percentage of the oil profits for his nation. In a book entitled *The Energy Cartel* by Norman Medvin, published in 1974, we can clearly see that the Shah was correct in his appraisal of the situation.

Iran had three operating oil companies at that time:

1.) Lavaan Petroleum Company, With the following partners:

Iran Oil Co.
Atlantic Richfield
Union oil
Murphy oil

2.) Iranian Oil Consortium, with the following partners:

BP
Shell
Mobil
Gulf
Exxon
CFP
American Independent
Texaco
Standard of CA

3.) Iranian Offshore Petroleum Co., with the following partners:

Atlantic Richfield
Cities Service
CFP
Superior
Sun
Kerr-McGhee
National Iranian Oil Co.

All this breaks down into seventeen American firms, two European firms, and two Iranian firms. It does seem to me that the Shah knew exactly what he was talking about. The Satori controlled 90% of the partnership and threw an occasional bone to Iran.[13] In 1979, several stories appeared in the LA *Herald Examiner* and the *London Express.* All claimed that the Ayatollah Khomeini, who was installed in Iran, was not the same person that was exiled in France. Amir Hoveida testified to this in court, was shouted down, taken outside and shot. The real Khomeini

[13]Given the ownership of Iran's oil companies in 1973, a good question would be, "Who really controlled OPEC?"

was missing the middle finger of his right hand, the impostor presented a full ten fingers. Khomeini had been replaced by an impostor.

The Panama Canal give-away was and still is opposed by a huge majority of the American people. It was instituted by the Satori for the same reason as the Mexican bail-out of 1995-1996. In 1977, the Panamanian government, through its dictator General Torrijos, was in hock to Satori NY bankers up to its proverbial neck. Like the Mexican deal, all the banks who were on the hook were Satori-owned institutions. The situation was so bad that Panama had allocated 40% of its tax revenues to service that debt. Panama's total debt had skyrocketed in the nine years of the Torrijos regime from $160 million to the astronomical sum of $1.45 billion. The Panama canal treaty was instituted by Carter in order to allocate funds to the Satori banks through American taxpayer subsidies.

This is exactly the same thing Clinton did in the Mexican bail-out in which $70 billion was confiscated by the Mandarins from the American treasury, and indirectly given to the Satori controlled and owned banks. Payments were made to Mexico whose government endorsed the check and sent it on to Wall Street to be cashed. The TC is the prominent figure in all these transactions because the Satori-owned banks are all staffed by Mandarins, the FRS.

Banks Involved in the Panamanian Deal Were:

Chase Manhattan — Rockefeller.
First National City Bank (Citybank)
First Bank of Chicago
Republic National
Bankers Trust
Marine Midland

Marine Midland was so badly on the hook at the time that there was considerable speculation that they might go bankrupt. Directly after the treaty was negotiated by the Carter administration, that fear evaporated. Half of the board of directors of the aforementioned banks are TC or CFR members.

Today over one fourth of the world's entire industrial output is controlled by multi-national corporations. Superficially, this may not appear to be a staggering amount, when you can argue that three quarters of the world's economy is not so controlled. There are several problems with this argument. First, it is not necessary to control everything in order to have actual control. Think of all the subcontractors, suppliers, and customers which these firms are able to influence. Second, although they represent only one fourth, they are organized. Third, they have uniformity of purpose, while the rest don't. The inescapable fact is that while the average international business grows at about 3%, these multi-national corporations exceed that by almost another 3%. The additional fact is that the Satori-controlled sectors of the world economy are more strategic than those not in their control. When we examine Mandarin presence in various sectors of economic endeavor, we come up with some startling information:

Membership Sector Participation

Sector	%
Media	18%
Academia	10%
Banking	19%
Law	12%
Government	20%
Manufacturing	12%
Miscellaneous	9%
Total	100%

The "membership" of all Mandarin organizations totals approximately 5,000 people. Therefore, using the media as an example, we find that of the many thousands of people employed in the media, only 900 are Mandarins (18% of 5,000). Yet, these 900 Mandarins have effective control of the mass media. Want proof? In October of 1997, one million "Promise Keepers" rallied in Washington D.C. and nary a photo in major newspapers. In addition, much of the coverage was negative, male chauvinistic diatribe. Compare this with the TV and newspaper coverage that would have been given were this a rally of one million of Jesse Jackon's, "Rainbow Coalition," or, one million "homeless," and there can be no doubt that the media is directed as to which social concepts to negate and which to promote.

An interesting fact relates to the present American executive branch of government. In the entire Clinton cabinet, there is not one single member outside of government, law or academia. This leads to many costly mistakes due to the unbalanced nature of the advisors. Participation by Mandarins in cabinet positions in the last six administrations is remarkable. (See list at end of this section). By concentrating their power on the aforementioned areas, the Satori exert an inordinate amount of pressure for non-participants to follow their lead. Bear in mind that most businesses are controlled by people who own less than 15% of the stock. David Rockefeller controls the Chase Manhattan Bank with an ownership of about 9% of the stock. Once you control the board of directors, you control where the meetings are held, who the CFO and CEO are, who the president is, how dividends are to be paid, and how funds are to be allocated. In fact you control the entire business lock, stock, and barrel. Over 75% of stockholders normally vote by proxy, and since most mutual funds (the largest share holders) are managed by Mandarins the Satori are able to control about $15 billion for every million invested.

The key to understanding TC policies and plans is the acceptance of the premise that the main thrust of all Satori plans at the present time is their concept of "Free Trade."

A dominant problem for the Satori has been the vast capital accumulated by Middle Eastern nations. The TC has tackled this problem from two differing directions. The first was the "Third Window" whereby large loans were made by OPEC nations to third world nations. These transactions went through the World Bank where the Satori took their cut. This allowed the third world nations to purchase more goods produced in the west with the following consequences: increased trade, increased profit, increased fees. From the minutes of a TC meeting comes the following quote: "A joint OPEC-TC initiative that brings forth more capital for development will serve TC interests very well."

Trilateral Commission (TC) membership is concentrated in Japan, Europe, and North America. The TC is a Satori organization. TC membership by region is as follows (as of February, 1996):

USA	99
Europe	151
Japan	68
Total:	318

See Appendix F for a complete listing of Trilateral Commission Members as of February, 1996.

Cabinet Members of the Last Six Presidents Associated with the Council on Foreign Relations, and/or the Trilateral Commisson, and the Bilderbergers:

William Clinton 93 (CFR, Tri, Bil)
state: Warren M. Christopher (CFR, Tri)
treasury: Lloyd Bentsen (CFR, Bil)
treasury: Robert E. Rubin (CFR, Bil)
defense: Les Aspin (CFR)
interior: Bruce Babbitt (CFR, Tri)
agriculture: Mike Espy (Bil)
commerce: Roland H. Brown (CFR)
health and human services: Donna E. Shalala (CFR, Tri)
housing and urban development: Henry G. Cisneros (CFR, Tri)

George Bush 89-93 (CFR, Tri, Bones)
state: Lawrence S. Eagleburger (CFR, Tri)
treasury: Nicholas F. Brady (CFR, Bil)
defense: Richard B. Cheney (CFR)
commerce: Robert A. Mosbacher (CFR)
commerce: Barbara H. Franklin (CFR)
labor: Lynn Martin (CFR)
attorney general: Richard Thornburg (CFR)

Ronald Reagan 81-89
state: Alexander M. Haig, Jr. (CFR)
state: George P. Shultz (CFR, Tri)
treasury: Donald T. Regan (CFR)
treasury: Nicholas F. Brady (CFR, Bil)
defense: Caspar W. Weinberger (CFR, Tri)
defense: Frank C. Carlucci (CFR, Tri)
commerce: Malcolm Baldrige (CFR)
labor: William E. Brock (CFR)
attorney general: Richard Thornburg (CFR)

Jimmy Carter 77-81 (CFR, Tri)
state: Cyrus R. Vance (CFR, Tri)
state: Edmund S. Muskie (CFR)
treasury: W. Michael Blumenthal (CFR, Tri)
treasury: G. William Miller (CFR)
defense: Harold Brown (CFR, Tri)
commerce: Juanita M. Kreps (CFR)
labor: F. Ray Marshall (CFR)
health, education and welfare: Joseph A. Califano, Jr. (CFR, Tri)
HEW Patricia Roberts Harris (CFR)
health and human services: Patricia Roberts Harris (CFR)
education: Shirley Hufstedler (CFR)
housing and urban development: Patricia Roberts Harris (CFR)
transportation: Neil E. Goldschmidt (CFR, Tri)

energy: James R. Schlesinger (CFR)
energy: Charles Duncan, Jr. (CFR, Tri)

Gerald Ford 74-77 (CFR, Bil)
state: Henry A. Kissinger (CFR, Bil)
treasury: William E. Simon (CFR)
defense: James R. Schlesinger (CFR)
defense: Donald H. Rumsfeld (CFR)
health, education and welfare: Caspar W. Weinberger (CFR)
housing and urban development: James T. Lynn (CFR)
HUD Carla Anderson Hills (CFR, Tri)
transportation: William T. Coleman, Jr. (CFR, Tri)

Richard Nixon 69-74 (CFR)
state: William P. Rodgers (CFR)
state: Henry A. Kissinger (CFR, Tri, Bil)
treasury: George P. Shultz (CFR, Tri)
treasury: William E. Simon (CFR)
defense: Melvin R. Laird (CFR)
defense: Eliott L. Richardson (CFR, Tri)
defense: James R. Schlesinger (CFR)
commerce: Peter G. Peterson (CFR)
labor: George P. Shultz (CFR, Tri)
labor: James D. Hodgson (CFR)
health, education and welfare: Eliott L. Richardson (CFR)
health, education and welfare: Caspar W. Weinberger (CFR)
housing and urban development: James T. Lynn (CFR)
attorney general: Eliot L. Richardson (CFR)

THE BILDERBERGERS

The Bilderberger Group is a secret establishment which functions as one of the major Mandarin organizations for the Satori. The association takes its name from an obscure hotel, the Hotel de Bilderberger in the Dutch town of Oosterbeek, where their first meeting was held 29-31 May 1954. In the strictly confidential minutes of that first meeting, the following statement may be found: ". . . To evolve an international order which will look beyond the present day crisis, when time is ripe for our present concepts of world affairs to be extended to the whole world . . ." (31 May 1954, Hotel de Bilderberg).[14] The third meeting was held in Bavaria, Germany at the resort of Garmisch-Patenkirchen. An important participant was the American ambassador to what was then West Germany, George McGee. Several days after the meeting, ambassador McGee made the following statement about the Bilderbergers: "The treaty of Rome, which brought the Common Market into being, was nurtured at various Bilderberger meetings."[15] At a more recent meeting held at Vouliagmeni, Greece, several notable British citizens participated, among them Kenneth Clarke (then Chancellor of the Exchequer) and Tony Blair (leader of the Labor Party since 1994 and current Prime Minister). A list of participants to that particular meeting is given below:[16]

United Kingdom of Great Britain

KeMeth Clarke	Chancellor of the Exchequer
Tony Blair	Leader, Labor Party
Lord Carrington	CEO Christies
Barbara Amiel	Columnist Sunday Times London
Conrad Black	Husband Amiel & CEO of London Telegraph

[14]*This England,* Fitu. 1995 Ed.
[15]*Treason at Maastricht,* Coupaprint Publications UK
[16]*The Global Manipulators,* 1980, Pentacle Books UK

Rodric Braithwaite	Foreign policy advisor to prime minister Majors
Andrew Knight	CEO New International
Eric Roll	Pres. Warburg Group
Sir Patrick Sheehy	CEO Bat Industries
Marilin Taylor	CEO Courtaulds Textiles

United States of America

Paul Allaire	CEO Xerox
George Ball	Former under-Sec, State
Kenneth Darn	Prof. U. of Chicago, former Dep. Sec. of State
Stephen Friedman	CEO Goldman Sacs
John Galvin	Prof. West Point; former Supr. Allied Commander SHAPE
James Hoagland	Correspondent Wash. Post
Lane Kirkland	Pres. AFL/CID
Samuel Lewis	Director planning State Dep.
William Odom	Former of Nat. Security Agency
Lany Pressler	US Senator
David Rockefeller	to much to list TC/CFRJChase./ etc.
Lynn Williams	United Steel Workers Pres.

The Federal Republic of Germany

Christopher Bertram	Diplo. Corresp. Die Zeit
Ulrich Cartellieri	Board Deutche Bank
Wolfgang Reizle	Board BMW
Volke Ruehe	Minister of Defense
Theo Sommer	Editor Die Zeit
Lothar Spaeth	CEO Jenopik; former minister Baden Wuertrenberg

Denmark

Uffe Ellemann	Former Foreign Minister

France

Patric Divedjian	Mem. Parliament

Thierry de Montbiral	Director French Institute of International Relations
Louis Schweizer	CEO Renault
Greece	
Stelios Argyros	CEO Federation of Greek Industries
Yanis Costopoulus	CEO Credit Bank
John Lyras	Vice Chair Greek Ship Owners
Stefanos Manos	Minister Nat. Economy
M. Papaconstantinous	Minister Foreign Affairs
T. Papalexopoulous	Deputy Chair Titan
Themistocles Voskos	CEO Seatrade
Thanos Veremis	Prof. U. Athens
Holland	
Elco Brinkman	Parliament leader Christian Democrats
Viktor Halberstadt	Prof. Leiden U. Bild. Hon. Sec. For Europe.
Wim Kok	Finance minister
Floris Maljeks	CEO Unilever NV
Ernst Van der Beugel	Prof Leiden U. Bild. Hon. Sec. Ret. Europe
Ireland	
Conor Brady	Editor Irish Times
Peter Sutherland	CEO Allied Irish Bank; former EC Commissioner
Austria	
Peter Jankowitsch	Chaie. Joint Parliamentary Committee
Paul Lendvai	Director Austrian Int. Radio
Franz Vranizky	Federal Chancellor
Sweden	
Percy Barnevik	Pres. & CEO Asea BBC
Carl Bildt	Prime minister
Italy	
Giovanny Agnelli	CEO Fiat

What a fascinating group. Consider that the CEO's of the five largest firms in the list employ over one million people. It is a fact that in Europe, membership in the Bilderberger group guarantees political success. Not surprisingly, opposition to Bilderberger dogma will result in loss of power and position. Just ask Baroness Margaret Thatcher about that. The removal of British Prime Minister Thatcher was of paramount importance to the Bilderbergers since she was opposed to European consolidation and especially to currency merger under the EC umbrella. This is the reason why most European politicians tote the Bilderberger philosophy. They know full well that any deviance from the association's dogma will result in severe repercussions. At a meeting held on the island of La Toia off the Atlantic coast of Spain on the weekend of 11 May 1989, the following phrase can be found in the minutes, ". . . emphasized the need to bring down the Thatcher government, because of her refusal to yield British sovereignty to a European super state that is to emerge in 1992." Thatcher was viciously attacked by every known media source within days of the meeting. She was denounced in almost all European newsprint, television, and radio as a "provisionalist" and an "Ultra-nationalist," and that was only the beginning. Within days, a parliamentary assault was initiated against her. Not even the Iron Lady could withstand all that. She had said no, no, no, to Eurofascism in the form of the EC and Maastricht, and within two years she was history.

Other Bilderberger meetings held include one in Montebello, Québec, Canada in May 1983. At this particular meeting a demand was made of the US President Reagan for a $50 billion cashflow to be provided to the third world from the US treasury. This was to be provided out of US taxpayers funds and to be paid out over the next eight years of Mr. Reagan's presidency. Surprise! Reagan was president for eight years, and $50 billion was provided to two organizations — the World Bank and the IMF. The plan was called the "Brady Plan."[17]

At their meeting held in Innsbruck, Austria in 1988, the Bilderbergers called for an American tax increase in order to increase funding of the IMF and World Bank, as well as some other international groups. The then sitting US president, George Bush, broke his "Read My Lips" pledge and gave the American taxpayer what was, up to then, the largest tax increase in the nation's history. He subsequently lost a second term, but I have been told that promises were made for his son.

During the 1992 meeting in Evian, France, it was decided to have the US taxpayer fund the so-called democratization of the former Soviet Union by providing it with hundreds of billions of dollars. Not long after that, the media started running stories of how we had to purchase plutonium from Russia to reduce their nuclear arsenal and that we had to provide funds to relocate Russian military. Then we provided funds for housing Russian soldiers. The rubbish produced by the media did not cease for weeks. To my knowledge, nothing has been transferred except billions of American tax dollars to Russia.

In a more recent meeting held on the Buergerschtock in Switzerland, military incursions were called for in Bosnia.

The following prominent EC politicians were all Bilderbergers prior to attaining prominence in their political field: Harold Wilson, Edward Heath, Helmut Schmidt, and Tony Blair. To succeed in world politics in the nineties, it is a foregone conclusion that one must subscribe to Satori ideology. Whether it's the Bilderbergers for Europeans, or the CFR and TC for the rest, if you want success, follow the line of the New World Order, single world government through the administration of the

[17]*The Barnes Review of History*, Jan. 1996

Mandarins under the guidance of the Satori. Bear in mind that it is not required that you know anything of the Satori, in my opinion they prefer it if as few people as possible are aware of their existence. It is not necessary for a soldier to know who gave the order, the only important matter is that the order is followed.

None other than NY Senator Jacob Javits, who was at the time a considerable force in the US Senate, stated in the congressional record, "Leading figures are invited who, through special knowledge and experience, can help the future of the Bilderberger objectives." The success of the Bilderbergers is unquestionably envied by their American counterpart, the CFR. Today's EC citizens travel with EC passports, own allegiance to the EC rather than an individual nation, are judicially represented in EC courts, have an EC parliament, and even an EC anthem.

To run this monolith, an enormous bureaucracy has been created which is seated in Brussels. One of the offices held in the EC is that of Commissioner of the EC. To hold this office, the commissioner elect must take a solemn oath of office as required by the Maastricht treaty. In every single instance this oath of office is in direct violation of the national duties otherwise held by the officer. This oath of office is made at the European Court of Justice and reads as follows:

> *"To perform my duties in compete independence, in general interest of the community; in carrying out my duties neither to seek nor to take instruction from any government or body; to refrain from any action incompatable with my duties."*

There is not one single instance where this oath does not directly conflict with the oath of office taken by that person in his home nation prior to departing for Brussels. In any event there you have it. Allegiance is not to the community which elected you, but to the bureaucracy of Mandarins which serve the Satori. In regards to the Americas, the question now becomes, how long will it be before the NAFTA secretariat, which is in the NAFTA accord, will require American, Canadian and Mexican participants to take a similar oath of office?

It is indisputable that there are numerous parallels between NAFTA and the EC. Furthermore, it is an undeniable fact that there is not only similarity but membership overlap between all the dominant international Mandarin organizations. The Bilderbergers, Bones, the CFR, and the TC all possess a substantial subset of members who are members in one of the other four groups. Some individuals are even members of all of them. You must understand that the Satori have devised a modus operandi through which national interests and internal government are supplanted by an external federalism. This external government is created in the form of a bureaucracy staffed by Mandarins who work under the control of a small number of administrators whose only allegiance is to the Satori. It comes to pass that a new external government actually takes over all governing aspects of society and thus controls all mankind within their sphere of influence. This will be a reality in the EC within the next five to eight years. In America, as well as Europe, the fact that most citizens think poorly of their political leaders is a tremendous help to the Satori.

The greatest stumbling block in EC integration has been monetary. This will likewise be the case with NAFTA. This was bound to occur because monetary integration attacks everyone's personal wealth. Citizens may pay little attention to political change, but when it affects their pocketbook they become very interested. Germany and the Benelux nations including Holland, are afraid they will get short-changed in any consolidation. To further compound the problem those nations are terrified at the possible prospect of a Greek, Italian, or Spaniard in charge of EC monetary policy. Let's face it — would Americans be happy if a Mexican or Brazilian were in charge of the Federal Reserve System (FRS)?

The NAFTA deal, which was instituted by a lame duck congress, represents the greatest betrayal of the public trust in this or in any other century, against the citizens of North America. This treaty, and that is exactly what it is, regardless of what politicians may call it, was passed by both houses of congress before one single member had ever read it. It is an historic fact that the final published version was not printed until after it had been ratified. It was rammed through Congress by a legislature who had already lost the election. The agreement was opposed by over 87% of the population. The amount of political payoffs during this time was unprecedented, even by Mexican standards. I was a member of the Connecticut District Export Council (CTDEC) at that time. DECs were an advisory board for trade policy to the Department of Commerce. Each major region in the country had a DEC usually consisting of about fifteen members who were prominent in international trade. As Brown took over Commerce, the entire operation became nothing more than a mouthpiece for Satori policy. Anyhow, the Department of Commerce was the lead organization for the Bush administration in assuring that this plan would be adopted by the congress and media. The Mexican government was partner to this effort and was the dispenser of gratuities to the political establishment while Commerce took care of organizational matters and the media. Believe me, we are not talking about peanuts here. The Mexican government, on a tour of major cities organized by Commerce, came with a war chest of some $30 million that was liberally lavished on politicos and the media. While this was going on, Commerce spent $14 million on the effort. As all the payoffs came from the Mexican side, Commerce could simply pretend that this was not taking place. The Commerce portion of the arrangement included a front group of 55 organizers which arrived in each destination two days before the tour and set up the entire circus. When I went to the NYC meeting with my friend, the Swiss Commercial Attache, he commented that he had never in his thirty years with the Consul seen such a circus. Now you know how a treaty with over three quarters of the population opposed can get passed. This treaty was to see the gradual installation of an EC-type market arrangement on this side of the Atlantic. Bear in mind that the Bilderbergers are North Atlantic, while the CFR is North American, and the Trilateralists are Pacific Rim as well as North American and North Atlantic. Not long after the inception of the agreement, the Mexican government announced difficulty in their finances. Ever-helpful Uncle Sam, via the US Treasury, immediately purchased US $20 billion in pesos. But that was just the beginning. A few short weeks after that, the Mexican government devalued the peso by about 50%. Thus, Uncle Sam took an immediate hit for $10 billion. Shortly after that, a Mexican delegation arrived in Washington and announced that they lacked the funds to repay the loan originally made by Goldman Sachs and other New York bankers. Our government (under the able leadership of Clinton (D), Dole (R), and Gingrich (R)) then promptly pushed through a Mexican bailout to the tune of $50 billion. So now we had spent $60 billion on NAFTA. The deal, by the way, was that the treasury would send a check to Mexico where it would be endorsed and sent on to Goldman Sachs. In other words, the US taxpayers were on the hook for a bad loan made by Goldman Sachs.*The fact that the ex-chairman of Goldman Sachs was Secretary of the Treasury had nothing whatsoever to do with this! Right!*

The G7 nations recently reached agreement on a debt relief proposal for the world's poorest nations. Sounds grand and magnanimous, does it not? The relief measure involves the tidy sum of US $7.7 billion. This debt to the World Bank was due in 1997 & 98. The agreement calls for the G7 nations to write off 80% of the amount due. This is US $6.16 billion. The un-elected to anything, Robert Rubin of Mexican bail-out fame, was the American representative at the G7 meeting held at the Blair

House in Washington DC. He stated the implementation would go forward on a case by case basis. This meeting took place just days before a World Bank meeting at which 181 nations were present. Previosly, Rubin had attempted to finance this bad debt through the sale of gold from the World Bank reserves. The Bundesbank put the kibosh on that.

What does all this have to do with you? The World bank is 80% financed by American taxpayers. This means that Rubin gave away 80% of US $6.16 billion or US $4.92 billion of your money. Another load of commissions and fees for the Satori.

It should be painfully clear to you by this time that everything is orchestrated from above. In my opinion anyone who still believes that all these acts are happenstance must also believe in the tooth fairy. We have now established, with reasonable proof, that there are links between the various Mandarin groups. Their authority overlaps, as does their membership. Thus we have established that the various Mandarins more or less act in unison at the pleasure of the Satori. Let's face facts: that various groups of people in organizations spread across four continents would function with identical goals without an overlord is completely ludicrous.

GATT stands for General Agreement on Tariffs and Trade. The WTO, or World Trade Organization, is what you would call the operating and controlling agency which administers GATT. The purpose of the treaty and its organization has little to do with trade and a great deal to do with "Economic Integration." You have probably not heard this phrase unless you work within the beltway,[18] but economic integration is what the EC, NAFTA, GATT, and WTO are all about. Economic Integration means the merging of economies under one authority. When

[18]"Inside the beltway" is American slang for Washington DC.

this happens, you can kiss the constitution, liberty, freedom, and the pursuit of happiness goodbye. At this writing, America has already lost its first WTO case which is currently under appeal. Venezuela and Brazil brought a complaint relating to the petroleum purity standards set by the Environmental Protection Agency (EPA). The WTO has informed the US that we will have to lower our environmental standards for fuel, because the complainants lacked the financial acumen to produce fuel that meets EPA standards.

A long time ago, Karl Marx figured out that to control a society, one first had to control the economic structure. This is a lesson that the Satori have taken to heart. Remember the sequence of events in the EC. First it was for peace, then came trade barriers, then currency fluctuation, and lastly economic integration. The exact same plan exists for NAFTA.

I fully realize that this part of the book is supposed to deal with the Bilderbergers, but as you can see, it is very difficult to separate Mandarin organizations and continents. The reason is, of course, that a universal plan renders the various parts inseparable.

In the name of "Free Trade" all Europeans who are part of the northern EC states have seen drastic loss of individual income, drastic unemployment, and a lowering of the standard of living. This is exactly the same as in North America. The Europeans, however, who are further along in Satori plans, are also faced with mandated EC laws, measurements, health codes, agrarian production, manufacturing standards, etc., etc. ad infinitum. The EC has gone so far as to attempt to impose transportation standards to non-member states like Switzerland. Within the EC, matters are no better. Germany, ever protective of its sovereignty, forced EC legislation to prevent Portuguese workers from working for German firms in Portugal because of lower pay-scales, regardless of the fact that German firms were paying more than Portuguese firms.

Let us recap. After seven separate GATT trade rounds and an elapse of over forty years, the World Trade Organization

(WTO) miraculously appeared out of thin air in 1994, and added into the GATT agreements. Who authored it remains a mystery to some, but it is very clear that the Mandarins were in charge of the addition. The why is also simple. WTO turns a contractual agreement between individual nations into a binding agreement to be arbitrated by WTO. It is, in essence, the first step toward world government. WTO has power over constituted nation states which sign on to the treaty. It can change, abrogate, or veto any act by any participant member. It controls all external policy of member states. In fact, a provision of the treaty states that the ". . . US must consult with other states for the purpose of achieving conformity of state laws and practices with the Uraguay agreements."

The Uraguay Round was the last of the seven GATT meetings before the adoption of the entire package. Please note that this treaty clearly violates the 10th amendment of the constitution as well as dozens of other American laws and the constitution in general. The 10th ammendment states:

> *. . . Congress does not have the authority, without the approval of a two-thirds majority of states, to abrogate or in any way change or alter the U.S. Constitution.*

As you can now see, this Satori-inspired entanglement of treaties basically destabilizes national entities. This is what it's all about — consolidation — social, economic, and military. Total integration into a one world government. This was part of the first Bilderbergers meeting way back in 1954.

In England, there has been considerable opposition to the EC and particularly to the Masstricht accord. One of the staunchest opponents was Baroness Thatcher. She paid dearly for her interference with Satori plans.

Americans have been deeply connected in the founding and the continuing operations of the Bilderbergers. Historically, most Americans have viewed Europe as a single political structure, except perhaps for the United Kingdom. The fact that this concept is totally wrong does not alter it as reality. The "League of Nations," along with its associate the "United States of Europe," were both American inspired ideas. The subsequently founded United Nations fits right in with this American concept. To foster ever increasing multi-nationalism, the "Marshall Plan" and "Lend Lease" were instituted. We must all clearly understand that the Bilderbergers, who act as surrogates for the Satori, are driven by an internationalist agenda which does not favor "We The People" of the United States.

In June of 1947, General George Marshall announced that if the European nations would jointly produce a plan for European recovery, the United States would help finance it. By providing the Europeans with a source of supply and funds with which to buy, credit as it were, the Satori, in one move, succeeded to:

1.) Consolidate power,
2.) Create economic dependence,
3.) Set the groundwork for the coming UN,
4.) Put themselves, through their banks, in charge of the entire cabal.

The Marshall Plan provided for:

1.) The removal of all trade barriers (EC),
2.) Political integration (EC),
3.) Economic integration (EC),
4.) Military integration (NATO).

Shortly thereafter, numerous new organizations appeared on the scene: The European Coal and Steel Community (ECSC), the European Organization for Economic Cooperation (OEC which later changed to OECD). The ECSC was subsequently supplanted by the European Economic Community (EEC) which then created the Treaty of Rome. This, then, evolved into the EC.

The Truman Doctrine of March 1947 stated that the United States would provide assistance to any nation for the combating of internal or external expansion threats. With this, the United States supplanted the United Kingdom as provider of military aid to Greece and Turkey. This was the event which actually lead to the creation of The North Atlantic Treaty Organization (NATO) as a separate UN entity. NATO is, after all, a treaty which binds all European members to assess their military needs and requirements jointly with those of the United States. In other words the military integration of all European, Canadian, and American assets. The present more expanded outcome is to accomplish this on a worldwide basis through the UN. As you can realize, military integration, which is to be used for coercive practice against participating members, is well on its way toward completion. The Satori plan is close to fruition. The first step in a takeover is the ability to enforce. The planned UN world-integrated military will become that force.

First we are separated into manageable trade blocks, then an enforcement apparatus is put into place. National sovereignty has already been compromised by WTO and numerous other treaties. All that remains is for the heavy hand of the military to enforce those treaties. Bearing in mind that the third world will be more then delighted to supply all the military personnel required to enforce the transfer of our wealth to them.

Dr. Joseph Retinger was the visionary who concocted the Bilderbergers. During the Second World War, he was the top aid to Polish general Sikorski, head of the Polish government in exile in London. After having met most European leaders, he suggested a regular meeting of ministers (continental only) with the goal of developing an association of leaders. At the close of the war, Retinger made a formal presentation for European unification at the British Institute of International Affairs, an organization which has close links to the CFR. In his presentation, he formally advised the representatives at the meeting that there were no European superpowers left — and that the solution to European problems rested with a federal union of all adjacent countries, each of which would surrender some of its sovereignty to the new union.[19] Shortly after this important meeting Dr. Retinger was introduced to the then American ambassador at Earls Court, none other then Averell Harriman. Harriman promptly invited him to the States where they would drum up support for his idea. His greatest support was to come from John Foster Dulles (Sec. of State to Eisenhower). He then met with and was introduced to virtually everyone who was anyone: L. Ingwell (senior partner J. P. Morgan), David Rockefeller (CEO Chase), Alfred Sloan (CEO Dodge), Charles Hood (Pres. Amer. Polly), Sir William Wiseman (partner Kuhn & Loeb & Co.), and George Franklin (CFR Secretary and TC coordinator). What a fascinating list, every last one of them a CFR member. Coincidentally the CFR had 2,500 members at that time.

Dr. Retinger drew up a list of people from Europe and America for consideration for membership in what was to become the Bilderbergers. Each person expressed a unanimity of political position, and equal numbers from all political spheres were chosen. Understand clearly that the members of all Mandarin organizations have no fixation with political affiliation or policy. Their goal has nothing to do with politics and everything to do with domination.

Facts about the Bilderbergers:

USA Address: As of 1995, None

Previously: Carnegie Endowment for International Peace
345 E. 46th St.
NYC. USA

No Telephone, Fax, or E-mail address exists.

[19]*The Nation*, July 1980

Meetings: Bi-annually at undisclosed locations. Different country each meeting. Bring own staff.
Present Chairman Emeritus: His Royal Highness, Prince Bernard of Holland.

See appendix G for a complete listing of the Bilderbergers.

SUPER MANDARINS

The following list of super Mandarins is composed of names of individuals who are active in numerous Mandarin organizations or who are otherwise classified as such. The list is not complete due to the secretive nature of the organizations involved. While it is possible to obtain (with difficulty) a list of the memberships of the CFR and the TC, this is not the case for the other organizations. Bones, for example, is located in New Haven CT. As for the Bilderbergers it is not even possible to locate headquarters.

Paul Arthur Allaire
Chairman Xerox

Graham Tillett Allison Jr.
Dir. Emer. CFR Ctr. For Nat. Policy

Dwayne Orville Andreas
CEO ADM

C. Fred Bergsten
Direct. Inst. For Int. Econ. Asst. Sec. Emer. Treasury

John Brademas
Dir. Texaco

Zbigniew Brzezinski
Center For Strategic & Int. Stud.

William F. Buckley Jr.
Ed. Nat. Review., PBS Firing Line.

William Jefferson Clinton
Pres. USA

Richard Newell Cooper
Prof. Harvard, Dir. CFR, Und. Sec. State. Econ. E.
Gerald Corrigan
Chair. Goldman Sachs, Pres. Emer. FRB of NY
Stephen James Friedman
CEO Goldman Sachs, Fed Res. Bnk.
Katharine Graham
Chair. Wash. Post, Brookings Inst.
Maurice R. Greenberg
Dep. Chair Fed. Res. NY, CEO Amer. Int. Grp., Dir. CFR
Vernon Eullon Jordan Jr.
Brookings Inst., Dir. RJR Nabisco
Heinrich Alfred Kissinger
Chair Kissinger Assoc.
Wilson Lord
State Dep. Eastern Affairs
Robert Strange McNamara
Pres. Emer. World Bank, Brookings Inst.
Walter Fritz Mondale
US Amb. Japan
Joseph S. Nye Jr.
Nat. Intel. Council
Rozanne Lejeanne
Ridgeway Atlantic, Coun. Amb. Emer., Dir. RJR Nabisco
Charles W. Robinson
Overseas Develop. Coic., Brookings Inst.
David Rockefeller
CEO Chase, Bon., Chair. CFR
Brent Scowcroft
Nat. Secur. Council, Dir. Emer. CFR
Robert B. Zoellick
Fed. Nat. Morg. Assoc., Und. Sec State., Dir. CFR

THE SATORI

You will, by now, be hoping for a list of the Satori. Unfortunately, that is not possible. I could most certainly make intelligent guesses about the membership of that very select group, but they would still be only guesses, and this work is about facts, not guesses. If I were to postulate even a partial list of Satori members without clear and concise proof, this book would wind up in the fiction section of the library.

I have made a concerted effort to show the master plan as I see it. I have stuck to facts which are not disputable. I have shown clearly that there is a conspiracy in this century and that it is controlled by a select small group of individuals. I have shown that there are Mandarin groups which act in unison and have identical agendas. I have shown that the Mandarins have overlapping memberships. I have proven beyond the shadow of a doubt that there is a conspiracy, and that it is guided by a group I call the Satori, and who Franklin Delano Roosevelt called "a financial element." I quote:

> *"The real truth of the matter is, as you and I know, that a financial element in the large centers has owned the government of the U.S. since the days of Andrew Jackson."*
>
> — Franklin Delano Roosevelt
> 11/23/31 letter to Colonel House
> Seymour: *The Intimate Papers of Colonel House*

CHAPTER SEVEN

WHAT YOU CAN DO

The inevitable question in your mind must be how can I tell if the candidate for office is in the hands of the Satori? The answer to that question lies in a series of questions to ask candidates depending on the office they are running for. From the answers you will easily be able to discern their allegiance to either the United States Constitution or the Satori. As you already know who the Mandarins are, you have disarmed much of their ability to do harm, in that you will suspect any action they take.

We have enumerated how our political world is manipulated by the Satori. We have seen that they influence every single aspect of our lives, from our children's education to products that we use in our daily lives. Indeed the present direction is toward control of our food supplies through the USDA, of food supplement products, vitamins and medicines through the FDA, right down to the type and size vehicle we drive through the USDT. In fact, a recent trade agreement may make it necessary to have a doctor's prescription to buy vitamins.

THE JUDICIARY

How did the federal government get such power over our lives? Easy. It was granted to them by the judiciary. Read the following words of Thomas Jefferson, the author of The Declaration of Independence, carefully:

> *". . . our government is now taking so steady a course as to show by what road it will pass to destruction, to wit: by consolidation first, and then corruption, its necessary consequence. The engine of consolidation will be the federal judiciary; the other two branches the corrupting and corrupted instruments."*

Consider that if Clinton completes his full second term, he will have appointed over 52% of all sitting federal judges. These people are appointed for life. This consequently means that the effect of his appointments will be with us for 20 years or more. The US senate has overview of judicial appointments but has neglected their duty for years. No federal judge can be appointed by the president without senatorial review. Unfortunately, in over 95% of all cases, the senate has lumped a group of appointees together in a package deal and then approved them through a process called unanimous consent. What this means is that they simply endorsed all of the candidates without even knowing their names. The first thing you can do is ask every candidate for the office of senator the following question: Will you allow the appointment by the president of federal judges to be made by the process of unanimous consent? If the candidate answers yes, vote against him.

The process called "judicial activism" is the perversion of our constitution under the philosophy that the constitution should be read based on application to present societal circumstance. What this would indicate is that the constitution is a document open to individual opinion. What I am saying is, according to advocates of "judicial activism," judges are allowed to read into the constitution what they perceive it to say, or want it to say, and not what it actually does say. This is absolute crap, and has resulted in such preposterous rulings as *Brown vs. Board of Education* 1954, in which the court ruled that the constitution requires the assignment of children to schools based on race. In fact, the supreme court, which under our constitution is not allowed to make laws, has in the past few years disallowed almost all distinction of citizens based on sex. It found the constitution gives the right of infanticide, protects the rights of child pornographers, allows virtually any public perversion, and permits citizens to desecrate national symbols at will. Under judicial wants: Judge James Dennis, US Court of Appeals Fifth Circuit, attempted to expand criminals rights to include the right to sue police for possible "psychological injuries" incurred while being arrested. Judge Rosemary Barkett, US Court of Appeals Eleventh Circuit, attempted to give fifth graders the right to sue their school for the misbehavior of one of their classmates. Judge Diane Wood, US Court of Appeals Seventh Circuit, construed the eighth amendment against cruel and unusual punishment to include a prison inmate who demanded to be placed in a "smoke free" prison environment. Judge Theodore McKee, US Court of Appeals Third Circuit, wanted to have the sentence for illegal immigrants, who had been deported for drug dealing and rearrested, reduced from fifteen to two years.

These are not rights enumerated in the constitution, so the second question of a candidate for senator is: Will you vote for a candidate to the judiciary who believes in judicial activism, or has a record of same? The very next question should be: Will you support a change to a maximum term of 10 years for federal judges, whereupon they must run for reappointment by the senate to the office they hold? If "We The People" want to change our constitution we have a vehicle to do so through the amendment process. This has been done numerous times. We do not need a despotic bunch of elitist lawyers making illegal laws for us, on behalf of the Satori. Allowing nine black-robed elitists to make new laws instead of congress is the way to serfdom at the hands of the Satori.

On the judicial front there is one other matter that should be pursued: the voiding of all laws enacted by judicial mandate. The First Article, Section one, of the constitution should not only be strictly adhered to, but should be retroactively enforced. The constitution is very specific in its first article, indeed in its first sentence after the preamble: "All legislative powers herein granted shall be vested in a congress of the United States, which shall consist of a Senate and a House of Representatives." Let's face it, even our judiciary should be able to understand that statement.

THE EXECUTIVE

On the executive side of the presidency, it is imperative that the candidate swear that he will not issue any executive orders, unless the nation is under attack by a foreign power, and to remove the perpetual state of emergency enacted by FDR and reinstituted by every president since. The constitution does not give the president the right to issue executive orders, or to institute law. President Clinton, in particular, has used executive orders as a means to circumvent the legislative authority of the congress. He has, by this act, violated his oath of office, and the congress by allowing it, has violated their oaths. Executive orders which I have seen (some have been made secret, not even congress has seen them) have authorized a dictatorship of the Executive under the auspices of FEMA. One particular order gives power to the director of FEMA to nationalize all farms, power companies, transport firms, tractors, farm equipment, highways, railroads, and even to dismiss locally elected school boards, mayors, sheriffs, select men, and officers of the court. There is no reason for any such order. It is unconstitutional, and a gross violation of the trust placed by the people in their elected president. The very first question to ask of any person running for the presidency is: Will you swear not to enact any executive orders if elected, unless the United States is militarily attacked, and will you void all previously issued executive orders? If he will not or avoids the questions, you will know that he is in the Satori's pockets.

THE HOUSE OF REPRESENTATIVES

This, then, brings us to the House of Representatives. For decades the House has avoided hard questions. This has been done in a number of devious ways. The best example is the latest pay increase they gave themselves, which was engineered in such a way as to achieve a pay increase without voting for it. They do things like this all the time, so they won't be held accountable. Therefore, the first question to ask a congressional candidate is: Will you swear not to allow, or to vote against, any legislative act allowing the passing of legislation without a roll-call vote? This will force responsibility of action upon congress

The entire issue of campaign reform, as presently under discussion in both houses of congress, is a sham. Therefore, the second question to ask the congressional candidate is: Will you swear to support a constitutional amendment restricting campaign contributions to the district of representation, and the total elimination of other than personal contributions? Currently, in many races, 90% of the campaign financing comes from outside the congressional district in question. This practice also exists in the financing of Senate campaigns. What we need is the total elimination of corporate, union, PAC, and business contributions to political campaigns. This would greatly reduce Satori influence in the electoral process.

THE UNITED NATIONS — GET *US* OUT

The guiding light of our nation for the duration of it's greatest success was, as Theodore Roosevelt expressed it, "Walk softly and carry a big stick." The elimination of current foreign entanglements goes right along with that advice. Today the US has troops in over 100 different nations. Every one of them is in violation of the constitution. All were sent by executive order. We are embroiled in hundreds, if not thousands, of treaties any one of which could involve us in another Vietnam-type war. We are not the policemen to the world, and we are not the arbitrator of world problems. Get us out of the United Nations.

When I was young I lived in New York City, and through an uncle I met an ambassador to the UN, and through him I met numerous UN aperatnicks and officials. Let me tell you, these people, when it comes to wasting money, would make congressmen blush. The worst part of the UN is not it's ability to waste money, but it's horrible record as an omnipotent world government. In our nation, all rights belong to our people through our constitution. In the UN charter, all rights vested are not in the people, but in the state. Other entities in which rights rested in the state were Nazi Germany, Fascist Italy, Communist USSR, and Imperial Japan. Does that give you any idea as to why the Satori prefer the UN type of structure? A fine example of this is Radio and TV. If the power is vested in the people (USA), you have independent, private broadcast stations, if the power is vested in government, you have state-controlled broadcast stations (GB, Germany, France, etc.). There is an enormous difference if the power in government is derived from the people or the state. To name but one: if the state obtains its powers (rights) from the people, the people can take them away, whereas, if the people get their rights from the state, the state can take them away whenever it chooses.

The UN is a many-headed hydra controlled by the Satori, whose aim is the control of our personal property, homes, money and education. Hitler said it best: ". . . why bother socializing banks and businesses? We socialize people." And on the socialization of people he said, "When I am told 'I will not support your efforts to socialize me!' I tell the respondent, we already have your children." This is why we have to get out of the UN. Do not think this to be an impossible task. In 1997 Congressman Dr. Ron Paul offered an amendment to get us out of the UN, and 34 congressmen supported the legislation.

GET *US* OUT OF NAFTA, ETC.

We, as a nation, have entered into numerous treaties. Of these, the worst by far are WTO and NAFTA. The operating principal of these agreements is "Free Trade." There is no such thing, and anyone who supports this premise is either stupid or a Satori dupe. What these treaties do is to provide STATE MANAGED TRADE. What would free trade actually be? It would mean that an American farmer could sell rice in Japan for what the market would bear, without duty, quotas, or governmental interference. It would further mean that this farmer received no government assistance in producing or selling his crop. It would mean that a Korean car manufacturer could sell his cars in Germany without quotas. Well, in the real world these things just don't occur. In fact, free trade does not even exist within America. In New Hampshire, for example, dairy farmers have price supports for milk and the milk they produce must be sold within a given marketing area. In California the citrus industry is strictly regulated as to growers and aspects of its sale. And, in Detroit auto manufacturers get R&D freebies and Department of Transportation grants, all of which are accompanied by regulation. "Free Trade" is the slogan of the Satori! It is their soundbite through which to develop worldwide managed trade and, with it, dominate the world.

REDUCE GOVERNMENT

Reducing the size of government must be a priority. As we have seen in corporate downsizing, a smaller bureaucracy results in better management and increased production. This is nowhere as true as in government. It is more then obvious that departments of the federal bureaucracy, without which we functioned for 200 years, are not required. The Departments of Education, Energy, and Commerce as well as Housing and Urban Development serve no purpose but to control people and private property. They should be abolished. This is only a small portion of the required downsizing. A complete hiring freeze for at least four years and a reduction of allotted funds per agency of 10% per year would reduce the bureaucracy and give current employees time to find productive jobs in the private sector. And last, but not least, a requirement that government spending be limited, in all expenditures, to a given percentage of the GNP.

TAXES

As we have seen, Foundations, through special privilege, have a status before tax authorities different from the rest of society. We have also shown that a majority of these foundations have been co-opted by political activists whose plan is to change our society into a Satori-invented feudal state. We must remove the tax exempt status of all foundations, before they wind up controlling the entire ball of wax. Why should Hanoi Jane's husband be allowed to donate $1 billion to a foundation which he controls, and give a percentage of the profits to an international body? It's a huge tax saving scheme. He avoids paying taxes and gains international power.

Demand that your congressman and senators investigate the legality of the Income Tax Amendment.[1] There is but one Constitutional way (article 1, section 9, paragraph 4) to fund the Federal government: an indirect, voluntary, proportionate tax on consumption levied by each State, who, in turn, pays the State's proportion of the Federal budget according to its population. Eliminate all unconstitutional Federal taxes via the amendment which institutes the new, Constitutional, taxing system.[2] The entire system of socialist-enacted tax statutes are an anchor on the entire economy, as well as our rights as citizens of the United States. Due to the US tax structure, I was forced to close my manufacturing business as it was suicide to continue producing machine tools in the US. This is an everyday occurrence in our country. There are three main causes: 1) income taxes; 2) estate taxes; 3) "Free Trade." The more we return taxation to the local level, the better off we are. It makes absolutely no sense to pay taxes to a bureaucracy in Washing-

[1]The Income Tax Amendment was put into effect illegally. Only 3 of the 48 States ratified it. *The Law That Never Was,* by Benson & Buckman.
[2]Taxpayers Association, Clearwater, Florida 33756-1220.

ton, and then have them return a small portion to the states. Washington is so inefficient that, for example, $.72 cents of every dollar collected for social security is spent on bureaucratic administration, rather then distributed to beneficiaries.

EDUCATION

As a past member of a local school board, I can surely inform you that it is imperative to return schools to total local control. Not federal, not state, but to local community control. And this is only a small portion of what must be done. We must foster competition in the educational process if we expect to educate our children. The concept of public schools, as we know them, stems from Germany in pre-nazi times. Just look where it got them. In any socialist system, market competition is virtually eliminated. The state monopoly takes over and this, in turn, gives rise to such organizations as the National Education Association (NEA) teachers union. The NEA leadership is an ultra-left elitist cabal. As they are also the supplier of most delegates to the Democrat party, and in large part responsible for writing the Democrat national platform, we have to reform education, by introducing free market competition.

SOCIAL SECURITY

The Ponzi scheme that is Social Security must be drastically changed, and along with that, so must federal and state healthcare entitlements. Although most people think of Social Security as insurance they have paid for, it is not. The Supreme Court has ruled that Social Security is a tax and only a tax. It does not owe any individual a dime. The "payout" is whatever congress decrees. Social Security must be privatized and made into personal insurance policies. This could be done along the same lines as the Chilean model. I have personally contacted several annuity insurance carriers, and learned the following: If I had been allowed to make my SS payments to a private carrier, in the same amounts I paid in SS taxes, I would receive from the private carrier a guarantee of a monthly allotment 40% higher then what I hope to get from SS when I retire. In addition, when I die, the residual value remaining in my policy would go to my heirs. In contrast, Social Security will pay my heirs the monumental sum of $300. Just enough cash for some flowers on the coffin. We can do nothing for those Americans that have been in the system for a long time such as myself, but we can certainly fix it for our children.

Your advocacy of the foregoing, as an individual and in association with others, can and will awaken fellow Americans to the imminent takeover by the New World Order via treaty agreements and the United Nation's many-headed hydra. A good starting point would be to tell friends about this book, and others mentioned in the bibliography.

I close with this thought written by John Stuart Mill, author of *Wealth of Nations*:

> "WAR IS AN UGLY THING, BUT NOT THE UGLIEST OF THINGS; THE DECAYED AND DEGRADED STATE OF MORAL AND PATRIOTIC FEELING WHICH THINKS THAT NOTHING IS WORTH WAR IS MUCH WORSE. A MAN WHO HAS NOTHING FOR WHICH HE IS WILLING TO FIGHT, NOTHING HE CARES ABOUT MORE THAN HIS OWN PERSONAL SAFETY, IS A MISERABLE CREATURE WHO HAS NO CHANCE OF BEING FREE, UNLESS MADE AND KEPT SO BY THE EXERTIONS OF BETTER MEN THAN HIMSELF."

APPENDICES

APPENDIX A

THE LIBRARY OF CONGRESS,
Washington, D.C., July 12, 1968.

HON. THOMAS J. DODD,
Chairman, Special Subcommittee To Investigate Juvenile Delinquency, U.S. Senate, Washington, D.C.

Dear Senator Dodd: Your request of July 2, 1968, addressed to the Legislative Reference Service, for the translation of several German laws has been referred to the Law Library for attention.

In compliance with your request and with reference to several telephone conversations between Miss Frank of your Office and Mr. Fred Karpf, European Law Division, we are enclosing herewith a translation of the Law on Weapons of March 18, 1938, prepared by Dr. William Sólyom-Fekete of that Division, as well as the Xerox copy of the original German text which you supplied.

The translation of the Decree implementing the Law on Weapons of March 19, 1938, and the pertinent provisions of the Federal Hunting Law of March 30, 1961, is in preparation and will be sent to you as soon as completed.

Sincerely yours,

LEWIS C. COFFIN,
Law Librarian.

APPENDIX B

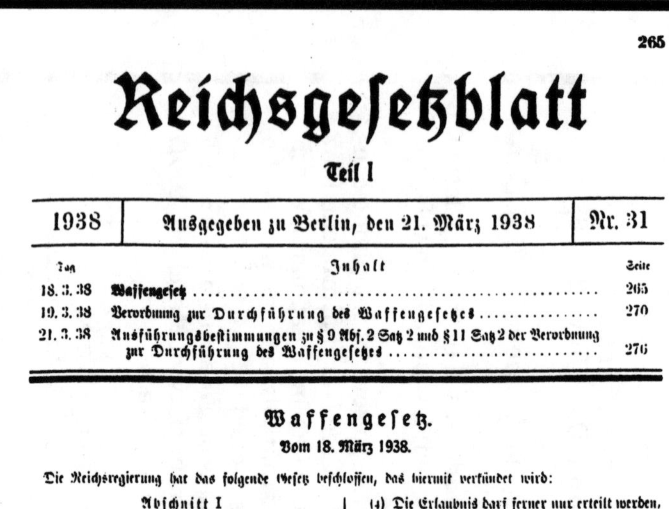

265

Reichsgesetzblatt

Teil I

1938	Ausgegeben zu Berlin, den 21. März 1938	Nr. 31

Tag	Inhalt	Seite
18. 3. 38	Waffengesetz	265
19. 3. 38	Verordnung zur Durchführung des Waffengesetzes	270
21. 3. 38	Ausführungsbestimmungen zu § 9 Abs. 2 Satz 2 und § 11 Satz 2 der Verordnung zur Durchführung des Waffengesetzes	276

Waffengesetz.

Vom 18. März 1938.

Die Reichsregierung hat das folgende Gesetz beschlossen, das hiermit verkündet wird:

Abschnitt I

Allgemeines

§ 1

(1) Schußwaffen im Sinne dieses Gesetzes sind Waffen, bei denen ein fester Körper durch Gas- oder Luftdruck durch einen Lauf getrieben werden kann.

(2) Als Munition im Sinne dieses Gesetzes gilt fertige Munition zu Schußwaffen sowie Schießpulver jeder Art.

(3) Fertige oder vorgearbeitete wesentliche Teile von Schußwaffen oder Munition stehen fertigen Schußwaffen oder fertiger Munition gleich.

§ 2

Hieb- oder Stoßwaffen im Sinne dieses Gesetzes sind Waffen, die ihrer Natur nach dazu bestimmt sind, durch Hieb, Stoß oder Stich Verletzungen beizubringen.

Abschnitt II

Herstellung von Schußwaffen und Munition

§ 3

(1) Wer gewerbsmäßig Schußwaffen oder Munition herstellen, bearbeiten oder instand setzen will, bedarf dazu der Erlaubnis. Als Herstellen von Munition gilt auch das Wiederladen von Patronenhülsen.

(2) Die Erlaubnis darf nur erteilt werden, wenn der Antragsteller die deutsche Staatsangehörigkeit besitzt und im Reichsgebiet einen festen Wohnsitz hat.

(3) Der Reichsminister des Innern kann im Einvernehmen mit den beteiligten Reichsministern Ausnahmen von den Vorschriften des Abs. 2 zulassen.

(4) Die Erlaubnis darf ferner nur erteilt werden, wenn der Antragsteller und die für die kaufmännische oder für die technische Leitung seines Betriebes in Aussicht genommenen Personen die für den Betrieb des Gewerbes erforderliche persönliche Zuverlässigkeit und wenn der Antragsteller oder die für die technische Leitung seines Betriebes in Aussicht genommene Person die für den Betrieb des Gewerbes erforderliche fachliche Eignung besitzen.

(5) Die Erlaubnis darf nicht erteilt werden, wenn der Antragsteller und die für die kaufmännische oder für die technische Leitung seines Betriebes in Aussicht genommenen Personen oder einer von ihnen Jude ist.

§ 4

(1) Bei der Erteilung der Erlaubnis kann eine Frist bis zur Dauer eines Jahres bestimmt werden, innerhalb deren das Gewerbe begonnen werden muß, widrigenfalls die Erlaubnis erlischt. Ist eine Frist nicht bestimmt, so erlischt die Erlaubnis, wenn das Gewerbe nicht innerhalb eines Jahres nach Erteilung der Erlaubnis begonnen wird. Die Fristen können verlängert werden, wenn ein wichtiger Grund vorliegt.

(2) Die Erlaubnis erlischt ferner, wenn der Gewerbetreibende das Gewerbe seit einem Jahr nicht mehr ausgeübt hat, ohne daß ihm darüber hinaus eine Frist gewährt worden ist, innerhalb deren das Gewerbe wieder aufgenommen werden muß. Diese Frist beträgt höchstens ein Jahr; sie kann verlängert werden, wenn ein wichtiger Grund vorliegt.

(3) Der Gewerbetreibende hat binnen einer Woche schriftlich anzuzeigen, daß er das Gewerbe begonnen hat oder nicht mehr ausübt.

Reichsgesetzbl. 1938 I 72

To procure the complete text of this German Law, contact your Congressman and/or the German Consulate.

APPENDIX C

80

1571

Reichsgesetzblatt

Teil I

1938	Ausgegeben zu Berlin, den 12. November 1938	Nr. 188

Tag	Inhalt	Seite
11. 11. 38	**Gesetz über die Ergänzungswahlen zum Großdeutschen Reichstag**	1571
8. 11. 38	Verordnung über die Herstellung orthopädischer Maßschuhe	1572
9. 11. 38	Verordnung über die Einführung des Gesetzes über die Beförderung der im unmittelbaren Reichsdienst stehenden Polizeivollzugsbeamten auf den öffentlichen regelmäßig verkehrenden Beförderungsmitteln im Lande Österreich	1572
10. 11. 38	Verordnung zur Ergänzung der Familienunterstützungsverordnung für Österreich	1573
11. 11. 38	Verordnung gegen den Waffenbesitz der Juden	1573
11. 11. 38	Verordnung über die Einführung des Hypothekenbankgesetzes und des Gesetzes über die Pfandbriefe und verwandten Schuldverschreibungen öffentlich-rechtlicher Kreditanstalten im Lande Österreich	1574
11. 11. 38	Anordnung über die Erfassung und Musterung 1938/39 für den aktiven Wehrdienst und Reichsarbeitsdienst im Lande Österreich	1578

Nr. 188 — Tag der Ausgabe: 12. November 1938 **1573**

Verordnung gegen den Waffenbesitz der Juden.

Vom 11. November 1938.

Auf Grund des § 31 des Waffengesetzes vom 18. März 1938 (Reichsgesetzbl. I S. 265), des Artikels III des Gesetzes über die Wiedervereinigung Österreichs mit dem Deutschen Reich vom 13. März 1938 (Reichsgesetzbl. I S. 237) und des § 9 des Erlasses des Führers und Reichskanzlers über die Verwaltung der sudetendeutschen Gebiete vom 1. Oktober 1938 (Reichsgesetzbl. I S. 1331) wird folgendes verordnet:

§ 1

Juden (§ 5 der Ersten Verordnung zum Reichsbürgergesetz vom 14. November 1935, Reichsgesetzbl. I S. 1333) ist der Erwerb, der Besitz und das Führen von Schußwaffen und Munition sowie von Hieb- oder Stoßwaffen verboten. Sie haben die in ihrem Besitz befindlichen Waffen und Munition unverzüglich der Ortspolizeibehörde abzuliefern.

§ 2

Waffen und Munition, die sich im Besitz eines Juden befinden, sind dem Reich entschädigungslos verfallen.

§ 3

Für Juden fremder Staatsangehörigkeit kann der Reichsminister des Innern Ausnahmen von dem im § 1 ausgesprochenen Verbot zulassen. Er kann diese Befugnis auf andere Stellen übertragen.

§ 4

Wer den Vorschriften des § 1 vorsätzlich oder fahrlässig zuwiderhandelt, wird mit Gefängnis und mit Geldstrafe bestraft. In besonders schweren Fällen vorsätzlicher Zuwiderhandlung ist die Strafe Zuchthaus bis zu fünf Jahren.

§ 5

Der Reichsminister des Innern erläßt die zur Durchführung dieser Verordnung erforderlichen Rechts- und Verwaltungsvorschriften.

§ 6

Diese Verordnung gilt auch im Lande Österreich und in den sudetendeutschen Gebieten.

Berlin, den 11. November 1938.

Der Reichsminister des Innern

Frick

To procure the complete text of this German Law, contact your Congressman and/or the German Consulate.

APPENDIX D

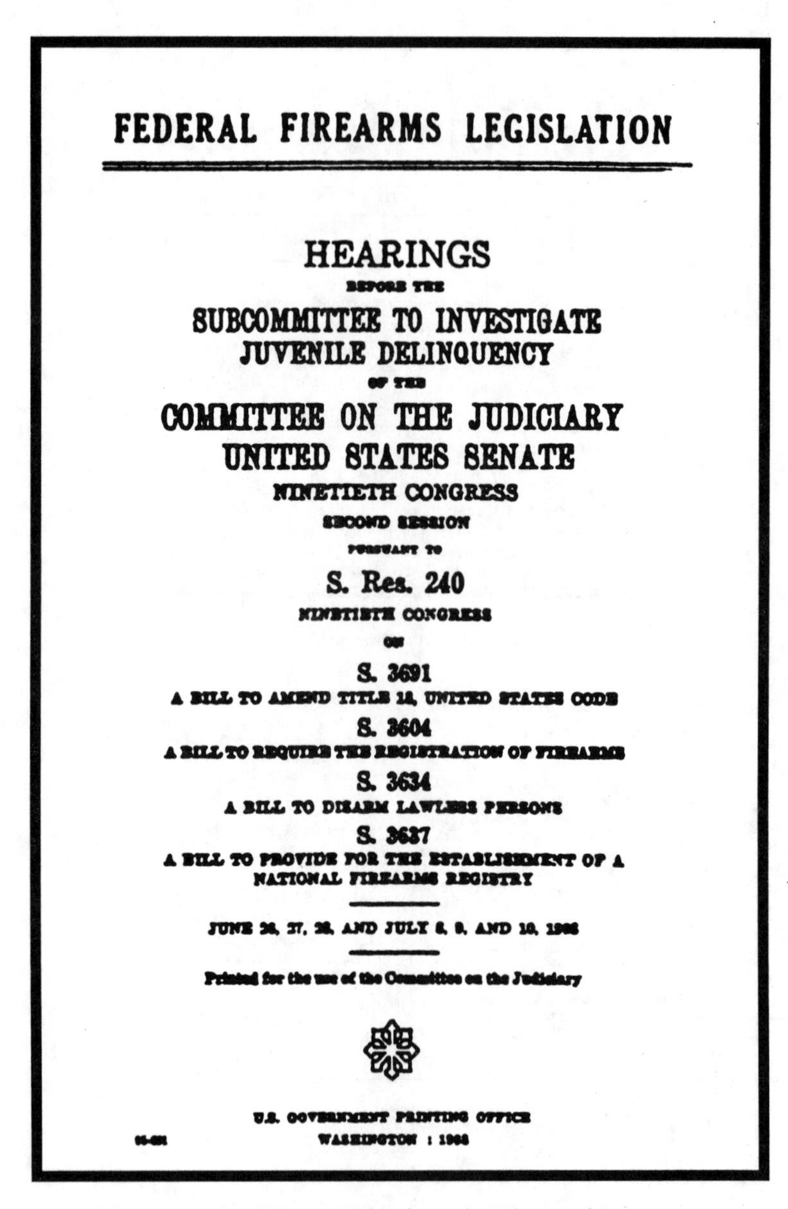

FEDERAL FIREARMS LEGISLATION

HEARINGS

BEFORE THE

SUBCOMMITTEE TO INVESTIGATE JUVENILE DELINQUENCY

OF THE

COMMITTEE ON THE JUDICIARY UNITED STATES SENATE

NINETIETH CONGRESS

SECOND SESSION

PURSUANT TO

S. Res. 240

NINETIETH CONGRESS

ON

S. 3691

A BILL TO AMEND TITLE 18, UNITED STATES CODE

S. 3604

A BILL TO REQUIRE THE REGISTRATION OF FIREARMS

S. 3634

A BILL TO DISARM LAWLESS PERSONS

S. 3637

A BILL TO PROVIDE FOR THE ESTABLISHMENT OF A NATIONAL FIREARMS REGISTRY

JUNE 26, 27, 28, AND JULY 8, 9, AND 10, 1968

Printed for the use of the Committee on the Judiciary

U.S. GOVERNMENT PRINTING OFFICE

WASHINGTON : 1968

This report should be available from the Library of Congress. If not, contact your Congressman and/or Senators.

APPENDIX E

CFR MEMBERSHIP ROSTER – 1995

** Elected to membership in 1995*
*** Elected to five-year term membership in 1995*

Aaron, David L.
Abboud, A. Robert
Abboud, Labeeb M.
Abdel-Meguid, Tarek
Abegglen, James C.
Abel, Elie
Abram, Morris B.
Abramowitz, Morton I.
Abrams, Elliot
Abshire, David M.
Aburdene, Odeh
Ackerman, Peter
Adams, Gordon M.
Adams, Robert McCormick
Adelman, Carol C.
Adelman, Kenneth L.
Agnew, Harold M.
Agostinelli, Robert F.
Agronsky, Martin
Aho, C. Michael
Aidinoff, M. Bernard
Ajami, Fouad
Akins, James E.
Albright, Alice Patterson
Albright, Madeleine
Alderman, Michael II
Aldrich, George II
Alexander, Robert J.
Alexander, Sarah Elizabeth
Alford, William P.
Allaire, Paul A.
Allbritton, Joe L.
Allen, Jodie T.*
Allen, Lew, Jr.
Allen, Robert E.
Allison, Grahan T., Jr.
Allison, Richard C.
Almond, Michael*
Alpern, Alan N.
Altman, Roger C.
Altman, Sidney
Altschul, Arthur G.
Alvarado, Donna M.
Alvarez, Jose E.
Ames, Oakes
Amos, Deborah
Andelman, David
Andersen, Harold W.
Anderson, Craig B
Anderson, David
Anderson, John B
Anderson, Lisa
Anderson, Marcus A.
Anderson, Paul F.
Anderson, Robert
Anderson, Robert O.
Andreas, Dwayne O.
Andreas, Terry*
Andrews, David R.
Ansour, M. Michael
Anthoine, Robert
Anthony, John Duke
Apgar, David P.
Apodaca, Jerry

Aponte, Mari Carmen
Appiah, Kwarne
Apter, David E.
Araskog, Rand V.
Arciniega Tornas A.
Arcos, Cresencio S.
Arledge, Roone
Armacost, Michael II.
Armstrong, Anne
Armstrong, C. Michael
Armstrong, John A.
Arnhold, Henry II
Arnold, Millard W.
Aron, Adam M.
Aronson, Bernard W.
Aronson, Jonathan D.
Art, Robert J.
Arthurs, Alberta
Artzt, Edwin L.
Asencio, Diego C.
Asher, Robert E.
Asmus, Ronald D.
Assevero, Vicki-Ann E.
Assousa, George E.
Atherton, Alfred L., Jr.
Atwood, J. Brian
Auer, James E.
Augustine, Norman R.
Auspitz, Josiah Lee
Ausubel, Jesse Huntley
Avedon, John F.
Avery, John E.
Ayers, H. Brandt.
Babbitt, Bruce
Bacot, J. Carter
Bader, William B
Baer, M. Delal
Baeza, Mario L.
Bailey, Charles W.
Bains, Leslie E.
Baird, Charles F.
Baker, Howard H., Jr.
Baker, James E.
Baker, James Edgar
Baker, Pauline H.
Baker, Stewart A.
Balaran, Paul
Baldwin, David A.
Baldwin, H. Furlong
Baldwin, Richard Edward
Baldwin, Robert E.
Baldwin, Sherman**
Bales, Carter F.
Balick, Kenneth D.
Baliles, Gerald L.
Ball, David G.
Barber, Charles F.
Barber, James A., Jr.
Bardel, William G.
Barger, Teresa C.
Barker, John P.
Barnds, William J.
Barnes, Harry G., Jr.
Barnes, Michael D.
Barnet, Richard J.
Barnett, A. Doak
Barnett, Michael N.
Barnett, Robert W.
Baroody, William J., Jr.
Barr, Thomas D.
Barrett, Barbara McConnell
Barrett, John A.
Barrett, Nancy Smith
Barry, John L.
Barry, Lisa B.
Barry, Thomas C.
Bartholomew, Reginald
Bartlett, Joseph W.
Bartlett, Thomas A.
Bartley, Robert L.

Barton, Christopher
Basek, John T.
Bashawaty, Albert C.
Basora, Adrian A.
Bass, James E.
Bass, Peter E.
Bassow, Whitman
Batkin, Alan R.
Bator, Francis M.
Battaglia, Charles*
Battle, Lucius D.
Bauman, Robert P.
Baumann, Carol Edler
Baumann, Roger R.
Bean, Atherton
Beard, Ronald S.
Beattie, Richard I.
Becherer, Hans W.
Beckler, David Z.
Beeman, Richard E.
Begley, Louis
Behrman, Jack N.
Beilenson, Anthony C.*
Beim, David O.
Beinecke, William S.
Beitler, Ruth Margolies**
Belfer, Robert A.
Bell, Devid E.
Bell, Gordon P.**
Bell, Holley Mack
Bell, J. Bowyer
Bell, Peter D.
Bell, Steve
Bell-Rose, Stephanie
Bellamy, Carol
Bellinger, John B., III
Bello, Judith Hippler
Benbow, Terence H.
Bender, Gerald J.
Benedict, Kennette M.*
Bennet, Douglas J., Jr.
Bennett, Andrew
Bennett, J. F.
Bennett, Susan J.
Benson, Lucy Wilson
Beplat, Tristan E.
Bereuter, Douglas K.*
Berger, Marilyn
Berger, Samuel R.
Berger, Suzanne
Bersten, C. Fred
Berkowitz, Bruce D.
Berman, Howard L.
Bernardin, Joseph Cardinal
Berndt, John F.
Bernstein, David S.
Bernstein, Peter W.
Bernstein, Robert L.
Bernstein, Tom A.*
Berresford, Susan Vail
Berris, Jan
Bessie, Simon Michael
Best, William A., III
Bestani, Robert M.
Bestor, Theodore C.
Betts, Richard K.
Beyer, John C.
Bialer, Seweryn
Bialkin, Kenneth J.
Bicksler, Barbara
Biel, Eric R.
Biemann, Betsy
Bienen, Henry S.
Bierley, John C.
Biggs. David J.
Bilder, Richard B.
Binger, James H.
Binkley, Nicholas B.
Binnendijk, Hans
Birkelund, John P.

Birnbaum, Eugene A.
Bissell, Richard E.
Bjornlund, Eric C.
Black, Joseph E.
Black, Shirley Temple
Black, Stanley Warren
Blacker, Coit Dennis
Blackwell, J. Kenneth
Blackwell, James A., Jr.
Blackwill, Robert D.
Blair, Sally Onesti
Blake, Robert O.
Blank, Stephen
Blechman, Barry M.
Bleier, Edward
Blendon, Robert J.
Blinken, Antony J.
Bloch, Julia Chang
Bloom, Evan Todd
Bloomfield, Lincoln P.
Bloomfield, Richard J.
Blum, John A.
Blumenthal, Sidney
Blumenthal, W. Michael
Blumrosen, Alexander B.**
Bob, Daniel E.
Bobbitt, Philip
Bodea, Sorin A.**
Bodie, William C.
Boeker, Paul H.
Bogert, Carroll R.
Boggs, Michael D.
Bohen, Frederick M.
Bohlen, Avis T.
Bohn, John A.
Bolling, Landrum R.
Bollinger, Martin J.
Bond, George C.
Bond, Jean Carey*
Bond, Robert D.
Bonime-Blanc, Andrea
Bonney, J. Dennis
Bonsal, Dudley B.
Bonsal, Philip W.
Booker, Salih
Bookout, John F.
Boone, Theodore S.
Boorda, Jeremy Michael*
Boren, David Lyle
Boschwitz, Rudy
Bossert, Philip A., Jr.
Bosworth, Stephen W.
Botts, John C.
Bouis, Antonina W.
Bouton, Marshall M.
Bovin, Denis A.
Bowen, William G.
Bower, Joseph L.
Bowie, Robert R.
Bowlin, Mike R.
Bowman, Richard C.
Boyd, Charles G.
Boyer, Ernest L.
Bracken, Paul
Brademas, John
Bradford, Zeb
Bradley, Edward R.
Bradley, William L.
Brady, Linda Parrish
Brady, Nicholas F.
Brainard, Lawrence J.
Brainard, S. Lael
Brand, Laurie A.
Branscomb, Lewis M.
Branson, William H.
Brauchli, Marcus W.
Breck, Henry R.
Breindel, Eric M.
Bremer, L. Paul, III
Breslauer, George W.

Bresnan, John J.
Brewer, John D.
Breyer, Stephen G.
Briggs, Everett Ellis
Brimmer, Andrew F.
Brimmer, Esther Diane
Brinkley, David
Brittenham, Raymond L.
Broadman, Harry G.*
Broda, Frederick C.
Brokaw, Tom
Bromley, D. Allan
Bronfman, Edgar M.
Brookins, Carol
Brooks, Harvey
Brower, Charles N.
Brown, Alice L.
Brown, Brian A.**
Brown, Carroll
Brown, Cynthia*
Brown, Frederic J.
Brown, Gwendolyn
Brown, Harold
Brown, L. Carl
Brown, L. Dean
Brown, Lester R.
Browrn, Richard P., Jr.
Brown, Ronald, II
Brown, Tobias Josef**
Browne, Robert S.
Bruce, Judith
Bruemmer, Melissa L.S.
Bruemmer, Russell J.
Bryan, Greyson L.
Bryant, Ralph C.
Bryson, John E.
Brzezinski, Zbigniew
Buchheim, Robert W.
Buchman, Mark E.
Buckley, William F., Jr.
Buergenthal, Thomas
Bugliarello, George
Bullard, Edward P.
Bullock, Mary Brown
Bundy, McGeorge
Bundy, William P.
Burand, Deborah K.
Burgess, James E.
Burke, James E.
Burkhalter, Holly J.
Burlingame, Edward L.
Burns, Haywood
Burns, Patrick Owen
Burns, R. Nicholas*
Burns, William F.
Burns, William J.
Burt, Richard R.
Burton, Daniel F., Jr.
Busbee, R. Christopher**
Bushner, Rolland
Bussey, Donald S.
Bussey, John
Busuttil, James
Butler, George Lee
Butler, Samuel C.
Butler, William J.
Buxbaum, Richard M.*
Cabot, Louis W.
Cabot, Thomas D.
Cabranes, Jose A.
Cahill, Kevin M.
Cahn, Anne H.
Calabia, Dawn T.
Calder, Kent Eyring
Caldwell, Dan
Caldwell, Philip
Calhoun, Michael J.
Califano, Joseph A., Jr.
Callahan, David L.**
Callander, Robert J.

Callen, Michael A.
Calleo, David P.
Callwood, Kevin R.
Campbell, Colin G.
Campbell, John C.
Campbell, Kurt M.
Campbell, W. Glenn
Canavan, Christopher
Canfield, Franklin O.
Cappello, Juan C.
Carbonell, Nestor T.
Carey, Hugh L.
Carey, John
Carey, Sarah C.
Carey, William D.
Carlos, Manuel Luis
Carlson, Steven E.
Carlucci, Frank C., III
Carmichael, William D.
Carnesale, Albert
Carothers, Thomas
Carpendale, Andrew
Carrington, Walter C.
Carrion Rexach, Richard L.
Carroll, J. Speed
Carruth, Reba Anne
Carson, C. W., Jr.
Carson, Edward M.
Carswell, Robert
Carter, Ashton B.
Carter, Barry E.
Carter, George E.
Carter, Hodding, III
Carter, Jimmy
Carter, Mark Andrew**
Carter, Marshall N.
Carter, Theodore N.**
Casper, Gerhard
Cattarulla, Elliot R.
Catto, Henry E., Jr.
Caulfield, Matthew P.
Cave, Ray
Cebrowski, Arthur K.
Celeste, Richard F.
Cerjan, Paul G.
Chace, James
Chafee, John H.
Chain, John T., Jr.
Challenor, Herschelle S.
Chambers, Anne Cox
Chan, Gerald L.*
Chan, Ronnie C.
Chancellor, John
Chanis, Jonathan A.
Chao, Elaine L.
Chapman, Margaret Holt
Charles, Robert B.
Charney, Jonathan I.
Charpie, Robert A.
Chasin, Dana
Chaudhry, Kiren Aziz
Chaves, Robert J.**
Chavez, Linda
Chavira, Rocardo*
Chayes, Abram J.
Chayes, Antonia Handler
Cheever, Darniel S.
Chen, Kimball C.
Chenault, Kenneth I.
Cheney, Richard B.
Cheremeteff, Kyra
Cherne, Leo
Chickering, A. Lawrence
Choharis, Peter Charles
Cholmondeley, Paula H. J.
Choucri, Nazli
Chow, Jack C.
Christiansen, John F.**
Christianson, Geryld B.
Christan, Daniel William

Christman, Walter L.
Christopher, Warren
Chubb, Hendon
Churchill, Buntzie Ellis
Cisneros, Henry G.
Cisneros, Marc A.*
Clapp, Priscilla A.
Clark, Dick
Clark, Howard L.
Clark, J. H. Cullum
Clark, Noreen
Clark, Susan Lesley
Clark, Wesley K.
Clarke, J. G.
Clarkson, Lawrence W.
Clemons, Steven C.**
Clendenin, John L.
Cleveland, Harlan
Cleveland, Peter M.
Clifford, Donald K., Jr.
Cline, Ray S.
Cline, William R.
Clinger, William F., Jr.
Clinton, Bill
Cloherty, Patricia M.
Cloud, Stanley Wills
Clough, Michael
Clurman, Richard M.
Cobb, Charles E., Jr.
Cobb, P. Whit, Jr.
Cochran, Barbara S.
Coffer, C. Shelby, III
Coffey, Joseph I.
Cohen, Benjamin J.
Cohen, Eliot A.
Cohen, Herman J.
Cohen, Jerome Alan
Cohen, Joel E.
Cohen, Patricia
Cohen, Roberta
Cohen, Stephen B.
Cohen, Stephen F.
Cohen, Stephen S.
Cohen, William S.
Colbert, Evelyn
Colby, Jonathan E.
Colby, William E.
Cole, Johnetta
Coleman, Isobel
Colerna, William T., Jr.
Coles, Julius E.*
Collier, David
Collins, Joseph J.
Collins, Paula J.
Combs, Richard E., Jr.
Comstock, Philip E., Jr.
Cone, Sydney M., III
Conners, Lelia**
Connolly, Gerald E.
Connor, John T., Jr.
Considine, Jill M.
Constable, Pamela
Conway, Jill
Cook, Frances D.
Cook, Gary M.
Cook, Howard A.
Cooke, Goodwin
Cooke, John F.
Coolidge, Nicholas J.
Coombe, George W., Jr.
Coombs, Philip H.
Coon, Jane Abell
Cooney, Joan Ganz
Cooper, Charles A.
Cooper, Chester L.
Cooper, James H.S.*
Cooper, John Milton
Cooper, Kerry
Cooper, Richard N.
Cordesman, Anthony H.*

Cornelius, Wayne A.
Corrigan, E. Gerald
Cott, Suzanne
Cotter, William
Courtney, William H.
Cowal, Sally Grooms
Cowan, L. Gray
Cowhey, Peter F.
Cox, Edward F.
Cox, Robert G.
Crahan, Margaret E.
Crawford, John F.
Cressey, Roger W., III**
Crile, George, III
Crittenden, Ann
Crocker, Chester A.
Cromwell, Adelaide
Cross, June V.
Cross, Sam Y.
Cross, Theodore
Crossette, Barbara
Crowe, William J.
Crystal, Lester M.
Cullum, Lee
Culver, John C.
Cummings, Robert L., Jr.
Cummiskey, Frank J.
Cuneo, Donald
Cuny, Frederick C.
Cuomo, Kerry Kennedy
Cuomo, Mario M.
Curran, R. T.
Curtis, Gerald L.
Cutler, Lloyd N.
Cutler, Walter L.
Cutter, W. Bowman
Cyr, Arthur
Dahlman, Michael K.
Dale, William B.
Dalley, George A.
Dallin, Alexander
Dallmeyer, Dorinda
Dalton, Gregory**
Dalton, James E.
Dam, Kenneth W.
Damrosch, Lori Fisler
Danforth, William H.
Daniel, Ana R.
Daniel, D. Ronald
Danner, Mark D.
DaSilva, Russell J.*
David, Jack
Davidson, Daniel L.
Davidson, Ralph K.
Davidson, Ralph P.
Davis, Evan A.*
Davis, Jacquelyn K.
Davis, Jerome
Davis, Kathryn W.
Davis, Lynn E.
Davis, Maceo N.
Davis, Nathaniel
Davis, Vincent
Davison, Daniel P.
Davison, Kristina Perkin**
Davison, W. Phillips
Dawisha, Karen Lea
Dawkins, Peter M.
Dawson, Christine L.
Dawson, Horace G., Jr.
Dawson, Horace G., III
Dawson, Marion M.
Day, Anthony
Day, Arthur R.
Day, Robert A.
Deagle, Edwin A., Jr.
Dean, Jonathan
Dean, Robert W.
Debevoise, Eli Whitney, II
de Borchgrave, Arnaud

Debs, Barbara Knowles
Debs, Richard A.
DeBusk, F. Amanda
DeCrane, Alfred C., Jr.
Decter, Midge
de Cubas, Jose
Dedrick, Pred T.
Deffenbaugh, Ralston H., Jr.
Deibel, Terry L.
de Janosi, Peter E.
de la Garza, Rodolfo O.
Delaney, Andrew John
del Olmo, Frank
de Menil, George
de Menil, Lois Pattison
Deming, Rust M.
Denison, Robert J.
Dennis, Everette E.
Denny, Brewster C.
Dernoon, David B. H.
Denton, E. Hazel
DePalma, Samuel
Dergham, Raghida
Derian, Patricia Murphy
Derryck, Vivian Lowery
Desai, Padma
Destlet, I. M.
Deutch, John M.
Deutch, Michael J.
DeVecchi, Robert P.
Devine, Caroline M.*
Devine, Thomas J.
de Vries, Rimmer
DeWind, Adrian W.
DeYoung, Karen
Dickey, Christopher S.
Dicks, Norman D.*
Didion, Joan
Diebold, John
Diebold, William, Jr.
Diehl, Jackson
Dilenschneider, Robert L.
Dillon, Douglas
Di Martino, Rita
Dine, Thomas A.
Dinkins, David N.*
Djerejian, Edward P.
Dobriansky, Pauls
Dodd, Christopher J.
Dodge, William S.**
Doebele, Justin**
Doerge, David J.*
Doherty, William C., Jr.
Dominguez, Jorge I.
Donahue, Thomas R.
Donaldson, Roert H.
Donaldson, William H.
Donnell, Ellsworth
Donnelly, H. C.
Donnelly, Sally B.
Doran, Charles F.
Dornbusch, Rudiger
Dougan, Diana Lady
Douglass, Robert R.
Downie, Leonard, Jr.
Doyle, James S.
Doyle, Michael William
Draper, William H., III
Drayton, William, Jr.
Drell, Sidney D.
Drew, Elizabeth
Dreyfuss, Joel
Drobnick, Richard
Drumwright, J. R.
Druyan, Ann
Duberstein, Kenneth M.
Dubin, Seth H.*
DuBrul, Stephen M., Jr.
Duderstadt, James J.
Duersten, Althea L.

Duffey, Joseph
Duffey, Gloria Charmian
Duffy, James H.
Dugan, Michael J.
Dukakis, Michael S.
Dulany, Peggy
Duncan, Cbarles W., Jr.
Duncan, John C.
Duncan, Richard L.
Dunigan, P. Andrew
Dunkerley, Craig G.
Dunlop, Joan Banks
Dunn, Kempton*
Dunn, Lewis A.
Dur, Philip A.*
Dutton, Frederick G.
Duval, Michael Raoul
Dyke, Nancy Bearg
Eagleburger, Lawrence S.
Earle, Ralph H.
East, Maurice A.
Easum, Donald B.
Eberhart, Ralph E.*
Eberle, William D.
Eccles, Peter W.
Echols, Marsha A.*
Ecton, Donna R.
Edelman, Albert I.
Edelman, Gerald M.
Edelman, Marian Wright
Edelstein, Julius C. C.
Edley, Christopher, Jr.
Edwards, Howard L.
Edwards, Jacquelyn Mitchell
Edwards, Robert H.
Edwards, Robert H., Jr.
Eggers, Thomas E.*
Ehrlich, Thomas
Eichengreen, Barry*
Eilts, Hermann Fredrick
Einaudi, Luigi R.
Einhorn, Jessica P.
Eisendrath, Charles R.
Eizenstat, Stuart E.
Eliason, Leslie Carol
Ellingwood, Susan K.**
Elliott, Inger Mccabe
Elliott, Osborn
Ellis, James R.
Ellis, Patricia
Ellison, Keith P.
Ellsberg, Daniel
Ellsworth, Robert F.
Ely, John Hart
Ely-Raphael, Nancy Halliday
Embree, Ainslie T.
Emerson, Alice F.
Enders, Thomas O.
Enthoven, Alain
Epstein, Jason
Epstein, Jeffrey E.*
Erb, Guy F.
Erb, Richard D.
Erbsen, Claude E.
Erburu, Robert F.
Ercklentz, Alexander T.
Estabrook, Rcnbert H.
Estrada, Alfredo
Esty, Daniel C.
Evans, Carol V.
Evans, Gordon W.
Evans, Harold M.
Evans, John C.
Evans, Rowland, Jr.
Everingham, Susan M. S.
Ewing, William, Jr.
Fabian, Larry L.
Fairbanks, Douglas, Jr.
Fairbanks, Richard M., III
Falco, Mathea

Falcoff, Mark
Falk, Pamela S.
Falk, Richard A.
Fallows, James
Fanning, Katherine W.
Fanton, Jonathan F.
Farer, Tom J.
Farmer, Thomas I.
Fascell, Dante B.
Fawaz, Leila
Feaver, Peter D.
Feierstein, Mark;
Feiner, Ava S.
Feinstein, Lee
Feissel, Gustave
Feith Dougal J.
Feldman, Mark B.
Feldstein, Martin S.
Feltman, Jeffrey
Ferguson, Glenn W.
Ferguson, James L.
Ferrari, Frank E.
Ferraro, Geraldine A.
Ferre, Maurice A.
Fesharaki, Fereidun
Feshbach, Murray
Fessenden, Hart
Fetter, Steve
Fierce, Milfred C.
Fife, Eugene V.*
Fifield, Russell H.
Finberg, Barbara D.
Finger, Seymour Maxwell
Finkelstein, Lawrence S.
Finlayson, Grant Ellis
Finn, James
Finnemore, Martha
Finney, Paul B.
Firmage, Edwin B.
Fischer, David J.
Fischer, Stanley
Fisher, Cathleen S.
Fisher, Peter Reyerson
Fisher, Richard W.
Fisher, Roger
Fishlow, Albert
Fitz-Pegado, Lauri J.
FitzGerald, Francos
Fitzgibbons, Harold E.
Flaherty, Peter
Flanagan, Stephen J.
Flanigan, Peter M.
Fleishmann, Alan H.**
Fletcher, Philip Douglas
Flournoy, Michele A.
Flynn, Stephen E.
Fogleman, Ronald R
Foley, S. R., Jr.
Foley, Thomas S.
Foote, Edward T., II
Ford, Gerald R.
Ford, Paul B., Jr.
Forester, Lynn
Forman, Shepard
Forstmann, Theodore J.*
Fort, Randall M.
Fosler, Gail
Foster, Brenda Lei
Fowler, Henry H.
Fox, Donald T.
Fox, Elanor M.C.
Fox, Joseph C.
Franck, Thomas M.
Francke, Albert, III
Frank, Charles R., Jr.
Frank, Isaiah
Frank, Richard A.
Frank, Francine R.
Frankel, Jeffrey A.*
Frankel, Barbara Hackman

Franklin, George S.
Frazer, Jendayi, E.**
Fredericks, I. Wayne
Freedman, Eugene M.*
Freeman, Bennett
Freeman, Harry L.
Freeman, Orville L.
Freidheim, Cyrus F., Jr.
Frelinghuysen, Peter H.B.
Fremont-Smith, Marion R.
Freund, Gerald
Frey, Donald N.
Freytag, Richard A.
Fribourg, Michel
Fribourd, Paul
Fried, Edward R
Friedberg, Aaron L.*
Friedman, Bart*
Friedman, Benjamin M.
Friedman, David S.
Friedman, Jordana D.**
Friedman, Stephen
Friedman, Stephen J.
Friedman, Thomas L.
Frieman, Wendy
Friend, Theodore
Fromkin, David
Fromm, Joseph
Froot, Kenneth A.
Frost, Ellen L.
Fry, Earl H.
Frye, Alton
Fukushima, Glen S.
Fukuyama, Francis
Fuller, Kathryn S.
Fuller, William P.
Fullerton, William Bewick
Furlaud, Richard M.
Futter, Ellen V.
Gabriel, Charles A.
Gaggis, John Lewis
Gaer, Felice
Gaines, James R.*
Galbraith, Evan G.
Gallagher, Dennis
Gallucci, Robert L.
Galpin, Timothy J.
Galvin, John R
Galvis, Sergio J.
Ganguly, Sumit
Gann, Pamela
Ganoe, Charles S.
Gantcher, Nathan*
Garcia-Passalacqua, Juan Manuel
Gard, Robert G., Jr.
Gardner, Nathan P.
Gardner, James A.
Gardner, Nina Luzzatto
Gardner, Richard N.
Garment, Leonard
Garment, Suzanne
Garrison, Mark
Gart, Murray J.
Garten, Jeffrey E.
Garthoff, Raymond L.
Garwin, Richard L.
Gates, Henry Louis, Jr.
Gates, Philomeme A.
Gates, Robert M.
Gati, Charles
Gati, Toby Trister
Gaudiana, Claire Lynn
Gause, F. Gregory, III
Gay, Catherine
Gebhard, Paul R. S.**
Geertz, Clifford
Geier, Philip O.
Geiger, Theodore
Gejdenson, Sam
Gelb, Leslie H.

Gelb, Richard L.
Gell-Mann, Murray
Gellman, Barton David
Georgescu, Peter A.
Gephardt, Rchard A.
Gerber, Louis
Gergen, David R
Gerhart, Gail M.
Germain, Adrierme
Gerschel, Patrick A.
Gershman, Carl
Gerson, Allan*
Gerson, Ralph J.
Gerstner, Louis V., Jr.
Getler, Michael
Geyelin, Henry R.
Geyelin, Philip L.
Geyer, Georgie Anne
Gfoeller, Joachim, Jr.
Ghiglione, Loren
Gibbons, John H.
Gibbs, Nancy Reid
Gibney, Frank B.
Giffen, James H.
Gilbert, Jackson B.
Gilbert, Jarobin, Jr.
Gilbert, Steven, J.
Gillespie, Michael J.
Gilmore, Kenneth O.
Gilmore, Richard
Gilpatric, Roswell L.
Gilpin, Robert G., Jr.
Gingrich, Newton L.
Ginsburg, David
Ginsburg, James
Ginsburg, Ruth Bader
Glauber, Robert R.
Glazer, Nathan
Gleysteen, William H., Jr.
Globerman, Norma
Gluck, Carol
Gluck, Frederick W.
Godchaux, Frank A., III
Godwin, I. Lamond
Goekjian, Samuel V.
Goheen, Robert F.
Goins, Charlynn
Goizueta, Roberto C.
Goldberg, Andrew C.
Goldberg, Ronnie Lee*
Goldberger, Marvin L.
Golden, James R
Golden, William T.
Goldgeier, James M.**
Goldin, Harrison J.
Goldman, Andrew
Goldman, Charles N.
Goldman, Emily O.
Goldman, Guido
Goldman, Marshall I.
Goldman, Merle
Goldmark, Peter C., Jr.
Goldring, Natalie J.
Goldschmidt, Neil
Goldsmith, Jack Landman, III
Goldstein, Gordon**
Goldwyn, David L.
Golightly, Neil L.
Golob, Paul D.
Gomory, Ralph E.
Gompert, David C.
Goodby, James E.
Goodman, George J. W.
Goodman, Herbert I.
Goodman, John B.
Goodman, Nancy F.**
Goodman, Roy M.
Goodman, Sherri Wassennan*
Goospaster, Andrew J.
Goodsell, James Nelson

Gordon, Lincoln
Gordon, Michael R.
Gordon, Philip H.
Gorman, Joseph T.
Gornick, Alan L.
Gotbaum, Victor
Gottemoeller, Rose E.
Gottfried, Kurt
Gottlieb, Gidon A.G.
Gottsegen, Peter M.
Gould, Peter G.
Gourevitch, Peter A.
Graff, Henry F.
Graff, Robert D.
Graham, Bob
Graham, Katharine
Graham, Thomas, Jr.
Graham, Thomas Wallace
Grant, Stephen A.
Graubard, Stephen R.
Graves, Howard D.
Gray, Charles D.
Gray, Hanna Holborn
Green, Bill
Green, Carl J.
Green, Ernest G.*
Green, Jerrold D.
Green, Michael Jonathan**
Greenberg, Arthur N.
Greenberg, Evan G.*
Greenberg, Karen J.*
Greenberg, Maurice R
Greenberg, Sanford D.
Greenberger, Robert S.
Greene, James C.
Greene, Joseph N., Jr.
Greene, Margaret L.
Greene, Wade
Greenfield, James L.
Greenfield, Meg
Greenspan, Alan
Greenwald, Joseph A.
Greenway, H. D. S.
Greenwood, Ted
Gregg, Donald P.
Gregorian, Vartan
Gregson, Wallace C.*
Grenier, Richard
Griffin, Anne-Marea**
Griffith, William E.
Grimes, Joseph A., Jr.
Grose, Peter
Gross, Patrick W.
Grove, Brandon H., Jr.
Groves, Ray J.
Grundfest, Joseph
Grune, George V.
Grunwals, Henry A.
Guerra-Mondragon, Gabriel
Guest, Michael E.
Guisinger, Stephen E.
Gullion, Edmund A.
Gutfreund, John H.
Guth, John H.J.*
Gutman, Edwin O.
Gutmann, Henning P.
Gwertzman, Bernard M.
Gwin, Batherine
Hass, Peter E.
Haas, Robert D.
Hasass, Richard N.
Habsburg-Lothringen, Immaculada Von
Haddad, Yvonne Yazbeck
Hadley, Stephen J.
Hafiner, Joseph A., Jr.
Haggard, Stephan
Hahn, Keith D.
Haig, Alexander M., Jr
Hakim, Peter

Halaby, Najeeb E.
Hall, John P.
Hallingby, Paul, Jr.
Halperin, Morton H.
Halsted, Thomas A.
Haltzel, Michael H.
Hamburg, David A.
Hamburg, Margaret Ann
Hamilton, Ann O.
Hamilton, Charles V.
Hamilton, Daniel
Hamilton, Doug N.
Hamilton, Edward K.
Hamilton, Lee H.*
Hamilton, Michael P.
Hamilton, Ruth Simms
Hancock, Ellen
Hand, Scott M.*
Handelman, Stephen*
Hanrieder, Wolfram F.
Hanscom, Patricia L.
Hansell, Herbert I.
Hansen, Carol Rae
Hansen, Keith Eric
Hanson, Thor
Hantz, Giselle P.
Harari, Maurice
Harding, Harry
Hardt, John P.
Hargrove, John Lawrence
Harleston, Bernard W.
Harman, Jane L.*
Harman, Sidney
Harpel, James W.
Harper, Conrad K.
Harriman, Pamela C.
Harris, Irving B.
Harris, John M.
Harris, Joseph E.
Harris, Martha Caldwell
Harrison, Selig S.
Harsch, Joseph C.
Harshberger, Edward R
Hart, Augustin S., Jr.
Hart, Gary*
Hart, Parker T.
Hartman, Arthur A.
Haskell, John H.F., Jr.
Haskins, Caryl P.
Hatfield, Robert S.
Hauge, John R
Hauser, Rita E.
Hauser, William L.
Hawkins, Ashton
Hawley, F. William
Hayek, Alexandre
Hayes, Margaret Daly
Haynes, Fred
Haynes, Ulric, Jr.
Hayward, Thomas B.
Healy, Harold H., Jr.
Heard, Alexander
Heck, Charles B.
Heckscher, August
Hedstrom, Mitchell W.
Heep-Richter, Barbara D.
Heginbotham, Stanley J.
Hehir, I. Bryan
Heifetz, Elaine F.
Heilbrunn, Jacob E.
Heimann, John G.
Heimbold, Charles A., Jr.*
Heimowitz, James B.
Heineman, Benjamin E., Jr.
Heintz, Stephen B.*
Heintzen, Harry L.
Heinz, Teresa*
Helander, Robert C.
Heldring, Frederick
Helfer, Ricki Rhodarmer

Heller, Richard M.
Hellman, F. Warren
Hellman, Donald C.
Helms, Richard
Helprin, Mark*
Hendrickson, David C.
Henkin, Alice H.
Henkin, Louis
Hennessy, John M.
Henninger, Daniel P.
Henrikson, Alan K.
Hentges, Harriet
Herberger, Roy A., Jr.
Herbst, Jeffrey
Hermann, Charles F.
Hernandez, Antonia
Herandez-Colon, Rafael
Herskovits, Jean
Herter, Christian A., Jr.
Herter, Frederic P.
Hertzberger, Arthur
Hertzberg, Hendrik
Herz, Barbara
HerzEeld, Charles M.
Herzstein, Jessica
Herzstein, Robert E.
Hesburgh, Theodore M.
Hess, John B.
Hessler, Curtis A.
Hester, James M.
Hewin, William A.
Hewlett, Sylvia Ann
Heyns, Roger W.
Hicks, Irvin
Hicks, Irvin, Jr.**
Hicks, John F.*
Higgins, Robert F.
Highet, Keith
Hight, B. Boyd
Hill, J. French
Hill, J. Tomlinson
Hill, Pamela
Hillenbrand, Martin J.
Hillgren, Sonja
Hills, Carla A.
Hills, Laura Hume
Hilsman, Roger
Hilton, Robert P.
Himes, James A.
Hinerfeld, Ruth J.
Hines, Rachel
Hinshaw, Randall
Hinton, Deane R.
Hirschman, Albert O.
Ho, Christine M.Y.**
Hoagland, Jim
Hoar, Joseph P.
Hoch, Frank W.
Hoeber, Amoretta M.
Hoehn, William E., Jr.
Hoenlein, Malcolm
Hoepli, Nancy L.
Hoffenberg, Mark R.**
Hoffman, Adonis Edward
Hoffman, Michael L.
Hoffman, Stanley
Hoge, James F., Jr.
Hoge, Warren
Hoguet, George R
Hohenberg, John
Hoinkes, Mary Elizabetn
Holbrooke, Richard C.
Holcomb, M. Staser
Holgate, Laura S. Hayes**
Holl, Jane E.
Holland, Mary S.
Hollick, Ann L.
Holloway, Dwight F., Jr.
Holmes, H. Allen
Holmes, Kim R.*

Holt, Pat M.
Holum, John D.*
Hooks, Benjamin L.
Hoopes, Townsend W.
Hope, Judith R.
Horelick, Arnold L.
Horlick, Gary N.
Hormats, Robert D.
Horn, Garfield H.
Horn, Karen N.
Horn, Mirian
Horn, Sally K.
Homer, Matina S.
Horowitz, Irving Louis
Horton, Alan W.
Horton, Frank B., III
Horton, Scott*
Hosmer, Germaine A.
Hottelet, Richard C.
Houghton, Amory, Jr.
Houghton, James K.
House, Karen Elliott
Hovey, Graham
Hovey, J. Allan, Jr.
Howard, A. E. Dick
Howard, John R.
Howell, Ernest M.
Hoyt, Mont P.
Huber, Richard L.
Huberman, Benjamin
Hudson, Manley O., Jr.
Hudson, Michael C.
Hudson, Stewart J.
Huebner, Lee W.
Hufbauer, Gary C.
Huffington, Roy M.
Hufstedler, Shirley
Hughes, Jeffrey L.
Hughes, John
Hughes, Justin**
Hughes, Thomas L.
Huizenga, John W.
Hultman, Tamela
Hume, Ellan
Hummel, Arthur W., Jr.
Hunsberga, Warren S.
Hunter, Robert E.
Hunter, Shirleen T.
Hunter-Gault, Charlayne
Huntington, Samuel P.
Huntsman, Jon M., Jr.
Hurewitz, J. C.
Hurford, John B.
Hurlock, James B.
Hurst, Robert J.
Hurwitz, Seth L.**
Hurwitz, Sol
Hutchins, Glenn H.
Hutzler, Charles**
Huyck, Philip M.
Hyde, Henry B.
Hyland, William G.
Hyman, Allen I.
Ignatius, David
Ikenbery, G. John
Ikle, Fred C.
Ilchman, Alice S.
Inderfurth, Karl F.
Ingersoll, Robert S.
Ink, Dwight
Inman, B. R.
Intriligator, Michael D.
Irish, Leon E.
Irvin, Patricia L.
Irwin, John N., II
Isaacson, Walter
Iselin, John Jay
Isenberg, Steven L.
Isham, Christopher
Ispahani, Mahnaz Z.

Istel, Yves-Andre
Izlar, William H., Jr.
Jabber, Paul
Jacklin, Nancy P.
Jackson, Bruce P.
Jackson, Eric K.**
Jackson, Jesse L.
Jackson, John H.
Jackson, Lois M.
Jackson, Sarah
Jackson, William E.
Jacob, John E.
Jacobs, Eli S.
Jacobs, Nehama
Jacobs, Norman
Jacobson, Harold K.
Jacobson, Jerome
Jacoby, Tamar
Janis, Mark W.
Janklow, Morton L.
Janow, Merit E.
Jansen, Marius B.
Jaquette, Jane S.
Jarvis, Nancy A.
Jastrow, Robert
Jebb, Cindy R**
Jeffries, Bradley C.
Jervis, Robert L.
Jessup, Alpheus W.
Jessup, Philip C., Jr.
Joffe, Robert D.
Johns, Lionel Shipwith
Johnson, Howard W.
Johnson, James A.
Johnson, L. Oakley
Johnson, Larry D.
Johnson, Lionel C.
Johnson, Nancie S.*
Johnson, Robbin S.
Johnson, Robert H.
Johnson, Robert W., IV
Johnson, Suzanne Nora
Johnson, Thomas S.
Johnson, W. Thomas
Johnson, Willard R.
Jones, David C.
Jones, James R
Jones, Sidney R
Jones, Thomas V.
Jordan, Amos A.
Jordan, Vernon E., Jr.
Jorden, William J.
Joseph, Geri M.
Joseph, Ira B.**
Joseph, James A.
Joseph, Richard A.
Josephson, William
Joyce, John T.
Jumper, John P.*
Junz, Helen B.
Juster, Kenneth I.
Kaden, Lewis B.*
Kahan, Jerome H.
Hanin, George McT.
Kaher, Miles
Kahn, Harry
Kaiser, Philip M.
Kaiser, Robert G.
Kalb, Bernhard
Kalb, Marvin
Kalicki, Jan
Kalil, Thomas A.**
Kamarack, Andrew M.
Kamarack, Elaine Ciulla
Kaminer, Peter H.
Kaminsky, Howard
Kampelman, Max M.
Kamsky, Virginia A.
Kanak, Donald Perry
Kandell, Jonathan

Kanet, Roger E.
Kann, Peter R
Kanter, Arnold
Kanter, Rosabeth Moss
Kaplan, Gilbert E.
Kaplan. Harold J.
Kaplan, Helene L.
Kaplan, Mark N.
Kaplan, Stephen S.
Kapp, Robert A.
Kapstein, Ethan B.
Karalekas, Anne
Karamanian, Susan L.
Karatnycky, Adrian*
Karis, Thomas G.
Karl, Terry Lynn
Karnow, Stanley
Karns, Margaret P.
Kartman, Charles*
Kasdin, Robert
Kass, Stephen L.
Kassof, Allen H.
Katz, Abraham
Katz, Daniel Roger**
Katz, Milton
Katz, Ronald S.
Katz, Stanley N.
Katzenstein, Peter J.
Kauffnan, Daniel J.
Kauffman, Henry
Kauffmann, William W.
Kaysen, Carl
Kazerni, Earhad
Kea, Charlotte G.**
Kean, Thomas H.
Kearney, Jude*
Kearns, David T.
Keel, Alton G., Jr.
Keene, Lonnie S.
Keeny, Spurgeon M., Jr.
Kelleher, Catherine M.
Kellen, Stephen M.
Keller, Edmond J.
Keller, Kenneth H.
Kellerman, Barbara
Kelley, P. X.
Kelly, James P.
Kelly, John H.
Kelman, Herbert C.
Kemble, Eugenia
Kemp, Geoffrey
Kempe, Frederick
Kempner, Maximilian W.
Kendall, Donald M.
Kenen, Peter B.
Keniston, Kenneth
Kennan, Christopher J.
Kennam, Elizabeth T.
Kennan, George F.
Kenney, F. Donald
Kent, William H.
Keohane, Nannerl O.
Keohane, Robert O.
Kern, Paul I.*
Kerr, Ann Z.
Kerry, John F.
Kesslar, Martha Neff
Kester, John G.
Kester, W. Carl
Khalilzad, Zalmay M.
Khuri, Nicola N.
Kiermaier, John
Kiernan, Robert Edward, III
Kiley, Robert R.
Kim, Andrew B.
Kim, Hanya Marie
Kimmitt, Robert M.
Kinde, Lawrence John**
King, Henry L.
King, John A., Jr.

King, Kay
Kinter, William R.
Kipper, Judith
Kirk, Grayson L.
Kirkland, Lane
Kirkpatrick, Jeane J.
Kirkpatrick, Melanie
Kissinger, Henry A.
Kitchen, Helen
Kitchen, Jeffrey C.
Kizer, Karin L.**
Kleiman, Robert
Klein, David
Klein, Edward
Klein, George*
Klein, Joe
Klissas, Nicholas S.
Klurfeld, James
Knight, Jessie J., Jr.
Knight, Robert Huntington
Knoppers, Antonie T.
Knowlton, William A.
Koch, Wendy M.
Kogan, Richard J.*
Kolodziej, Edward A.
Kolt, George
Koltai, Steven R
Komisar, Lucy
Kondracke, Morton
Korb, Lawrence J.
Korconski, Andrzej
Korry, Edward M.
Kotecha, Mahesh K.
Kraar, Louis
Kraemer, Lilian E.
Kraeutler, Kirk**
Kramer, Helen M.
Kramer, J. Reed
Kramer, Jane
Kramer, Mark Nathan
Kramer, Michael
Kramer, Steven Philip
Krasner, Stephen D.
Krasno, Rchard M.
Krause, Lawrence B.
Krauss, Clifford
Krauthammer, Charles
Kravis, Henry R.
Kreisberg, Paul H.
Krens, Thomas
Krepinevich, Andrew F.
Krepon, Michael
Kreps, Juanita M.
Krisher, Bernard
Kristoff, Sandra Jeanne
Kristol, Irving
Kross, Walter*
Krueger, Anne O.
Krueger, Harvey*
Kruidenier, David
Kruzel, Joseph
Ku, Charlotte
Kubarych, Roger M.
Kubisch, Jack B.
Kuchins, Andrew Carrigan
Kuniholm, Bruce R.
Kunstadter, Geraldine
Kuntz, Carol R.
Kupchan, Charles A.
Kupperman, Robert H.
Kurth, James R
Kurtzer, Daniel C.
Kwoh, Stewart*
Kyle, Robert D.
Laber, Jeri
Labrecque, Thomas G.
Ladner, Joyce A.
Lagon, Mark P.
Laipson, Ellen
Laird, Vanessa*

Lake, W. Anthony
Lake, William T.
Lall, Betty Goetz
Lamb, Denis
Lambeth, Benjamin S.
Lamm, Donald S.
Lamont, Lansing
Lampley, Virginia A.
Lampton, David M.
Lancaster, Carol J.
Landau, Christopher
Landau, George W.
Landers, James M.
Landy, Joanne
Lane, Charles M.
Laney, James T.
Langdon, George D., Jr.
Lansner, Kermit I.
LaPalombara, Joseph
Lapham, Lewis H.
Lapidus, Gail W.
Larrabee, F. Stephen
Larson, Charles R.
Lash, Jonathan
Lateef, Noel V.
Lauder, Leonard A.
Laudicina, Paul A.
Lauinger, Philip C., Jr.
Lautenbach, Ned C.
Laventhol, David A.
Lawrence, Richard D.
Lawrence, Robert Z.
Lawson, Eugene K.
Layne Christopher
Lazarus, Steven
Leach, James
Lederberg, Joshua
Lederer, Ivo John
Lee, Ernest S.
Lee, Janet
Lee, William L.
Lee-Kung, Dinah*
Leeds, Roger S.*
Lefever, Ernest W.
Leghorn, Richard S.
Legvold, Robert H.
Lehman, John F.
Lehman, Orin
Lehman, Ronald F., II
Lehrer, Jim
Leich, John Foster
Leigh, Monroe
Leland, Marc E.
Lelyveld, Joseph
LeMelle, Tilden J.
LeMelle, Wilbert J.
Lempert, Robert I.
Lenzen, Louis C.
LeoGrande, William M.
Leonard, James F.
Leonard, James G.
Leone, Richard C.
Lescaze, Lee
Lesch, Ann Mosely
Lesser, Ian O.
Levin, John A.*
Levin, Michael S.
Levine, Irving R.
Levine, Mel
Levine, Susan B.
Levinson, Marc*
Levitas, Mitchel
Levy, Marion J., Jr.
Levy, Reynold
Levy, Walter J.
Lewis, Anthony
Lewis, Bernard
Lewis, David A.**
Lewis, Edward T.
Lewis, Flora

Lewis, John P.
Lewis, John Wilson
Lewis, Loida Nicholas*
Lewis, Samuel W.
Lewis, Stephen R.
Lewis, W. Walker
Lewy, Glen S.
Li, Lehmann
Li, Victor H.
Libby, I. Lewis
Lichtblau, John H.
Lichtenstein, Cynthia C.
Lieber, James Edmund**
Lieber, Robert J.
Lieberman, Jodi B.**
Lieberman, Joseph I.
Lieberman, Nancy A
Lieberthal, Kenneth
Lief, Louis
Lifton, Robert K.
Light, Timothy
Lilienthal, Sally
Lincoln, Edward J.
Lind, Michael E.
Lindquist, Warren T.
Lindsay, Franklin A.
Lindsay, George N.
Lindsay, John V.
Lindsay, Robert V.
Linen, Jonathan S.*
Link, Troland S.
Linowes, David F.
Linowitz, Sol M.
Lipper, Kenneth
Lippman, Thomas W.
Lipscomb, Thomas H.
Lipset, Seymour Martin
Lipsky, John P.*
Lipsky, Seth
Lipson, Eon
Lissakers, Karin M.
Litt, David G.**
Little, David
Litwak, Robert S.
Liu, Eric**
Livingston, Robert Gerald
Llewellyn, J. Bruce
Lodal, Jan M.
Lodge, George C.
Loeb, Frances Lehman
Loeb, John L.
Loeb, Marshall
Logan, Francis D.
Long, Susan M.**
Longstreth, Bevis
Loomis, Henry
Loranger, Dornld E., Jr.
Lord, Bette Bao
Lord, Winston
Louis, William Roger
Lovejoy, Thomas E.
Lovelace, Jon B.
Low, Stephen
Lowenfeld, Andreas F.
Lowenstein, James G.
Lowenthal, Abraham F.
Loy, Frank F.
Lozano, Ignacio E., Jr.
Lubin, Nancy
Lubman, Stanley B.
Lucas, C. Payne
Luce, Charles F.
Luck, Edward C.
Lucy, William
Luers, Wendy W.
Luers, William H.
Luke, John A., Jr.
Lumpe, Lora
Lustick, Ian S.
Luttwak, Edward N.

Lyall, Katharine C.
Lyman, Princeton Nathan
Lyman, Richard W.
Lynch, Edward S.
Lynch, William, Jr.*
Lynk, Myles V.
Lynn, James T.
Lynn, Laurence E., Jr.
Lyon, David W.
Lyons, Gene M.
Lyons, James E.
Lyons, Richard K.
Ma, Christopher Yi-Wen
MacCorrnack, Charles F.
MacDonald, Gordon J.
MacDonald, Shawn A.**
MacDougal, Gary E.*
MacFarquhar, Emily
Mack, Kathryn S.
Mackay, Leo S., Jr.
MacLaury, Bruce K.
Macomber, John D.
Macomber, William B.
Macy, Robert M., Jr.
Madrid, Arturo
Maguire, John D.
Mahaney, Mark S.
Mahnken, Thomas G.
Mahoney, Catherine F.
Mahoney, Margaret E.
Mahoney, Thomas H., IV
Mai, Vincent A.
Maier, Charles S.
Makins, Christopher J.
Mako, William P.
Malek, Frederic V.
Malin, Clement B.
Mallery, Richard
Malmgren, Philippa
Malmgren, Harald B.
Manca, Marie Antoinette
Mandelbaum, Michael E.
Manilow, Lewis
Mann, Michael D.
Mann, Thomas E.
Manning, Bayless
Mansfield, Edward D.**
Marans, J. Eugene
Marcum, John Arthur
Marder, Murrey
Margolis, David I.
Mark, Davis E.
Mark, Gregory A.
Marh, Hans M.
Marks, Leonard H.
Marks, Paul A.
Marks, Russell E., Jr.
Marlin, Alice Tepper
Marmor, Theodore R.
Marr, Phebe A.
Marron, Donald B.
Marshall, Andrew W.
Marshall, Anthony D.
Marshall, C. Burton
Marshall, Dale Rogers
Marshall, Katherine
Marshall, Ray
Martin, Daniel R
Martin, Edwin M.
Martin, Lisa L.**
Martin, Lynn
Martin, Malcolm W.
Martin, Susan Forbes
Martin, William F.
Martin, William McC., Jr.
Martin-Brown, Joan
Martinez, Annando Bravo**
Martinuzzi, Leo S., Jr.
Marton, Kati
Marx, Anthony

Masin, Michael T.
Mason, Elvis L.
Massie, Suzanne
Mathews, Jessica T.
Mathews, Michael S.
Mathews, Charles McC., Jr
Mathis, Brian Pierre
Matlock, Jack F.
Matsui, Robert T.
Matteson, William B.
Mattox, Gale A.
Matuszewski, Daniel C.*
Maxwell, Kenneth
May, Ernest R.
Mayer, Claudette
Mayer, Gerald M., Jr.
Mayer, Lawrence A.
Mayhew, Alice E.
Maynes, Charles William
Mazarr, Michael J.
Mazur, Jay
McAfee, W. Gage
McAllister, Jer Olivarius
McCaffrey, Barry R.
McCall, H. Carl
McCann, Edward
McCartan, Patrick F.*
McCarthy, James P.
McCarthy, John G.
McCauley, John F.
McCloy, John J., II
McCormack, Elizabeth J.
McCouch, Donald G.
McCracken, Paul W.
McCurdy, Dave K
McDermott, James A.*
McDonald, Alonzo L.
McDonough, William J.
McDougal, Myres S.
McDougall, Gay J.
McEntee, Joan M.*
McFarlane, Robert C.
McFate, Patricia Ann
McGhee, George C.
McGiffert, David E.
McGillicuddy, John F.
McGovern, George S.
McGowan, Alan
McGrath, Eugene R.
McGuire, Raymond J.
McHale, Thomas R
McHenry, Donald F.
McKinney, Robert
McLaughlin, David T.
McLean, Shelia Avrin
McLin, Jon B.
McManus, Jason D.
McNamara, Robert S.
McNeill, John H.
McNeill, Robert L.
McPeak, Merrill A.
McPherson, M. Peter
McQuade, Lawrence C.
McWade, Robert S.
Mead, Dana G.
Meagher, Robert F.
Mearsheimer, John J.
Medish, Mark C.
Meers, Sharon I.
Mehta, Ved
Meissner, Charles F.
Meissner, Doris M.
Meister, Irene W.
Melby, Eric D.K.*
Mello, Judy Hendren
Melloan, George R.
Melville, Richard A.
Mendlovitz, Saul H.
Menke, John R
Merkling, Christian

Meron, Theodor
Merow, John E.
Merill, Philip
Merritt, Jack N.
Merszei, Zoltan
Mesa-Lago, Carmelo
Meselson, Matthew
Messner, William Curtis, Jr.
Metcalf, George R.
Mettler, Ruben F.
Meyer, Cord
Meyer, Edward C.
Meyer, John R.
Meyer, Karl E.
Meyerman, Harold J.
Meyerson, Martin
Michaels, Marguerite
Mickelson, Sig
Miekiewiez, Ellen P.
Midgley, Elizabeth
Mihaly, Eugene B.
Mikell, Gwendolyn
Miles, Edward L.
Miller, Charles D.
Miller, Christopher D.
Miller, David Charles, Jr.
Miller, Debra L.*
Miller, Franklin C.*
Miller, J. Irwin
Miller, Judith
Miller, Linda B.
Miller, Marcia E.
Miller, Matthew L.
Miller, Paul David
Miller, Roberta Balstad
Miller, William Green
Miller-Adams, Michelle Beth
Millett, Allan R.
Millington, John A.
Mills, Bradford
Mills, Karen Gordon*
Mills, Susan
Min, Nancy-Ann
Minow, Newton N.
Miranda, Lourdes R.
Mirsky, Yehudah**
Mitchell, George H., Jr.
Mitchell, George J.
Mitchell, Wandra
Mize, David M.*
Mochizuki, Kichi
Mochizuki, Mike Masato
Moe, Sherwood G.
Molano, Walter Thomas**
Mondale, Walter F.
Monroe, Hunter
Montgomery, George Cranwell
Montgomery, Parker G.
Montgomery, Philip O'Bryan, III
Moock, Joyce Lewinger
Moody, Jim
Moody, William S.
Moore, John M.
Moore, John Norton
Moore, Johnathan
Moore, Julia A.
Moore, Paul, Jr.
Moorman, Thomas S., Jr.
Moose, George E.
Moose, Richard M.
Mora, Alberto J.*
Maragoda, Milinda**
Moran, Theodore H.
Morley, James William
Morrell, Gene P.
Morris, Bailey
Morris, Max K.
Morris, Milton D.
Morrisett, Lloyd N.
Morse, Edward L.

Morse, Kenneth P.
Mortimer, David
Mosbacher, Robert A.*
Moses, Alfred H.
Mosettig, Michel
Moskow, Kenneth A.
Moss, Ambler H., Jr.
Motley, Joel W.
Mottahedeh, Roy
Motulsky, Dan T.
Moynihan, Daniel P.
Mroz, John Edwin
Mudd, Margaret F.
Mujal-Leon, Eusebio
Mulford, David C.
Mulholland, William D.
Muller, Henry
Muller, Steven
Mundy, Carl E., Jr.
Munger, Edwin S.
Munroe, George B.
Munyan, Winthrop R.
Murase, Emily Moto**
Muravchik, Joshua*
Murdoch, Rupert
Murphy, Caryle Marie
Murphy, Joseph S.
Murphy, Richard W.
Murphy, Sean Davis
Murphy, Thomas S.
Murray, Allen E.
Murray, Douglas P
Murray, Ian P.**
Murray, Lori Esposito
Muse, Martha T.
Muskie, Edmund S.
Myerson, Toby S.
Nachmanoff, Arnold
Nacht, Michael
Nadiri, M. Ishaq
Nagorski, Andrew
Nagorski, Zygmunt
Namkung, K. A.
Nasher, Raymond D.
Nathan, James A.
Nathoo, Raffiq A.**
Natt, Ted M.
Nau, Henry R.
Navab, Alexander
Naylor, Rosamond Lee
Neal, Stephen J.*
Negroponte, John D.
Neier, Aryeh
Nelson, Anne
Nelson, Daniel N.
Nelson, Jack
Nelson, Merlin E.
Nenneman, Richard A.
Neuman, Stephanie G*
Neustadt, Richard E.
Newburg, Andre W.G.
Newell, Barbara W.
Newhouse, John
Newman, Constance B.*
Newman, Prisciila A.
Newman, Richard T.
Newson, David D.
Newton, Ouigg
Ney, Edward N.
Nicholas, N. J., Jr..
Nichols, Nancy Stephenson*
Nichols, Rodney W.
Niehuss, John M.
Niehuss, Rosemary Neaher
Nielsen, Waldema A.
Nierenberg, Claudia
Nilsson, A. Kenneth
Nimetz, Matthew
Nitze, Paul H.
Nitze, William A.

Nix, Crystal
Nolan, Janne E.
Noland, Marcus
Nolte, Richard H.
Nooter, Robert H.
Norman, William S.
Norton, Augustus Richard
Norton, Eleanor Holmes
Noto, Lucio A.
Novak, Michael
Novicki, Margaret A.
Nuechterlein, Jeffrey D.
Nugent, Walter
Nussbaum, Bruce
Nye, Joseph S., Jr.
Oakes, John B.
Oakes, John G.H.
Oakley, Phyllis E.
Oakley, Robert B.
Oberdorfer, Don
O'Brien, Dennis J.
O'Cleireacain, Carol
O'Connel, Mary Ellen
O'Connor, Sandra Day
O'Connor, Walter F.
Odeen, Philip A.
Odell, John S.
Odom, William E.
Oettinger, Anthony G.
Offit, Morris W.
O'Flaherty, J. Daniel
Ogden, Alfred
Ogden, William S.
Oh, Kongdan*
O'Hare, Joseph A.
Okawara, Merle Aiko
Oksenberg, Michel
Okun, Herbert S.
Oliva, L. Jay
Oliver, April
Oliver, Covey T.
Olmstead, Cecil J.
Olson, William C.
Olvey, Lee D.
O'Malley, Cormacc K.H.
Omestad, Thomas E.
O'Neill, Michael J.
Opel, John R.
Oppenheimer, Franz M.
Oppenheimer, Michael F.
Orlins, Stephen A.
Ornstein, Norman J.
Osborne, Richard de J.
O'Shaughnessy, Elise
Osmer-McQuade, Margaret
Osnos, Peter
Osnos, Susan Sherer
Ostrander, F. Taylor
Ovitz, Michael S.*
Owen, Henry
Owen, Roberts B.
Owens, James W.
Owens, William A.
Oxman, Stephan A.
Oxnam, Robert B.
Paal, Douglas H.
Pachon, Harry P.
Packard, George R.
Paine, George C., II
Pais, Abraham
Pakula, Hannah C.
Palmer, Norman D.
Palmer, Robbie Mark
Palmer, Ronald D.
Palmieri, Victor H.
Panofsky, Wolfgang K.H.
Pardee, Scott F.*
Parker, Barrington D., Jr.
Parker, Jason H.
Parker, Maynard

Parker, Richard B.
Parkinson, Roger
Parsky, Gerald L.
Parsons, Richard D.
Passer-Muslin, Juliette M.
Passin, Herbert
Patrick, Hugh T.
Patrikis, Ernest T.
Patterson, Gardner
Patterson, Hugh B., Jr.
Paul, Michael G.**
Paul, Roland A.
Payne, Donald M.
Pearce, William R
Pearlstein, Norman
Pearson, John E.
Pearson, Scott D.
Pedersen, Richard F.
Pederson, Rena
Pell, Claiborne
Pelletreau, Robert H., Jr.
Pelson, Victor A.
Penfield, James K.
Percy, Charles H.
Perella, Joseph Robert
Peretz, Don
Peretz, Antonio F.
Perkin, Linda J.
Perkins, Edward J.
Perkins, James A.
Perkins, Roswell B.
Perkovich, George
Perle, Richard N.
Perlman, Janice E.
Perlmutter, Arnos
Perlmutter, Louis*
Perry, Robert C.
Peters, Arthur King
Peters, Aulana L.
Petersen, Howard C.
Petersen, Erik R
Peterson, Holly
Peterson, Peter G.
Peterson, Rudolph A.
Petree, Richard W.
Petree, Richard W., Jr.
Petri, Thomas E.
Petschek, Stephen R.
Pettibone, Peter J.
Petty, John R
Peyronnin, Joseph
Pezzullo, Lawrence A.
Pfaltzgraff, Robert L., Jr.
Pfeiffer, Jane Cahill
Pfeiffer, Steven B.
Pham, Kien D.
Pharr, Susan J.
Phelan, John J., Jr.
Phillips, Christopher H.
Phillips, Russell A., Jr.
Picker, Harvey
Pickering, Thomas R.
Pieczenik, Steve R.
Piel, Gerald
Pierce, Lawrence W.*
Pierce, Ponchitta
Pierre, Andrew J.
Pifer, Alan
Pigott, Charles M.
Pike, John E.
Pilling, Donald L.
Pilliod, Charles J., Jr.
Pincus, Lionel I.
Pincus, Walter H.
Pinkerton, W. Stewart
Pino, John A.
Pipes, Daniel
Pipes, Richard E.
Pisano, Jane G.
Platt, Alan A.

Platt, Alexander Hartley
Platt, Nicholas
Plepler, Richard*
Plimpton, Calvin H.
Ploumpis, Valerie
Poats, Rutherford M.
Pocalyko, Michael N.
Podhoretz, Norman
Pogue, Richard W.
Polk, William R.
Pollack, Gerald A.
Pollack, Lester
Polsby, Nelson W.
Pond, Elizabeth
Poneman, Daniel B.
Pool, Marquita I.
Pope, Clara A.
Popkin, Anne Brandeis**
Popoff, Frank P.
Porter, John Edward*
Portes, Richard D.
Porzecanski, Arturo C.
Posen, Barry R.
Posner, Michael H.
Posvar, Wesley W.
Potter, William C.
Powell, Colin L.
Powell, Jerome H.*
Powell, Michael K.**
Power, Hilip H.
Powers, Averill L.
Powers, Thomas Moore
Pranger, Robert J.
Precht, Henry
Press, Frank
Pressler, Larry
Preston, Lewis T.
Prewitt, Kenneth
Price, Daniel M.
Price, Hugh
Price, John R., Jr.
Price, Robert
Pritzker, Penny
Pryce, Jeffrey F.
Puchala, Donald J.
Puckett, Allen E.
Puckett, Robert H.
Purcell, Susan Kaufman
Pursley, Robert E.
Pusey, Nathan M.
Pustay, John S.
Putnam, Robert D.
Pye, Lucian W.
Pyle, Cassandra A.
Pyle, Kenneth B.
Quandt, William B.
Quester, George H.
Quigley, Kevin F. F.
Quigley, Leonard V.
Quinn, Jane Bryant
Rabb, Maxwell M.
Rabinowitch, Alexander
Rabinowitch, Victor
Rademaker, Stephen G.
Radway, Laurence I.
Ragone, David V.
Raines, Franklin D.
Raisian, John
Ralph, Regan Elisabeth
Ralston, Joseph W.*
Ramierz, Lilia L.
Ramo, Simon
Rangel, Charles B.*
Ranis, Gustav
Raphael, Robin L.*
Rasmussen, Nicholas J.**
Ratchford, J. Thomas
Rather, Dan
Rathjen, George W.
Ratner, Steven R.

Rattner, Steven L.
Rattray, Gregory J.**
Rauch, Rudolph S.
Raul, alan Charles*
Ravenal, Earl C.
Ravenholt, Albert
Ravitch, Richard
Faymond, David a.
Raymond, Jack
Raymond, Lee R.
Reback, Sanford C.
Reed, Charles B.
Reed, John S.
Reed, Joseph Verner
Reese, William S.*
Regan, Edward V.*
Riechert, Douglas D.
Reichert, William M.*
Reid, Ogden
Reinhardt, John E.
Reinke, Fred W.
Reisman, W. M.
Reiss, Mitchell B.
Renfrew, Charles B.
Rennie, Milbrey
Rennie, Renate
Reppy, Juidth V.
Resor, Stanley R.
Rey, Nicholas a.
Rhinelander, John B.
Rhodes, Edward
Rhodes, Frank H. T.
Rhodes, John B., Sr.
Rhodes, Thomas L.
Rhodes, William R.
Ribicoff, Abraham A.
Rice, Condeleezza
Rice, Donald B.
Rice, Donald S.
Rice, Joseph A.
Rice, Susan E.
Rich, John H., Jr.
Rich, Michael D.
Richard, Anne C.**
Richards, Paul G.
Richards, Stephen H.
Richardson, David B.
Richardson, Eliot L.
Richardson, Henry J., III
Richardson, John
Richardson, Richard W.
Richardson, William B.
Richardson, William R.
Richardson, Yolonda
Richman, Joan F.
Richter, Anthony H.
Ridgway, Rozanne L.
Rieff, David*
Rielly, John E.
Ries, Hans A.
Riley, Jack
Rindskopf, Elizabeth R.
Riordan, Michael L.
Ritch, John B., III
Rivers, Richard R.
Rivkin, Donald H.
Rivlin, Alice M.
Rizopoulos, Nicholas X.
Robb, Charles S.
Robbins, Carla Anne
Robert, Stephen
Roberts, Chalmers M.
Roberts, John J.
Roberts, Walter R.
Robinson, Barbara Paul*
Robinson, David Z.
Robinson, Davis R.
Robinson, Elizbeth L.
Robinson, Eugene Harold*
Robinson, James D., III

Robinson, Leonard H., Jr.
Robinson, Linda S.
Robinson, Marshall A.
Robinson, Pearl T.
Robinson, Randall
Robinson, Olin C.
Roche, James G.
Rocke, Mark D.
Rockefeller, David
Rockefellr, David, Jr.
Rockefeller, John D., IV
Rockefeller, Nicholas
Rockefeller, Rodman C.
Rockwell, Hays H.
Rodman, Peter W.
Rodriguez, Rita M.
Rodriguez, Vincent A.
Roett, Riordan
Roff, J. Hugh, Jr.
Rogers, William D.
Rogers, William P.
Rogoff, Natasha Lance
Rogovin, Mitchell
Rohatyn, Felix G.
Rohlen, Thomas P.
Rokke, Ervin J.
Romberg, Alan D.*
Romero, Philip J.
Romero-Barcelo, Carlos
Roney, John H.
Roosevelt, Theodore, IV
Rosberg, Carl G.
Rose, Daniel
Rose, Elihu
Rose, Frederick P.
Rosecrance, Richard
Rosen, Arthur H.
Rosen, Jane K.
Rosen, Robert L.*
Rosenberg, Tina
Rosenblatt, Lionel
Rosenblatt, Peter R.
Rosenblum, Mort
Rosenfeld, Stephen S.
Rosenfield, Patricia L.
Rosenstock, Robert
Rosenthal, A. M.
Rosenthal, Douglas E.
Rosenthal, Jack
Rosenthal, Joel H.
Rosenzweig, Robert M.
Rosin, Axel G.
Roskens, Ronald W.
Rosovsky, Henry
Ross, Alison K.
Ross, Arthur
Ross, Christopher W.S.*
Ross, Dennis B.
Ross, James D.
Ross, Roger
Ross, Thomas B.
Rosso, David J.
Rossotti, Charles O.
Rostow, Elspeth Davies
Rostow, Eugene V.
Rostow, Nicholas
Rostow, Walt W.
Rotberg, Robert I.
Roth, Kenneth
Roth, Stanley Owen*
Roth, William M.
Roth, William V., Jr.
Rothkopf, David J.
Rovine, Arthur W.
Rowen, Henry S.
Rowny, Edward L.
Rubin, Barnett R.
Rubin, James P.
Rubin, Nancy H.
Rubin, Robert E.

Rubin, Seymour J.
Rubin, Trudy
Ruckelshaus, William D.
Rudenstine, Neil L.
Rudman, Warren B.
Rudolph, Barbara
Rudolph, Lloyd L.
Rudolph, Susanne Hoeber
Ruebhausen, Oscar M.
Ruenitz, Robert M.
Ruggie, John G.
Runge, Carlisle Ford
Runstow, Dankwart A.
Ruttan, Vernon W.
Rutzen, Douglas**
Ryan, Arthur F.
Ryan, John T., Jr.
Ryan John T., III
Sachs, Jeffrey D.
Sacks, Paul M.
Safran, Nadav
Sagan, Carl E.
Sagan, Scott D.
Said, Edward
Sakoian, Carol Knuth
Salacuse, Jeswald W.
Salerno, Frederic V.
Salomon, Richard E.
Salomon, William R.
Sample, Steven B.
Samuels, Barbara C., II
Samuels, Michael A.
Samuels, Nathaniel
Samuels, Richard J.
Sanchez, Miguel A.
Sanchez, Nestor D.
Sandel, Michael J.*
Sander, Alison
Sanders, Edward G.
Sanders, J. Stanley
Sanford, Charles S., Jr.
Sanford, Terry
Santos, Charles E.
Sapiro, Miriam
Sapolsky, Harvey M.
Satloff, Robert Barry**
Sato, Kumi
Saul, Ralph S.
Saunders, Harold H.
Savage, Frank
Sawhill, John C.
Sawoski, Mark*
Sawyer, David H.
Sawyer, Diane
Scalapino, Robert A.
Schacht, Henry B.
Schachter, Oscar
Schaetzel, J. Robert
Schaffer, Howard B.
Schake, Kori
Schaufele, William E., Jr.
Schecter, Jerrold
Scheffer, David J.
Scheinman, Lawrence
Schell, Orville H.
Schick, Thomas
Schiff, Frank W.
Schifter, Richard
Schilling, Warner R.
Schlesinger, Arthur, Jr.
Schlesinger, James R
Schlesinger, Stephen
Schlosser, Herbert S.
Schmertz, Herbert
Schmidt, Benno Jr.
Schmoke, Kurt L.
Schneider, Jan
Schneider, William
Schneier, Arthur
Schoettle, Enid C.B.

Schorr, Daniel L.
Schrage, Elliot J.
Schroeder, Christopher M.*
Schubert, Richard F.
Schuh, G. Edward
Schuker, Jill*
Schulhof, Michael P.
Schumer, Charles E.*
Schwab, Susan C.
Schwartz, Eric Paul
Schwarz, Frederick A. O., Jr.
Schwarzer, William W.
Schwarzman, Stephen A.
Schwebel, Stephen M.
Sciolino, Elaine F.
Scowcroft, Brent
Scranton, William W.
Seaborg, Glenn T.
Seagrave, Norman P.
Seamans, Robert C., Jr.
Segal, Sheldon J.
Segal, Susan L.
Seib, Gerald
Seibold, Frederick C., Jr.
Seidman, Herta Lande
Seigenthaler, John L.
Seitz, Frederick
Sekulow, Eugene A.
Selin. Ivan
Semple, Robert B., Jr.
Serfaty, Simon*
Sesno, Frank*
Sestanovich, Stephen R
Sewall, John O.B.
Sewall, Sarah Bulkeley
Sewell, John W.
Seymour, Frances J.
Shafer, D. Michael
Shaffer, Gail S.
Shalala, Donna E.
Shalikashvili, John M.*
Shapiro, Eli
Shapiro, Harold T.
Shapiro, Isaac
Sharp, Daniel A.
Shattuck, John*
Shayne, Herbert M.
Sheffield, James R.
Sheffield, Jill W.
Sheinbaum, Stanley K.
Sheinkman, Jack
Sheldon, Eleanor Bernert
Shelley, Sally Swing
Shelp, Ronald K.
Shelton, Joanna Reed
Shelton, Sally A.
Shenk, George H.
Shepard, Stephen B.*
Sherman, Michael*
Sherry, George L.
Sherwood, Ben
Sherwood, Elizabeth D.
Shestack, Jerome J.
Shiner, Josette
Shinn, James I.*
Shipley, Walter V.
Shirk, Susan L.
Shlaes, Amity
Shoemaker, Alvin V.
Shoemaker, Christopher Cole
Shoemaker, Don
Shriver, Donald W., Jr.
Shubert, Gustave H.
Shultman, Colette
Shulman, Marshall D.
Shultz, George P.
Shuman, Stanley S.*
Sick, Gary G.
Siegman, Henry
Sifton, Elisabeth

Sigal, Leon V.
Sigmund, Paul E.
Silas, C. J.
Silberman, Laurence H.
Silkenat, James R.
Silver, Daniel B.
Silver, Ron
Silvers, Robert B.
Simes, Dimitri K.
Simmons, Adele Smith
Simon, Francoise L.*
Simon, William E.
Sims, Albert G.
Sims, Robert B.*
Sinclair, Paula
Sinding, Steven W.
Sinkin, Richard N.
Sisco, Joseph J.
Sisk, Timothy D.**
Sitrick, James B.
Skidmore, Thomas E.
Skinner, Elliott P.
Skolnikoff, Eugene B.
Slade, David R.*
Slater, Joseph E.
Slaughter, Anne-Marie
Slawson, Paul S.
Sloane, Ann Brownell
Slocombe, Walter B.
Sloss, Leon
Small, Lawrence M.
Smalley, Patricia T.
Smart, S. Bruce., Jr.
Smith, Andrew F.
Smith, Clint E.
Smith, David S.
Smith, DeWitt C., Jr.
Smith, Edwin M.
Smith, Gaddis
Smith, Gare A.
Smith, Hedrick L.
Smith, Jeffrey H.
Smith, John T., II
Smith, Larry
Smith, Leighton W., Jr.
Smith, Malcolm B.
Smith, Michael B.
Smith, Perry M.
Smith, Peter B.
Smith, Peter Hopkinson
Smith, R. Jeffrey
Smith, Raymond W.
Smith, Richard M.
Smith, Stephen G.
Smith, Theodore M.
Smith, Tory
Smith, W. Y.
Smith, Wayne S.
Smith, Winthrop H., Jr.
Smythe, Mabel M.
Snow, Robert Anthony
Snowe, Olympia J.
Snyder, David M.
Snyder, Jack L.
Snyder, Jed C.
Snyder, Richard E.
Sobol, Dorothy Meadow
Soderberg, Nancy E.
Sofaer, Abraham Davi
Sohn, Louis B.
Solarz, Stephen J.
Solbert, Peter O.A.
Solnick, Steven I.
Solomon, Anne G.K.
Solomon, Anthony M.
Solomon, Peter J.
Solomon, Richard H.
Solomon, Robert
Sonenshine, H. Marshall
Sonenshine, Tara

Sonne, Christian R.
Sonnenberg, Maurice
Sonnenfeldt, Helmut
Sonnenfeldt, Richard W.
Sorensen, Gillian Martin
Sorensen, Theodore C.
Soros, George
Soros, Paul
Sovern, Michael I.
Spain, James W.
Spalter, Jonathan
Spangler, Scott M.*
Spar, Debora L.
Spector, Leonard S.
Speidel, Kirsten Elizabeth
Spencer, Edson W.
Spencer, John H.
Spencer, William C.
Spero, Joan E.
Speth, James Gustave
Speyer, Jerry I.
Spielvogel, Carl
Spiers, Ronald I.
Spiro, Herbert J.
Spiro, Peter J.
Spratt, John M., Jr.
Squadron, Howard M.
Stacks, John
Staheli, Donald L.
Stalson, Helena
Stamas, Stephen
Stankard, Francis X.
Stanley, Peter W.
Stanley, Timothy W.
Stanton, Frank
Staples, Eugene S.
Starobin, Herman
Starr, John Bryan
Starr, S. Frederick
Stassen, Harold E.
Steadman, Richard C.
Stedman, Louellen**
Steel, Ronald
Steiger, Paul E.
Stein, David Fred
Stein, Eliot, Jr.
Stein, Eric
Stein, Mark B.**
Stein, Paul E.*
Steinberg, David J.
Steinberg, James B.
Steinberg, Richard H.**
Steinbruner, John D.
Steiner, Daniel
Steiner, Joshua L.
Stempel, John D.*
Stent, Angela E.
Stepan, Alfred C.
Stephanopoulos, George R.
Stern, Ernest
Stern, Fritz
Stern, H. Peter
Stern, Paula
Stern, Walter P.
Sterner, Michael E.
Sternlight, David
Stevens, Charles R
Stevens, James W.
Stevens, Norton
Stevens, Paul Schott
Stevenson, Adlai E., III
Stevenson, Charles A.
Stevenson, Jonn R.
Stewart, Donald M.
Stewart, Gordon C.
Stewart, Patricia Carry
Stewart, Ruth Ann
Stiehm, Judith Hicks
Stith, Kate
Stobaugh, Robert B.

Stockman, David A.
Stoessinger, John G.
Stofft, William A.
Stoga, Alan
Stokes, Bruce
Stokes, Donald E.
Stokes, Louis
Stone, Jeremy J.
Stone, Roger D.
Straus, Donald B.
Straus, Oscar S., II
Straus, R. Peter
Straus, Robert S.
Strauss, Simon D.
Strausz-Hupe, Robert
Stremlau, John J.
Strock, James M.
Stromseth, Jane E.
Stroock, Thomas F.
Strossen, Nadine
Stroud, Joe H.
Studeman, William O.
Styron, Rose
Sudarkasa, Michael E.M.
Sudarkasa, Niara
Sughrue, Karen M.
Suleiman, Ezra N.
Sullivan, Gordon Russell
Sullivan, Leon H.
Sullivan, Margaret C.
Sullivan, William H.
Summers, Harry G., Jr.
Summers, Lawrence H.
Sunderland, Jack B.
Suslow, Leo A.
Sutterlin, James S.
Sutton, Francis X.
Swank, Emory C.
Swanson, David H.
Sweitzer, Brandon W.
Swenson, Eric P.
Swid, Stephen C.
Swiers, Peter Bird
Swing, John Temple
Szanton, Peter L.
Szporluk, Roman
Taft, Julia V.
Taft, William H., IV
Tagliabue, Paul
Tahir-Kheli, Shirin R.
Talbot, Phillips
Talbott, Strobe
Tang, David K.Y.
Tanham, George K.
Tannenwald, Theodore, Jr.
Tanner, Harold
Tanter, Raymond
Tapia, Raul R.
Tarnoff, Peter
Tasco, Frank J.
Taubman, William
Taylor, Arthur R.
Taylor, Kathryn Pelgrift
Taylor, William J., Jr.
Tedstrom, John E.
Teece, David J.
Teeley, Peter B.
Teeters, Nancy H.
Teitelbaum, Michael S.
Telhami, Shilbey
Tempelsman, Maurice
Tennyson, Leonard B.
Terraccino, Anthony P.
Terry, Sarah M.
Thayer, A. Bronson
Theobald, Thomas C.
Thoman, G. Richard
Thomas, Barbara S.
Thomas, Brooks
Thomas, Evan W., III

Thomas, Franklin A.
Thomas, Lee B., Jr.
Thompson, Robert L.*
Thompson, W. Scott
Thomson, James A.
Thomson, James C., Jr.
Thornburgh, Dick
Thornell, Richard P.
Thornton, Thomas P.
Thoron, Louisa
Thurman, M. R.
Tierney, Paul E., Jr.
Tillinghast, David R.
Tillman, Seth P.
Timothy, Kristen
Timpson, Sarah L.
Tipson, Frederick S.
Tisch, Laurence A.
Tobias, Randall L.
Todaro, Michael P.
Todd, Maurice Linwood
Todman, Terence A.
Toll, Maynard J., Jr.
Tomlinson, Alexanda C.
Topping, Seymour
Torano, Maria Elena*
Torres, Art
Torres, Raidza M.
Torricelli, Robert G.
Toth, Robert C.
Trachtenberg, Stephen Joel
Train, Harry D., II
Train, John
Train, Russell E.
Trainor, Bernard E.
Trani, Eugene P.
Travis, Martin B., Jr.
Treat, John Elting
Trebat, Thomas J.
Treverton, Gregory F.
Trezise, Philip H.
Trooboff, Peter D.
Trowbridge, Alexanda B.
Truitt, Nancy Sherwood*
Truman, Edwin M.
Tsipis, Kosta
Tucher, H. Anton
Tuck, Edward Hallam
Tucker, Nancy Bankopf
Tucker, Richard F.
Tucker, Robert W.
Tung, Ko-Yung
Turck, Nancy B.
Turkevich, John
Turner, J. Michael
Turner, Robert F.
Turner, Stansfield
Turner, William C.
Tuthill, John Wills
Tyrrell, R. Emmett, Jr.
Tyson, Laura D'Andrea
Udovitch, A. L.
Uhlig, Mark
Ullman, Richard H.
Ulman, Cornelius M.
Ulrich, Marybeth Peterson
Ungar, Sanford J.
Unger, David
Unger, Leonard
Upton, Maureen
Urban, Thomas N.*
Uriu, Robert M.
Usher, William R.
Utgoff, Victor A.
Utley, Garrick
Utton, Albert E.
Vagliano, Alexander M.
Vagliano, Sara
Vagts, Detlev F.*
Vaky, Viron P.

Valdez, Abelardo Lopez
Valenta, Jiri
Valentine, Debra A.
Valenzuela, Arturo
Vance, Cyrus R.
Van Cott, Donna Lee**
Vande Berg, Marsha
Van de Mark, Brian
vanden Heuvel, Katrina
vanden Heuvel, William J.
Van Dusen, Michael H.
Van Dyk, Ted
Van Evera, Stephan W.
Van Fleet, James A.
Van Vlierden, Constant M.
van Voorst, L. Bruce
Varela, Marta B.*
Veblen, Tom C.
Vecchio, Mark S.
Veit, Carol M.
Veit, Lawrence A.
Veliotes, Nicholas A.
Vermilye, Peter H.
Vernon, Raymond
Verstandig, Toni Grant*
Verville, Elizabeth G.
Vessey, John W.
Vest, George S.
Viccellio, Henry
Viederman, Stephen
Viets, Richard Noyes
Vila, Adis Maria
Villar, Arturo
Viorst, Milton
Viscusi, Enzo
Vitale, Alberto
Voell, Richard A.
Vogel, Ezra F.
Vogelgesang, Sandy
Vojta, George J.
Volcker, Paul A.
Volk, Stephen R
von Eckartsberg, K. Gayle**
von Hippel, Frank N.*
von Klemperer, Alfred H.
von Mehren, Robert B.
Votaw, Carmen Delgado
Vuono, Carl E.
Wachner, Linda Joy
Waddell, Rick
Wadsworth-Darby, Mary
Waggoner, Robert C.
Wahl, Nicholas
Wais, Marshall Ivan, Jr.
Wakeman, Frederic E., Jr.
Wales, Jane
Walker, Charles E.
Walker, G. R
Walker, Jenonne
Walker, John L.
Walker, Mary Lynn
Walker, Nancy J.
Walker, William N.
Wallander, Celeste A.
Wallerstein, Mitchel B.
Wallison, Peter J.
Walsh, Michaela
Walters, Barbara
Walton, Anthony J.
Waltz, Kenneth N.
Ward, Jennifer C.*
Ward, John W.
Ward, Katherine T.
Ward, Patrick Joseph
Ware, Carl
Warner, Edward L., III
Warner, Volney J.
Warnke, Paul C.
Warren, Gerald L.
Washburn, Abbott M.

Washburn, John L.
Wasserstein, Bruce
Waterbury, John
Waters, Cherri D.
Watson, Alexander F.
Wattenberg, Ben J.
Watts, Glenn E.
Watts, John H.
Watts, William
Way, Alva O.
Weatherstone, Dennis
Weaver, David R.
Weaver, George L-P
Weber, Vin*
Webster, William H.
Wedgwood, Ruth
Wehrle, Leroy S.
Weidenbaum, Murray L.
Weigel, George
Weiksner, George B., Jr.
Weil, Frank A.
Weinberg, John L.
Weinberg, Steven
Weinberger, Caspar W.
Weiner, Myron
Weinert, Richard S.
Weinrod, W. Bruce
Weinstein, Michael M.
Weintraub, Sidney
Weisman, Steven
Weiss, Charles, Jr.
Weiss, Cora
Weiss, Edith Brown
Weiss, Stanley A.*
Weiss, Thomas G.
Weitz, Peter R
Welch, C. David
Welch, Jasper A., Jr.
Welch, John F., Jr.
Welch, Larry D.
Wells, Damon, Jr.
Wells, Herman B.
Wells, Louis T., Jr.
Wells, Samuel F., Jr.
Wender, Ira T.
Wendt, E. Allan
Wertheim, Mitzi M.
Wesely, Edwin J.
Wessel, Michael R.
West, J. Robinson
West, Togo D., Jr.*
Weston, Burns H.
Wexler, Anne
Weymouth, Lally G.
Whalen, Charles W., Jr.
Whalen, Richard J.
Wharton, Clifon R., Jr.
Wheat, Francis M.
Wheeler, John K.
Whitaker, C. S.
Whitaker, Jennifer Seymour
Whitaker, Mark
White, John P.
White, Julia A.
White, Peter C.
White, Robert J.
White, Robert M.
White, Walter H., Jr.
Whitehead, John C.
Whitehouse, Charles S.
Whitman, Christine Todd*
Whitman, Marina V. N.
Whitney, Craig R.
Whittemore, Frederick B.
Whyman, William E.
Wiarda, Howard J.
Widner, Jennifer
Wiener, Carolyn Seely
Wiener, Jonathan Baert*
Wiener, Malcolm H.

Wiesel, Elie
Wiesel, Torsten
Wieseltier, Leon
Wildenthal, C. Kern
Wilds, Walter
Wiley, Maya
Wiley, Richard A.
Wilhelm, Harry E.
Wilhelm, Robert E.
Wilkerson, Thomas L.*
Wilkie, Edith B.
Wilkins, Roger W.
Wilkinson, Sharon
Williams, Aaron S.
Williams, Avon N., III
Williams, Christine*
Williams, Earle C.
Williams, Eddie Nathan
Williams, H. Roy
Williams, Harold M.
Williams, Haydn
Williams, Reba White
Williamson, Edwin A.*
Williamson, Irving A.
Williamson, Thomas S., Jr.
Willrich, Mason
Wilmers, Robert G.
Wilson, Donald M.
Wilson, Don M., III*
Wilson, Ernest James, III
Wilson, Gretchen**
Wilson, Serena Lynn**
Wimpfheimer, Jacques D.
Wing, Adrien Katherine
Winner, Andrew C.
Winokur, Herbert S., Jr.
Winship, Thomas
Winston, Michael R.
Winterer, Philip S.
Winters, Francis X.
Wirth, John D.
Wirth, Timothy E.
Wisner, Frank G.
Wisner, Graham G.
Witkowsky, Anne A.**
Witunski, Michael
Woerner, Fred F.
Wofford, Harris L.
Wohl, Richard H.
Wohlforth, William C.
Wohlstetter, Albert
Wohlstetter, Roberta
Wolf, Charles, Jr.
Wolf, Milton A.
Wolfensohn, James D.
Wolff, Alan W-m.
Wolfowitz, Paul D.
Wolin, Neal S.
Wolpe, Howard
Wood, Joseph R.
Woods, Ward W., Jr.*
Woodward, Susan L.
Woolf, Harry
Woolsey, R. James
Woon, Eden*
Wray, Cecil, Jr.
Wriggins, W. Howard
Wright, L. Patrick*
Wright, Robin
Wright-Carozza, Paolo G.
Wyatl-Walter, Holly**
Yacoubian, Mona
Yalman, Nur
Yang, James Ting-Yeh
Yankelovich, Daniel
Yanney, Michael B.*
Yarmolinsky, Adam
Yergin, Daniel H.
Yochelson, John N.
Yoffie, David B.

Yordan, Jaime E.*
Yoshihara, Nancy Akemi
Yost, Casimir A.
Young, Alice
Young, Andrew
Young, Edgar B.
Young, George H., III
Young, Joan P.
Young, M. Crawford
Young, Michael K.*
Young, Nancy
Young, Peter Joel C.
Youngblood, Kneeland C.*
Yu, Frederick T.C.
Yudkin, Richard A.
Yzaguirre, Raul H.*
Zagoria, Donald S.
Zakheim, Dov S.
Zarb, Frank G.
Zartman, I. William
Zeidenstein, George
Zelikow, Philip D.
Zelnick, C. Robert
Zemmol, Jonathan
Zikha, Ezra K.
Zimmerman, Edwin M.
Zimmerman, Peter D.
Zimmerman, William
Zimmermann, Warren
Zinberg, Dorothy S.
Zinder, Norton D.
Zoellick, Robert B.
Zogby, James J.
Zolberg, Aristide R.
Zonis, Marvin
Zorthian, Barry
Zraket, Charles A.
Zuckerman, Harriet
Zuckerman, Mortimer B.
Zumwalt, Elmo R., Jr.
Zwick, Charles J.
Zysman, John

APPENDIX F

THE TRILATERAL COMMISSION

(As of 15 February 1996)
**Executive Committee*
*** Life Member of Executive Committee*

Otto Graf Lambsdorff, *European Chairman*
Carlos Ferrer, *European Deputy Chairman*
Paul Révay, *European Director*
Paul A. Volcker, *North American Chairman*
Allan E. Gotlieb, *North American Deputy Chairman*
David Rockefeller, *Founder and Honorary Chairman*
Charles B. Heck, *North American Director*
Kiichi Miyazawa, *Japanese Chairman (Acting)*
Shijuro Ogata, *Japanese Deputy Chairman*
Yotaro Kobayashi, *Japanese Deputy Chairman*
Tadashi Yamamoto, *Japanese Director*

North American Members

Paul A. Allaire, *Chairman and Chief Executive Officer, Xerox Corporation*

Dwayne O. Andreas, *Chairman of the Board and Chief Executive, Archer Daniels Midland Company*

Rand V. Araskog, *Chairman, President and Chief Executive Officer, ITT Corporation*

Michael Armascot, *President, The Brookings Institution*

*C. Fred Bergsten, *Director, Institute for International Economics; former U.S. Assistant Secretary of the Treasury for International Affairs*

Conrad M. Black, *Chairman and Chief Executive Officer, Holinger, Inc., Toronto*

Stephen W. Bosworth, *President, The Korean Peninsula Energy Development Organization (KEDO)*

Jacques Bougie, *President and Chief Executive Officer, Alcan Aiuminum Limited, Montreal*

John Brademas, *President Emeritus, New York University; former Member of U.S. House of Representatives*

Harold Brown, *Counselor, Center for Strategic and International Studies; former U.S. Secretary of Defense*

*Zbigniew Brzezinski, *Counselor, Center for Strategic and International Studies; Robert Osgood Professor of American Foreign Affairs, Paul Nitze School of Advanced International Studies, Johns Hopkins University; former U.S. Assistant to the President for National Security Affairs*

M. Anthony Burns, *Chairman, President and Chief Executive Officer, Ryder System, Inc.*

John H. Chafee, *Member United States Senate*

Marshall A. Cohen, *President and Chief Executive Officer, the Molson Companies Ltd., Toronto*

William S. Cohen, *Member of United States Senate*

*William T. Coleman, Jr., *Senior Partner, O'Melveny & Myers; former U.S. Secretary of Transportation*

E. Gerald Corrigan, *Chairman, International Advisors, Goldman, Sachs & Co.; former President, Federal Reserve Bank of New York*

Gerald L. Curtis, *Professor of Political Science, East Asian Institute, Columbia University*

Ian Deans, *Chairperson, Public Service Staff Relations Board of Canada, Ottawa; former Member of the Canadian House of Commons*

Paul Desmarais, *Chairman and Chief Executive Officer, Power Corporation of Canada, Montreal*

Peter C. Dobell, *Director, Parliamentary Centre for Foreign Affairs and Foreign Trade, Ottawa; Vice-President, Institute for Research on Public Policy*

Marie-Josée Drouin, *Adjunct Senior Fellow, Council on Foreign Relations, New York; former Executive Director, Hudson Institute of Canada, Montreal*

*Jessica P. Einhorn, *Managing Director for Finance and Resource Mobilization, World Bank*

Roger A. Enrice, *Vice Chairman, PepsiCo, Inc.*

Jeffrey E. Epstein, *President, J. Epstein & Company, Inc.; President, Wexner Investment Co.*

Robert F. Erburu, *Chairman and Chief Executive Officer, Times Mirror Company*

Trevor Eyton, *Member of Canadian Senate; President and Chief Executive Officer, Brascan Limited, Toronto*

Dianne Feinstein, *Member of the United States Senate; former Mayor of San Francisco*

Martin S. Feldstein, *President, National Bureau of Economic Research, Inc.; George F. Baker Professor of Economics, Harvard University; former Chairman, President's Council of Economic Advisors*

George M. C. Fisher, *Chairman of the Board and Chief Executive Officer, Eastman Kodak Company*

Richard B. Fisher, *Chairman, Morgan Stanley Group, Inc.*

Thomas S. Foley, *Partner, Akin, Gump, Strauss, Hauer & Feld; former Speaker of the U.S. House of Representatives*

*L. Yves Fortier, *Senior Partner, Ogilvy Renault, Barristers and Solicitors, Montreal; former Canadian Ambassador to the United Nations*

*Paolo Fresco, *Vice Chairman of the Board and Executive Officer, the General Electric Company (U.S.A.)*

Stephen Friedman, *Senior Chairman and Limited Partner, Goldman, Sachs & Co.*

Leslie H. Gelb, *President, Council on Foreign Relations*

John A. Georges, *Chairman and Chief Executive Officer, International Paper*

David R. Gergen, *Editor-at-Large,* U.S. News and World Report; *former Special Advisor to the U.S. President and Secretary of State*

Louis V. Gerstner, Jr., *Chairman and Chief Executive Officer, International Business Machines*

Joseph T. Gorman, *Chairman, President and Chief Executive Officer, TRW Inc.*

*Allen E. Gotlieb, *former Canadian Ambassador to the United States*

Bill Graham, *Member of the Canadian House of Commons and Vice Chairman of the Standing Committee on Foreign Affairs and International Trade, Ottawa*

William H. Gray, III, *President and Chief Executive Officer, United Negro College Fund; former Member of U.S. House of Representatives*

Maurice R. Greenberg, *Chairman and Chief Executive Officer, American International Group, Inc.*

John H. Gutfreund, *former Chairman of the Board and Chief Executive Officer, Salomon Brothers Inc.*

*Robert D. Haas, *Chairman and Chief Executive Officer, Levi Strauss & Co.*

Lee H. Hamilton, *Member of U.S. House of Representatives*

Carla A. Hills, *Chairman, Hills & Company; former U.S. Trade Representative*

Robert D. Hormats, *Vice Chairman, Goldman Sachs International; former U.S. Assistant Secretary of State for Economic and Business Affairs*

James R. Houghton, *Chairman of the Board and Chief Executive Officer, Corning Incorporated*

W. Thomas Johnson, *President, Cable News Network*

Vernon C. Jordan, *Partner, Akin, Gump, Strauss, Hauer & Feld*

Donald R. Keough, *Chairman of the Board, Allen & Co., Inc; former President and Chief Operating Officer, The Coca-Cola Company*

*Henry A. Kissinger, *Chairman, Kissinger Associates, Inc.; former U.S. Secretary of State; former U.S. Assistant to the President for National Security Affairs*

Thomas G. Labrecque, *Chairman and Chief Executive Officer, The Chase Manhattan Bank, N.A.*

Jim Leach, *Member of U.S. House of Representatives*

Gerald Levin, *Chairman and Chief Executive Officer, Time Warner*

Whitney MacMillan, *Chairman of the Board and Chief Executive Officer, Cargill, Inc.*

Jessica Tuchman Mathews, *Columnist,* The Washington Post; *Senior Fellow, Council on Foreign Relations*

Deryck C. Maughan, *Chairman of the Board and Chief Executive Officer, Salomon Brothers, Inc.*

Jay Mazur, *President, UNITE*

Hugh L. McColl, Jr., *Chairman, President and Chief Executive Officer NationsBank Corporation*

**Robert S. McNamara, *former President, The World Bank; former U.S. Secretary of Defense*

Allen E. Murray, *former Chairman of the Board, President and Chief Executive Officer, Mobil Corporation*

Michael Oksenberg, *Asia Pacific Research Center, Stanford University; former Staff Member (China), U.S. National Security Council*

Henry Owen, *Senior Advisor, Salomon Brothers; former U.S. Ambassador-at-Large and Special Representative of the President for Economic Summits*

James A. Pattison, *Chairman, President and Chief Executive Officer, Jim Pattison Group Inc., Vancouver*

Michael E. S. Phelps, *Chairman and Chief Executive Officer, Westcoast Energy Inc., Vancouver*

Robert D. Putnam, *Director of the Center for International Affairs and Clarence Dillon Professor of International Affairs, Harvard University*

Charles B. Rangel, *Member of U.S. House of Representatives*

Lee R. Raymond, *Chairman and Chief Executive Officer, Exxon Corporation*

Rozanne Ridgway, *Co-Chair, Atlantic Council; former U.S. Assistant Secretary of State for European and Canadian Affairs*

Charles S. Robb, *Member of United States Senate; former Governor of Virginia*

**David Rockefeller, *Founder and Honorary Chairman, Trilateral Commission*

John D. Rockefeller IV, *Member of United States Senate; former Governor of West Virginia*

Henry Rosovsky, *Lewis P & Linda L. Geyser University Professor of Economics, Harvard University*

William V. Roth, Jr., *Member of U.S. Senate*

William D. Ruckelshaus, *Chairman, Browning-Ferris Industries; former Administrator, U.S. Environmental Protection Agency; former U.S. Deputy Attorney General*

Kurt L. Schmoke, *Mayor of Baltimore*

Albert Shanker, *President, American Federation of Teachers*

Walter Shanker, *Chairman and Chief Executive Officer, Chemical Banking Corporation*

George P. Shultz, *Honorary Fellow, Hoover Institution, Stanford University; former U.S. Secretary of State; former U.S. Secretary of the Treasury; former U.S. Secretary of Labor; former Director. U.S. Office of Management and Budget*

C. J. Silas, *former Chairman of the Board and Chief Executive Officer, Phillips Petroleum Co.*

Ronald D. Southern, *Chairman, President and Chief Executive Officer, ATCO Ltd., Calgary; Chairman Canadian Utilities Ltd., Edmonton*

Paula Stern, *Senior Fellow, The Progressive Policy Institute; President, The Stern Group; former Chairwoman, U.S. International Trade Commission*

Wilson H. Taylor, *Chairman, President and Chief Executive Officer, CIGNA Corporation*

Ko-Yung Tung, *Chairman, Global Practice Group, O'Melveny & Meyers, New York*

*Paul A. Volcker, *Chairman and Chief Executive Officer, James D. Wolfensohn Inc.; Frederick H. Schultz Professor of International Economic Policy, Princeton University; former Chairman, Board of Governors, U.S. Federal Reserve System*

Glenn E. Watts, *President Emeritus, Communications Workers of America*

Henry Wendt, *former Chairman, SmithKline Beecham*

L. R. Wilson, *Chairman, Chief Executive Officer, BCE Inc., Montreal*

Robert N. Wilson, *Vice Chairman, Board of Directors, Johnson & Johnson*

Robert C. Winters, *Chairman Emeritus, Prudential Insurance Co. of America*

Robert B. Zoellick, *Executive Vice-President, General Counsel and Secretary, Federal National Mortgage Association; former U.S. Under Secretary of State for Economic Affairs*

Former Members in Government Service

Bruce Babbitt, *U.S. Secretary of the Interior*

Warren Christopher, *U.S. Secretary of State*

Henry Cisneros, *U.S. Secretary of Housing and Urban Development*

Bill Clinton, *President of the United States*

Richard N. Cooper, *Chairman, National Intelligence Council, Central Intelligence Agency*

William J. Crowe, Jr., *U.S. Ambassador to the United Kingdom*

Lynn E. Davis, *U.S. Under Secretary of State for International Security Affairs*

John M. Deutch, *Director, Central Intelligence Agency*

Richard N. Gardner, *U.S. Ambassador to Spain*

Alan Greenspan, *Chairman, Board of Governors, U.S. Federal Reserve System*

Richard Holbrooke, *U.S. Assistant Secretary of State for European and Canadian Affairs*

James R. Jones, *U.S. Ambassador to Mexico*

Winston Lord, *U.S. Assistant Secretary of State for East Asian and Pacific Affairs*

Walter F. Mondale, *U.S. Ambassador to Japan*

Roy MacLaren, *Canadian Minister of International Trade*

Alice M. Rivlin, *Director, U.S. Office of Management and Budget*

Donna E. Shalala, *U.S. Secretary of Health and Human Services*

Joan Edelman Spero, *U.S. Under Secretary of State for Economic and Agricultural Affairs*

Strobe Talbott, *U.S. Deputy Secretary of State*

Peter Tarnoff, *U.S. Under Secretary of State for Political Affairs*

European Members

Carl Johan Åberg, *Managing Director, AP-Fonden, Stockholm*

Lionello Adler, *Chairman, Banca Commerciale Italiana, Milan; Chairman, Cartiere Burgo, San Mauro Torinese*

Umberto Agnelli, *Chief Executive Officer and Vice Chairman, IFI; Chairman, IFIL, Turin*

Krister Ahlström, *Chairman, Ahlström Group, Helsinki*

*Michel Albert, *Membre de l'Institut de France, Paris; Honorary Chairman, Assurances Générales de France*

Lord Armstrong of Ilminster, *Director, The R.T.Z. Corporation, London; former Chief Cabinet Secretary to the Prime Minister*

Giovanni Auletta Armenise, *Chairman, Banca Nazionale dell'Agricoltura, Rome*

Raymond Barre, *Member of the National Assembly, former Prime Minister of France*

Hans Bartelds, *Chairman of the Board of Managing Directors, Amev, Utrecht; Chairman of the Executive Board of Fortis*

Piero Bassetti, *Chairman, Chamber of Commerce and Industry of Milan; former Member of Chamber of Deputies*

Erik Belfrage, *Senior Vice President, Skandinaviska Enskilda Banken, Stockholm*

Jean Bergougnoux, *Chairman, S.N.C.F. (French Railways), Paris*

*Georges Berthoin, *International Honorary Chairman, European Movement; Honorary European Chairman, The Trilaterial Commission, Paris*

Kurt Biedenkopf, *Minister President of the Free State of Saxony; former Member of the German Bundestag*

Ritt Bjerregaard, *Member of the European Commission, Brussels; former Member of Danish Parliament; former Minister of Education and Minister for Social Affairs*

Marcel Boiteux, *Honorary Chairman, French Electricity Board (EDF), Paris*

Michel Bon, *Chairman, France Telecom, Paris*

Peter Bonfield, *former Chairman and Chief Executive Officer, ICL, London*

Jorge Braga de Macedo, *Associate Professor of Economics, Nova University of Lisbon; former Portuguese Minister of Finances*

Arne Olav Brundtland, *Senior Researcher, Norwegian Institute of International Affairs, Oslo*

Richard Burrows, *Chairman, Irish Distillers, Dublin*

Pierre Callebaut, *Chairman, Amylum, Brussels; former Chairman, Belgian Federation of Agricultural and Food Industries*

Victoria Camps, *Member of the Spanish Senate; Professor of Philosophy, Barcelona University*

Umberto Cappuzzo, *Member of the Defense Committee, Italian Senate; former Chief of Staff of the Army, Italy*

*Hervé de Carmoy, *Chairmarn, Banque Industrielle et Mobilière Privée (B.I.M.P.), Paris; former Chief Executive, Société Générale de Belgique, Brussels*

Jaime Carvajal Urquijo, *Chairman Iberfomento; Chairman, Ford Espaiña, Madrid*

Jean-Claude Casanova, *Professor of Economics, Institute of Political Studies, Paris; Editor,* Commentaire

Fausto Cereti, *Chairman and Chief Executive Officer, Alenia, Rome*

José Luis Cerón Ayuso, *former Spanish Minister of Trade; Chairman of Astea, Madrid*

Willy de Clercq, *Member of the European Parliament; Chairman, Commission on Foreign Economic Relations; former Vice-President, Commission of European Communities, Brussels; former Belgian Minister of State*

Bertrand Collomb, *Chairman, Lafarge-Coppée, Paris*

*Umberto Collomb, *Chairman, LEAD Europe (Leadership for Environment and Development), Rome; former Italian Minister for Universities, Science and Technology*

Richard Conroy, *Chairman and Chief Executive, Conroy; Member of Senate, Irish Republic*

Alain Cotta, *Professor of Economics and Management, University of Paris*

Michel David-Weill, *Senior Partner, Lazard Frères, Paris & New York*

Viscount Etienne Davignon, *Chairman, Société Générale de Belgique; former Vice President of the Commission of the European Communities*

Baron Guido Declerq, *Chairman, Fidisco, Investco and Benevent, Brussels; Honorary General Administrator, Kath University, Lewen*

Jean Deflassieux, *Chairman, Banque des Echanges Internationaux; Honorary Chairman, Crédit Lyonnais, Paris*

Bengt Dennis, *Senior Advisor, Skandinaviska Enskilda Banken, Stockholm; former Governor of the Central Bank of Sweden*

Bill Emmott, *Editor,* The Economist, *London*

Aatos Erkko, *Chairman, Sanoma Corporation, Helsinki*

*Oscar Fanjul, *Chairman, Repsol, Madrid*

Julio Feo, *Chairman, Consultores de Communicacion y Direccion, Madrid; Chairman, Holmes & Marchant*

Carlos Ferrer, *President, Economic and Social Committee of the European Union; Chairman, Ferrer International Group; Chairman, Bank of Europe, Barcelona; Chairman, International Vienna Council*

*Garret FitzGerald, *former Prime Minister and Foreign Minister of Ireland; Member of the Irish Dail*

Michael Fuchs, *President, National Federation of German Wholesale & Export Traders, Bonn*

Tristan Garel-Jones, *Member of British Parliament, former Minister of State at the Foreign Office (European Affairs)*

Antonio Garrigues Walker, *Senior Partner, J & A Garrigues, Abogados, Madrid*

Giuseppe Gazzoni Frascara, *Chairman and Managing Director, Gazzoni; President, Federation of Italian Food Industries, Bologna*

John Gilbert, *Member of British Parliament; former Treasury, Transport and Defense Minister; Chairman of John Gilbert & Associates, London*

Marcello Guidi, *Chairman, ISPI, Milan; former Ambassador of Italy*

Uwe Haasen, *Chairman, Allianz Versicherungs-Aktiengesellschaft, Munich*

Carl Hahn, *Member of the Supervisory Board, Volkswagen, Wolfsburg*

Sirkka Hämäläinen, *Chairman of the Board, Bank of Finland, Helsinki*

Gerhard Heiberg, *Partner, Norscan Consulting, Oslo; Chairman of the Board, Aker, Oslo; President, C.O.J. Lillehammer '94 Olympic Games*

*Miguel Herreo de Miñon, *Lawyer, International Consultant; Member of the Royal Spanish Academy of Political and Moral Sciences; former Member of Spanish Parliament*

Jan Hinnekens, *Chairman, Belgian Boerenbond (Farmers Union); Member, Board of Directors, National Bank of Belgium*

Niels W. Holm, *Chairman, National Institute of Animal Science and of the Danish Standards Association; Vice Chairman, J. Lauritzen Holding; Director, Teledanmark, Copenhagen*

Karl-Heinz Hornhues, *Member of the German Bundestag (CDU) Chairman of the Foreign Affairs Committee*

David Howell, *Member of British Parliament (Cons.) Chairman of the Foreign Affairs Committee; Former Cabinet Minister*

Carmen Iglesias, *Member of the Royal Spanish Academy of History; Professor at the Complutense University, Madrid*

Claude Imbert, *Editor-in-Chief and Managing Director,* Le Point, *Paris*

Thorbjørn Jagland, *Member of the Norwegian Parliament; Chairman, Labour Party Parliamentary Group, Oslo*

*Max Jakobson, *Independent Consultant and Senior Columnist, Helsinki; former Finnish Ambassador to the United Nations; former Chairman of the Council of Economic Organizations*

*Baron Daniel Janssen, *Chairman, Executive Committee, Solvey & Co., Brussels*

Baron Paul Emmanuel Janssen, *Chairman of the Board of Directors, Générale de Banque, Brussels*

*Sir Michael Jenkins, *Executive Director, Kleinwort Benson, London; former British Ambassador*

Reimut Jochimsen, *President, Central Bank of Northrhine-Westphalia, Dusseldorf; Member of the Central Bank Council of the Deutsche Bundesbank*

Josef Joffe, *Foreign Editor,* Süddeutsche Zeitung, *Munich*

Alain Joly, *Chairman and Chief Executive Officer, L'Air Liquide, Paris*

Jacques Julliard, *Associate Director,* Le Nouvel Observateur, *Paris*

Karl Kaiser, *Director, Research Institute of German Society for Foreign Affairs (DGAP); Professor of International Relations, University of Bonn*

Justin Keating, *former Irish Minister of Industry and Commerce; former Leader of the Labour Party in the Senate, former Dean, Faculty of Veterinary Medicine, University College, Dublin*

Horst Köhler, *President, Deutscher Sparkassen-und Giroverband, Bonn; former State Secretary at the Federal Ministry of Finances*

Max Kohnstamm, *former President, European University Institute, Florence*

Manfred Lahnstein, *Member of the Supervisory Board Bertelsmann AG, Gütersloh; former Federal Minister of Finance*

Martin Laing, *Chairman, John Laing, London*

*Count Otto Lambsdorff, *Member of German Bundestag; Honorary Chairman and Chief Economic Spokesman, Free Democratic Party; former Federal Minister of Economy and President of the Liberal International*

Liam Lawlor, *Member of Irish Dail*

Cees van Lede, *Chairman and Chief Executive Officer, Akso Nobel, Arnheim; former President, Federation of Netherlands Industry*

Klaus Dieter Leister, *Member of the Board, Westdeutsche Landesbank Girozentrale, Dusseldorf; former State Secretary, Ministry of Defense*

Pierre Lellouche, *Member of the National Assembly; Defense Spokesman of the RPR Party and Advisor to the President of the French Republic*

Arrigo Levi, *Political Columnist,* Corriere Della Sera, *Rome*

Maurice Levy, *Chairman, Publicis, Paris*

André Leysen, *Chairman, Agfa Gevaert, Antwerp; Chairman, Supervisory Board, Hapag Lloyd, Hamburg*

*Cees Maas, *Member of the Executive Board of the Internationale Nederlanden Group, Amsterdam; former Treasurer of the Dutch Government*

Roderick MacFarquhar, *Professor of Government, Harvard University; Director, Fairbank Center for East Asian Research; former Member of British Parliament*

José Vila Marsans, *Chairman, Rhône Poulenc Fibras, Barcelona; Director, Banco Central, Madrid*

Gilles Martinet, *Ambassadeur de France; President, Association for the European Cultural Community, Paris*

Eberhard Martini, Spokesman, *Bayerische Hypotheken-und Weschel Bank, Munich*

Count Albrecht Matuschka, *Chairman, Matuschka Group, Munich*

Cesare Merlini, *Chairman of the Executive Committee, Council for the United States and Italy; Chairman, Institute for International Affaires, Rome*

Peter Mitterbauer, *Chairman, MIBA, Laakirchen, Austria*

Thierry de Montbrial, *Membre de l'Iustitut de France; Professor, Ecole Polytechnique; Director, French Institute for International Relations (IFRI), Paris*

*Mario Monti, *Member of the European Commission, Brussels; former President & Rector, Bocconi University, Milan*

Gian Marco Moratti, *Chairman, Saras-Raffinerie Sarde, Milan; Chairman, Unione Petrolifera Italiana, Rome*

Klaus Murmann, *Chairman, Federation of German Employers' Association (BDA), Cologne*

Antonio Lorenzo Necci, *Chief Executive Officer, PS-Ferrovie dello Stato*

Heinrich Neisser, *Member of Austrian Parliament; Second President of the National Assembly*

Sir Edwin Nixon, *Deputy Chairman, National Westminster Bank, London*

Lord Owen, *former Co-Chairman (EU) of the Steering Committee of the International Conference on Former Yugoslavia; former Member of British Parliament; former Foreign and Commonwealth Secretary*

Sir Michael Palliser, *Vice Chairman, Samuel Montagu & Co., former Permanent Under-Secretary of State, Foreign and Commonwealth Office, London*

Jacques Thierry, *Honorary Chairman, Banque Bruxelles Lambert; Chairman of the Board, Artois Piedboeuf Interbrew, Brussels*

Gaston Thorn, *Chairman, Banque Internationale à Luxembourg; former President of the Commission of the European Communities; former Prime Minister and Minister of Foreign Affairs of Luxembourg*

*Niels Thygesen, *Professor of Economics, Economics Institute, University of Copenhagen*

*Otto Grieg Tidemand, *Shipowner, Oslo; former Norwegian Minister of Defense and Minister of Economic Affairs*

Maarten Van Traa, *Member of Dutch Parliament (Labour); Chairman, Foreign Affairs Committee*

Marco Tronchetti Provera, *Deputy Chairman and Chief Executive Officer, Pirelli, Milan*

*António Vasco de Mello, *Chairman, Sociedade de Reparaçao e Montagem de Equipamentos Industriais, Lisbon; former Member of Portuguese Parliament*

Simone Veil, *former Minister of State for Social, Health and Urban Affairs, France*

Fredrich Verzetnitsch, *Member of Austrian Partiament (SPOe); President, Austrian Federation of Trade Unions, Vienna; President, European Trade Union Confederation (ETUC)*

Karsten D. Voigt, *Member of the German Bundestag; Spokesman on Foreign Affairs of the SPD Parliamentary Group; Chairman, North Atlantic Assembly*

Karel Vuursteen, *Chairman of the Executive Board, Heineken, Amsterdam*

Serge Weinberg, *Member of the Board and Director General, Pinault-Printemps-Redoute Group, Paris; former Chairman and Chief Executive Officer, Rexel*

Heinrich Weiss, *Chairman, SMS Company, Dusseldorf*

*Norbert Wieczorek, *Member of the German Bundestag and Chairman of the Committee for European Union Affairs*

Alan Lee Williams, *Director, The British Altantic Council; former Member of British Parliament*

*Otto Wolff von Amerongen, *Chairman, East Committee of the German Industry; Officer, Otto Wolff Industrieberatung und Beteiligung, Cologne*

Emilio Ybarra, *Chairman of the Board of Directors, Banco Bilbao-Vizcaya, Madrid*

Arie van der Zwan, *Chairman, World Software Group, The Hague*

Former Members in Public Service

Alain Lamassoure, *Budget Minister & Government Spokesman, France*

José Lamego, *Secretary of State for Foreign Affairs and Cooperation, Portugal*

Joris Voorhoeve, *Minister of Defense, The Netherlands*

Sir Michael Perry, *Chairman, Unilever, London*

Heinrich von Pierer, *Chairman of the Board, Siemens, Munich*

Ilidio de Pinho, *Chairman, Colep, Lisbon*

Lord Rippon of Hexham, *Chairman, Unichem and Dun & Bradstreet, London; former British Cabinet Minister*

Gianfelice Rocca, *Chairman, Techint, Milano*

Lord Roll of Ipsden, *President, S.G. Warburg Group, London*

Sergio Romano, *Editorialist,* La Stampa; *former Italian Ambassador to USSR, Milan*

John Roper, *Associate Fellow, The Royal Institute of International Affairs, London; former Director, Institute for Security Studies, Western European Union; former Member of British Parliament*

H. Onno Ruding, *Vice Chairman, Citicorp/Citibank, New York; former Dutch Minister of Finance*

Renato Ruggiero, *Director General, World Trade Organization (WTO/OMC), Geneva; former Italian Minister of Foreign Trade*

Antxón Sarasquent, *President, Multimedia Capital; Editor,* Hechos, *Madrid*

Willem Scherpenhuijsen Rom, *Former Chairman, Internationale Nederlanden Group, Amsterdam*

Jorgen Schleimann, *Senior Columnist,* Berlingske *Group of Newspapers, Denmark*

*Guido Schmidt-Chiari, *Chairman, Creditanstalt Bankverein, Vienna*

Ellen Schneider-Lenné, *Member of the Board, Deutsche Bank, Frankfurt*

Pedro Schwartz, *Vice President, FINCORP, Madrid; Professor of Economics, Madrid University*

Louis Schweitzer, *Chairman and Managing Director, Régie Renault, Paris*

José Segurado, *Chairman, Jasinas, Madrid; Honorary Chairman of CEIM (Madrid Employer's Confederation); former Member of Spanish Parliament*

*Peter Shore, *Member of British Parliament*

Umberto Silvestri, *Chairman, Telecom Italia, Rome*

David Simon, *Chairman, BP, London*

*Myles Staunton, *Member of Senate, Irish Republic*

*Thorvald Stoltenberg, *Co-Chairman (UN) of the Steering Committee of the International Conference on the former Yugoslavia; former Foreign Minister of Norway*

Peter Sutherland, *Chairman and Managing Director, Goldman Sachs International, London; former Director General, GATT/ WTO, Geneva; former Member of the European Commission; former Attorney General of Ireland*

Poul Johan Svanholm, *President and Group Chief Executive Officer, Carlsberg, Copenhagen*

*Björn Svedberg, *President and Group Chief Executive, Skandinaviska Enskilda Banken, Stockholm*

El Marquès de Tamaron, *Director, Instituto de Cuestiones Internacionales y Politica Exterior (INCIPE), Madrid*

Sir Peter Tapsell, *Member of British Parliament*

Carlos Tavares, *Chairman, Banca Nacional Ultramarino, Lisbon*

Horst Teltschik, *Member of the Board, BMW, Munich; former Head of the Foreign & Security Office in the Federal Chancellery*

Japanese Members

Joichi Aoi, *Chairman, Toshiba Corporation*

Yoshitoki Chino, *Honorary Chairman, Daiwa Securities Co., Ltd.*

*Koichiro Ejiri, *Chairman, Mitsui & Co., Ltd.*

Shinji Fukukawa, *Chairman and Chief Executive Officer, Dentsu Institute for Human Studies*

Yoichi Funabashi, *Washington Bureau Chief and Diplomatic Correspondent,* The Asahi Shimbun

*Toyoo Gyohten, *Chairman of the Board of Directors, The Bank of Tokyo; former Vice Minister of Finance for International Affairs*

Toru Hashimoto, *President, Fuji Bank, Ltd.*

Tetsuya Horie, *Director and Senior Counsellor, The Long-Term Credit Bank of Japan, Ltd.*

*Takashi Hosomi, *Chairman, NLI Research Institute; former Chairman, The Overseas Economic Cooperation Fund*

Shin'ichi Ichimura, *Vice-Chancellor, Osaka International University*

Rokuro Ishikawa, *Chairman, Kajima Corporation*

Takeru Ishikawa, *Chairman, Mitsui Marine & Fire Insurance Co., Ltd.*

Tadashi Ito, *Chairman, Sumitomo Corporation*

Kin'ichi Kadono, *Senior Advisor, Toshiba Corporation*

Motoo Kaji, *Vice President, The University of the Air; Professor Emeritus, University of Tokyo*

Fuji Kamiya, *Dean, Social Science Department, Toyo-Eiwa Women's University*

Ken'ichi Kamiya, *Director and Counsellor, The Sakura Bank, Ltd.*

Hisashi Kaneko, *President, NEC Corporation*

Koichi Kato, *Member of the House of Representatives; former Chief Cabinet Secretary*

Kenji Kawakatsu, *Chairman, Sanwa Bank, Ltd.*

Shoichiro Kobayashi, *Chairman of the Board of Directors, Kansai Electric Power Company, Ltd.*

*Yotaro Kobayashi, *Chairman and Chief Executive Officer, Fuji Xerox Co., Ltd.*

Akira Kojima, *Deputy Chief Editorial Writer,* The Nihon Keizai Shimbun

Yutaka Kosai, *President, Japan Center for Economic Research*

Yukata Kume, *Chairman, Nissan Motor Company, Ltd.*

Toru Kusukawa, *Chairman, Fuji Research Institute Corporation*

*Minoru Makihara, *President, Mitsubishi Corporation*

Michiya Matsukawa, *Senior Advisor to the President, Nikko Securities Co., Ltd.*

Seiji Matsuoka, *Special Advisor, The Nippon Credit Bank, Ltd.*

Isamu Miyazaki, *Chairman, Daiwa Institute of Research, Ltd.*

*Kiichi Miyazawa, *Member of the House of Representatives; former Prime Minister of Japan*

Masaya Miyoshi, *President and Director General, Keidanren (Japan Federation of Economic Organizations)*

Yuzaburo Mogi, *President, Kikkoman Corporation*

Toshio Morikawa, *President, Sumitomo Bank, Ltd.*

Kazuo Morita, *Vice President, Hitachi, Ltd.*

Moriyuki Motono, *Advisor to the Board, Nomura Securities Co., Ltd.*

Jiro Murase, *Managing Partner, Marks & Murase*

*Minoru Murogushi, *President and Chief Executive Officer, ITOCHU Corporation*

Nobuyuki Nakahara, *Honorary Chairman, Tonen Corporation*

Kaneo Nakamura, *Counsellor, The Industrial Bank of Japan, Ltd.*

Toshio Nakamura, *Counsellor, Mitsubishi Bank, Ltd.*

Masashi Nishihara, *Director of the First Research Department, National Institute for Defense Studies; Professor of International Relations, National Defense Academy*

Toshiaki Ogsawara, *Publisher-Chairman,* The Japan Times, *Ltd.; President, Nifco Inc.*

*Shijuro Ogata, *Senior Advisor, Yamaichi Securities Company, Ltd.*

Mitsuyoshi Okano, *President, The Suruga Bank, Ltd.*

*Yoshio Okawara, *Executive Advisor, Keidanren (Japan Federation of Economic Organizations); former Ambassador to the United States*

Ariyoshi Okumura, *President and Chief Executive, IBJNW Asset Management Co., Ltd.*

Masafumi Ohnishi, *Chairman, Osaka Gas Co., Ltd.*

*Kiichi Saeki, *Senior Advisor, Institute for International Policy Studies*

Yutaka Saito, *Chairman and Chief Executive Officer, Nippon Steel Corporation*

Seizaburo Sato, *Professor, Keio University, Research Director, Institute for International Policy Studies*

Masahide Shibusawa, *Director, East-West Seminar*

Motoo Shiina, *Member of the House of Councillors; Japanese Chairman, UK-Japan 2000 Group*

Takeo Shiina, *Chairman and Chief Executive Officer, IBM Japan, Ltd.*

Atsushi Shimokobe, *Chairman, The Tokyo Marine Research Institute*

Tsuyoshi Takagi, *General Secretary, ZENSEN (The Japanese Textile, Garment, Chemical, Mercantile, and Allied Industry Workers' Unions)*

Akihiko Tanaka, *Associate Professor, Institute of Oriental Culture, University of Tokyo*

Tatsuro Toyoda, *Vice Chairman of the Board, Toyota Motor Corporation*

Keiya Toyonaga, *Vice President, Matsushita Electric Industrial Co., Ltd.*

Seiji Tsutsumi, *Chairman, Saison Corporation*

Hisamitsu Uetani, *Chairman Emeritus, Yamaichi Securities Co., Ltd.*

Shoji Umemura, *Chairman of the Board, Nikko Securities Co., Ltd.*

Etsuya Washio, *General Secretary, Japanese Trade Union*

Confederation (RENGO)

Takeshi Watanabe, *Chairman, The Non-Life Insurance Institute of Japan; former President, Asian Development Bar*

Taizo Yakushiji, *Professor of Political Science, Keio University*

Tadashi Yamamoto, *President, Japan Center for International Exchange*

Masamoto Yashiro, *Executive Vice President and Country Corporate Officer, Citicorp/Citibank, N.A.*

Bunkroku Yoshino, *Chairman, Institute for International Economic Studies; former Ambassador to the Federal Republic of Germany*

Former Members in Public Service

Sadako Ogata, *United Nations High Commissioner for Refugees*

APPENDIX G

The Bilderbergers: The Best List Currently Available

Acheson, Dean G – US
Achilles, Theodore C – US
Agnelli, Giovanni – Italy
Agnelli, Umberto – Itlay
Ahistrom, Krister Harry – Finland
Aho, Esko – Finland
Ahtisarri, Martti – Finland
Aird, John B. – Canada
Airey, Sir Terence – UK
Akbil, Semih – Turkey
Allaire, Paul Arthur – US
Allison, Graham Tillett Jr. – US
Alp, Ali Hikmet – Turkey
Alphand, Herve – France
Ambrosetti, Alfredo – Italy
Amiel, Barbara – UK
Andersen, K. B. – Denmark
Anderson, Robert Orville – US
Andreas, Dwayne Orville – US
Androsch, Hannes – Austria
Argyros, Stelios – Greece
Arliotis, Charles C. – Greece
Armgard, Beatrix Wilhelmina – Netherlands
Arrogard, Johan Frisco Bernhard – Netherlands
Arsenis, Gerasimos – Greece
Attali, Jacques – France
Ball, George Wildman – US
Balsemao, Francisco Pinto – Portugal
Banck, Maja – Nether
Barbour, Walworth – US
Barnevik, Percy – Sweden
Barrosso, Jose Manuel Durao – Portugal
Bartley, Robert Leroy – US
Baumgartner, Wilfred S. – France
Becker, Kurt – Germany
Beebe, Frederick Sessions – US
Bell, David Elliott – US
Bell, Elliott Vance – US
Bennet, Douglas Joseph Jr. – US
Bennett, Frederic, Sir – UK
Bentsen, Lloyd – US
Bergsten, C. Fred – US
Bergstrom, Hans – Sweden
Bernabe, Franco – Italy
Bertram, Christoph(er) – Germany
Bettiza, Enzo – Italy
Beyazit – Turkey
Bildt, Carl – Sweden
Bingham, Barry – US
Birgi, M. Nuri – Turkey
Bjarnason, Bjorn – Iceland
Bjerregaard, Ritt – Denmark
Black, Conrad – UK / Canada
Black, Eugene – US
Blackwell, Robert D – US
Blair, Tony – UK
Blum, Robert – US
Bolling, Richard – US

Boskin, Michael Jay – US
Bourassa, Robert – Canada
Bowie, Robert R. – US
Boveri, Walter E. – Switzerland
Boyazit, Selattin – Turkey
Brademas, John – US
Brady, Conor – Ireland
Brady, Nicolas Frederick – US
Braithwaite, Rodric – UK
Brandt, Karl – US
Brautigam, Hans-Otto – Germany
Breuel, Birgit – Germany
Brewster, Kingman Jr. – US
Brinkhorst, Laurend-Jan – Nether
Brinkman, Elco – Nether
Brooke, Edward – US
Brown, Gordon – UK
Brown, Irving – US
Bruce, David K. E. – US
Brundtland, Arne Olav – Norway
Brzezinski, Zbigniew – US
Buckley, William Frank Jr. – US
Bundy, McGeorge – US
Burgess, W Randolph – US
Cabot, Louis Wellington – US
Cadieux, Jean-Louis – Belgium
Caglayangil, Ihsan S. – Turkey
Camps, Miriam – US
Camu, Louis – Belgium
Cantoni, Giampiero – Italy
Carli, Guido – Italy
Carras, Costa – Greece
Carrington, Lord (Peter Rupert) – UK
Cartellieri, Ulrich – Germany
Carvajal Urquijo, Jaime – Spain
Case, Clifford Philip – US
Catroux, Diomede – France
Cavasse, Felicia – France
Cavendish, Bentnick, Victor – UK
Chace, James – US
Chafee, John N. – US
Chalandon, Albin – France
Christodou, Efthymios – Greece
Christensen, Hakon – Denmark
Cipollette, Innocenzo – Italy
Cisler, Walker Lee – US
Cittadini, Cesil Marchese – Italy
Claes, Willy – Belgium
Clarke, Kenneth – US
Cleveland, James Harlan – US
Cleveland, Harold van B. – US
Clinton, William – US
Cole, David Lee – US
Coleman, John S. – US
Collado, Emelio G. – US
Collomb, Bertrand – France
Colonna di Paliano, Don Guido – Italy
Cook, Donald C. – US
Cooper, Richard Newell – US
Copeland, Lammot du Pont – US
Cordier, Andrew Wellington – US
Corrigan, E. Gerald – US
Cortines, Ramon C – US
Cotti, Flavio – Switz
Cowles, Gardner – US
Cradock, Percy – UK
Costopoulos, Yanis – Greece
Cowles, Gardner – US
Currie, R. T. – US
Dahrendorf, Ralf – International
Dallara, Charles H. – US
Dalma, Alfons – Austria
Dam, Kenneth – US
Davingnon, Viscounte Etienne – Belgium
de Lacharriere, Marc Ladreit – France
de Montbrial, Thierry – France
Dean, Arthur H. – US

Deleuran, Aage – Denmark
Delorme, Jean-Claude – Canada
Deming, Frederick Lewis – US
Demirel, Suleyman – Turkey
Deutch, John H. – Canada
Dewey, Thomas Edmund – US
Dicke, Gunter F. W. – Germany
Diebold, John – US
Dieter, Werner H. – Germany
Dillon, C. Douglas – US
Ditlev-Simonsen – Norway
Divedjian, Patric – France
Dodge, Joseph N. – US
Dogramaci, Ihsan – Turkey
Dohnanyi, Klaus von – Germany
Donovan, Hedley Williams – US
Draghi, Mario – Italy
Drouin, Marie-Joseph – Canada
Ducci, Roberto – Italy
Dunkel, Arthur – International
Duncan, James S. – Canada
Dupuy, Michel – Canada
Ecevit, Bulent – Turkey
Ehrnrooth, Georg – Finland
Eliot, Theodore Lyman Jr. – US
Ellemann(-Jensen), Uffe – Denmark
Engholm, Bjorn – Germany
Erkko, Aatos – Finland
Erler, Fritz – Germany
Espy, Mike – US
Fabius, Laurent – France
Fanfari, Amitore – Italy
Faure, Edgar – France
Faure, Lucie, Madam – France
Feinstein, Dianne – US
Ferguson, John Henry – US
Feyzioglu, Turan – Turkey
Finletter, Thomas Knight – US
FitzGerald, Garret – Ireland
Flanders, Ralph E. – US
Florio, James J .– US
Fontaine, Andre – France
Ford, Gerald Rudolph Jr. – US
Ford, Henry II – US
Forte, Francesco – Italy
Foster, William Chapman – US
Frankel, Max – US
Frazer, Donald – US
Freedman, Lawrence – UK
Frelinghuysem, Peter H. B. – US
Friedman, Stephen (James) – US
Fulbright, James William – US
Gallagher, Cornelius E. – US
Galvin, John (Rogers) – US
Gardner, Robert L. – US
Gasteyger, Curt – Switz
Gerber, Fritz – Switz
Gerson, Emelio Gabriel – US
Gerstner, Louis V. Jr. – US
Giersch, Herbert – Germany
Giles, Frank T. R. – UK
Gilpatric, Roswell Leavitt – US
Giovani, Agnelli (see Agnelli, G) – Italy
Giscard d'Estaing, Valery – France
Gokmen, Oguz – Turkey
Golden, Clinton S. – US
Goodpaster, Andrew Jackson – US
Gordon, Duncan – Canada
Gordon, Lincoln – US
Gossett, William T. – US
Goudswaard, Johan M. – Netherlands
Graham, Katharine – US
Greenberg, Maurice R. – US
Greenhill, Lord – UK
Gruenther, Alfred M – US
Grunwald, Henry Anatole – US
Guindey, Guillaume – France
Grunwald, Henry A. – US

Gustafsson, Stan – Sweden
Gysling, Erich – Switzerland
Hafstad, Lawrence R – US
Halberstadt, Viktor – Netherlands
Halefoglu, Vahit – Turkey
Hall, Arnold, Sir – UK
Hallgrimsson, Geir – Iceland
Hamalainen, Sirkka – Finland
Harris, Fred R. – US
Harsch, Joseph C. – US
Hartman, Arthur A. – US
Hauge, Gabriel – US
Hauge, Jens C. – Norway
Hays, Brooks – US
Healy, Denis – UK
Heath, Edmund – UK
Heilperin, Michael A. – US
Heinz, Henry J. – US
Henderson, Nicholas – UK
Herkstroter, Cor A. J. – Netherlands
Herter, Christian A. Jr. – US
Herzog, Maurice – France
Hesburgh, Theodore Martin – US
Hewitt, Williarn Alexander – US
Hickenlooper, Bourke Blakemore – US
Hochschild, Harold K – US
Hoagland, James – US
Hoegh, Leif – Norway
Hoegh, Westye – Norway
Hoffman, Paul Gray – US
Hoffmann, Stanley H. – US
Hojdahl, Odd – Norway
Holifield, Chet – US
Home, Lord of the Hirsel – UK
Horam, John – UK
Horning, Donald Frederick – US
Houthuys, Jozef – Belgium
Huber, Robert W. – US
Hunter, Robert E. – US
Huyghebaert, Jan – Belgium
Igler, Hans – Austria
Ihamuotila, Jaako – Finland
Iloniemi, Jaako – Finland
Imbert, Claude – France
Inan, Kamuran – Turkey
Irwin, Donald J. – US
Isik, Hasan F. – Turkey
Jaans, Pierre – Luxembourg
Jackson, C. D. – US
Jackson, Henry M. – US
Jackson, William H. – US
Jaffre, Philippe – France
Jakobson, Max – Finland
Jankowitsch, Peta – Austria
Janssen, Baron Daniel E. – Belgium
Janssen, Daniel E. – Belgium
Jarimo-Lehtinen, Marja – Finland
Javits, Jacob K. – US
Jay, Nelson Dean – US
Johnson, J. Bennett – US
Johnson, Joseph E. – US
Jones, Aubrey – UK
Jonung, Lars – Sweden
Jordan, Vernon Eulion Jr. – US
Justman Jacob, Poul Louis – Netherlands
Kaiser, Karl – Denmak
Karsten, C. Fritz – Netherlands
Kastrup, Dieter – Germany
Katz, Milton – US
Kaysen, Carl – US
Kazgan, Gulten (Mrs.) – Turkey
Keenan, George F. – US
Kennedy, David Michael – US
Keener, Jefferson Ward – US
Kennedy, David Michael – US
Kiep, Walter Leisler – Germany
Kissinger, Henry Alfred – US
Kirkland, Lane – US
Knapen, Ben – Netherlands

Knight, Andrew – UK
Knoppers, Antonie T. – US
Koc, Rahmi M. – Turkey
Kogg, Christopher – UK
Kohler, Jarl – Finland
Kohnstamm, Max – Italy
Kopper, Hilmar – Germa
Korteweg, Pieter – Netherlands
Kok, Wim – Netherlands
Kothbauer, Max – Austria
Kraft, Joseph – US
Krauer, Alex – Switz
Krogh, Peter F. – US
La Malfa, Giorgio – Italy
Lambert, Baron – Belgium
Lamping, Arnold T. – Netherlands
Larre, Rene – France
Larsson, Stig – Sweden
Lauk, Kurt – Germany
Lendvai, Paul – Austria
Leprince-Ringuet, Louis – France
Levi, Arrigo – Italy
Levy, Walter James – US
Levy-Lang, Andre – France
Lewis, Samuel – US
Lindsay, Franklin Anthony – US
Liotard-Vogt, Pierre – Switz
Litchfield, Lawrence Jr. – US
Littlejohn, Edward – US
Lloniemi, Jaako – Finland
Lorck, Karl – Norway
Lord, Winston – US
Lubbers, Ruud F. M. – Netherlands
Lundvall, D. Bjorn H. – Sweden
Luns, Joseph M. A. H. – International
Lyras, John – Greece
MacDonald, William A. – Canada
MacLaren, Roy – Canada
Maillard, William S. – US
Majesty, Her Royal, Sofia – Spain
Malfatti, Franco Maria – Italy
Maljers, Floris – Netherlands
Manos, Stefanos – Greece
Martens, Wilfried – Belgium
Martin, Edwin McCammon Jr. – US
Mason, Edward S. – US
Mathias, Charles McCurdy Jr. – US
Matlock, Jack Foust Jr. – US
Maudling, Reginald – UK
Maynes, Charles William – US
McCloy, John J. II – US
McConald, David J. – US
McCormack, James – US
McCracken, Paul Winston – US
McGee, Gale W. – US
McGhee, George Crews – US
McGill, Ralph E. – US
McKenna, Frank – Canada
McLaughlin, David Thomas – US
McNamara, Robert Strange – US
McNaughton, John T. – US
Meynen, Johannes – Netherlands
Mondale, Walter Fritz – US
Monjardino, Carlos A. P. V. – Portugal
Monnier, Claude – Switzerland
Monroney, A. S. Mike – US
Montbrial, de, Thierry – France
Monti, Mario – Italy
Morali, Veronique – France
Morris, Joseph – Canada
Morse, F. Bradford – US
Mosley, Philip E. – US
Moyers, Bill D. – US
Mueller, Rudolph – Germany
Muller, Charles W. – US
Murphy, Robert D. – US
Myrvoll, Ole – Norway
Nash, Frank C. – US
Neal, Alfred C. – US

Nebolsine, George – US
Newhouse, John – US
Niarchos, Stavros Spyros – Greece
Nitze, Paul H. – US
Noir, Michel – France
Norstad, Lauris – US
Nye, Joseph S. Jr. – US
Odom, William – US
O'Donnell, Anthony G. S. – Canada
Oddsson, David – Iceland
Olechowski, Andrzej – Poland
Olivetti, Roberto – Italy
Ollila, Jorma – Finland
Oort, Conrad J. – Netherlands
Ozceri, Tugay – Turkey
Palme, S. Olaf – Sweden
Papaconstantinou, Michalis – Greece
Papalexopoulous, Theodore – Greece
Parker, Cola G. – US
Patterson, Morehead – US
Payne, Frederick B. – US
Perkins, George William II – US
Perkins, James A. – US
Pesmazoglu, John S. – Greece
Petersen, Howard C. – US
Peterson, Rudolph A. – US
Pickering, Thomas R. – US
Piel, Gerald – US
Pimenta, Carlos – Portugal
Piore, Emanuel Rubin – US
Pirelli, Alberto – Italy
Pirelli, Leopoldo – Italy
Pohl, Karl Otto – Germany
Polanyi, John – Canada
Pompidou, Georges Jean R. – France
Ponto, Jergen – Germany
Pressler, Larry – US
Price, Donald K. – US
Prideaux, John Francis Sir – UK
Pritchard, Joel McFee – US
Pujol, Jordi – Spain
Pury, David de – Switz
Quandt, William Bauer – US
Quaroni, Pietro – Italy
Rabi, Isidor Isaac – US
Raimond, Jean-Bernard – France
Ramfors, Bo C. E. – Sweden
Rato Figaredo, Rodrigo de – Spain
Reed, John Shedd – US
Reizle, Woligang – Gamany
Reston, James Barrett – US
Retinger, Joseph H. – Poland
Reuss, Henry – US
Reuther, Walther Philip – US
Richardson, Gordon – UK
Ridgeway, Rozanne Lejeanne – US
Riegle, Donald W. – US
Ringier, Michael – Switzerland
Rippon of Hexham, Lord – UK
Roberts, Henry Lithgow – US
Robinson, Charles W. – US
Rockefeller, David – US
Rockefeller, Nelson Aldrich – US
Rodgers, William – UK
Rognoni, Virginia – Italy
Roll (of Ipsden, Lord), Eric – UK
Ronchey, Alberto – Italy
Roosa, Robert V. – US
Rossi, Reino – Finland
Rostow, Eugene Victor – US
Rothschild de, Baron Edmond – France
Rubin, Robert E. – US
Ruggiero, Renato – Italy
Ruehe, Volker – Germany
Ruhnau, Heinz – Germany
Rumsfeld, Donald Henry – US
Rusk, Dean – US

Ryan, John T. – US
Rykens, Paul – Nether
Samuelson, Paul Anthony – US
Santer, Jacques – Luxembourg
Sarmento Rodrigues, Manuel M – Portugal
Sauve, Jeanne (Mrs.) – Canada
Scalapino, Robert A. – US
Schleimann, Jorgen – Denmark
Schmid, Carlo – Germany
Schrnidheiny, Stephan – Switzerland
Schmidt, Adolph William – US
Schmidt, Helmut – Germany
Schmidt-Chiari, Guido – Italy
Schnitzler, William F. – US
Schrempp, Jurgen E. – Germany
Schroder, Gerhard – Germany
Schurer, Wolfgang – Switzerland
Schweizer, Louis – France
Scidenfaden, Toger – Denmark
Scott, Hugh – US
Scowcroft, Brent – US
Serra, Narcis – Spain
Shad, John S. R. – US
Sheinkman, Jack – US
Sheehy, Sir Patrick – UK
Shulman, Marshall D. – US
Sim(m)ons, Thomas W. – US
Simonet, Henri – International
Smith, John – UK
Smith, Harold Page – US
Smith, Gen. Walter Bedell – US
Snoy, et d'Oppuers, Baron – Belgium
Sommer, Theo – Germany
Sonnenfeldt, Helmut – US
Sorensen, Svend O. – Denmark
Soros, George – US
Spaeth, Lothar – Germany
Spang, Joseph P. Jr. – US
Sparkman, John – US
Spitaels, Guy – Belgium
Spofford, Charles M. – US
Steeg, Helga – International
Steinberg, James B. – US
Stevenson, Adlaii E. III – US
Stoleru, Lionel – France
Stoltenberg, Thorvald – Norway
Stone, Shepard – US
Strube, Jurgen – Germany
Sulzberger, Arthur Hays – US
Sulzberger, Cyrus Leo – US
Sutherland, Peter – Ireland
Taverne, Dick – UK
Taylor, Marlin – UK
Taylor, J. Martin – UK
Terkelsen, Terkel M. – Denmark
Teufel, Erwin – Germany
Thatcher, Margaret – UK
Thompson, Gerald FMP – UK
Thorsell, William – Canada
Thygensen, J. V. – Denmark
Tidemand, Otto Grieg – Norway
Trowbridge, Louis V. Jr. – US
Trudeau, Pierre – Canada
Tuke, Anthony – UK
Tunc, Halil – Turkey
Tuthill, John Willis – US
Umbricht, Victor H. – Switzerland
Uri, Pierre – France
Vaarvik, Dagfinn – Norway
Valletta, Vittorio – Italy
Van der Beugel, Ernst H. – Netherlands
van Kleffens, Eelco N. – ECSC
Van Lennep, Jonkheer Emile – International
Veiga, Miguel – Portugal
Veremis, Thanos – Greece
Vernon Raymond – US
Victor, Alice – US

Vogt, John W. – US
Von Amerongen, Otto Wolf – Denmark
Voreys, John M. – US
Voskos, Themistocles – Greece
Vranizky, Franz – Austria
Wallenberg, Marcus – Sweden
Warburg, Eric – US
Warburg, Sir Siegmund George – UK
Warring, Niels – Norway
Wegener, Henning – International
Weinberg, Sidney – US
Wendt, Gerhard M. H. – Finland
White, Peter G. – Canada
Whitehead, John Cunningham – US
Wicker, Thomas Grey – US
Wickman, Mrister – Sweden
Widmer, Siegmund – Switz
Wilbur, Brayton Jr. – US
Wilcox, Francis O. – US
Wilde, Frazar B. – US
Wilder, Lawrence Douglas – US
Wiley, Alexander – US
Wilhjelm, Nils – Denmark
Williams, Lynn (Russell) – US
Wilson, Michael – Canada
Winthrop, Grant F. – US
Wischnewski, Hans-Jurgen – Germany
Wisner, Frank G. II – US
Wohlstetter, Albert J. – US
Wolff von Amerongen, Otto – Germany
Wolfensohn, James David – US
Wolfowitz, Paul D. – US
Worner, Manfred – International
Wright, Patrick – UK
Wriston, Walter Bigelow – US
Yasa, Memduh – Turkey
Yasar, Selcuk – Turkey
Yost, Casimir A. – US
Zannoni, Paolo – Italy
Zellerback, James D – US
Zijlstra, Jelle – Netherlands
Zoellick, Robert B. – US
Zombanakis, Minos – Greece
Zuckerman, Mortimer Benjamin – US

APPENDIX H

Dr. Adrian H. Krieg CfMgE
Curriculum Vita

Updated July 1997

Patents:

4,094,612 Tool Mounting Apparatus:

Abstract: A base for mounting a magnetic base drill to any pipe, for drilling of holes into said pipe at an exact 90 degrees to the axis of said pipe, including mounting and holding mechanism.
7 claims 2 drawing June 1978 available for license

4,064,771 Automatic Torque Controller for Air Impact Wrenches:

Abstract: A device attaching to the square drive on any pneumatic impact wrench, which will automatically limit the torque applied based on the size of the socket tool used, through the reduction or increase of the amount of air supplied to the drive motor.
10 claims 6 drawing Dec. 1977 available for license

3,845,655 Press Brake Unloading System:

Abstract: A device that can be attached to any break press, which will allow the immediate unhindered unloading on a horizontal plain of any deep formed sheet.
4 claims 2 drawings Nov. 1974 available for license

3,788,192 Metal Forming Tool:

Abstract: An electrically or pneumatically driven tool for the beveling of steel and stainless steel in preparation for welding.
15 claims 9 drawings Jan. 1974 obsolete

3,787,970 Beveling Tool:
Abstract: A hydraulically driven tool for beveling ferrous and non-ferrous metals in preparation for welding.
15 claims 4 drawings Jan. 1974 available for license

4,192,487 Apparatus for Oxy-Fuel Cutting of Plate:
Abstract: A wire of rod guided four track vehicle which can cut plate in a strait line without the use of guidance track. Can also be used with plasma and water jet.
5 claims 3 drawings Mar. 1980 available for license

4,216,945 Apparatus for the automatic controlling of the angle of attack on a pipe or plate, utilizing oxy-fuel, plasma, or water jet:
Abstract: An automatic control means for cutting heads requiring to cut a bevel on an orbital axis around a pipe. Said head automatically compensates angle of attack for saddle as well as angle cuts while maintaining a constant bevel.
11 claims 6 drawings Aug. 1980 available for license

4,143,862 Orbital Pipe Cutting Robot:
Abstract: A device which is controlled either from a blue print line tracing, or a computerized program, which allows an orbital pipe cutting robot to cut saddle angles, as well as straight cuts, while maintaining a constant to the center line bevel in preparation for welding.
10 claims 14 drawings Mar. 1979 available for license

4,317,280 Power Feed Apparatus for Power Tools:
Abstract: A power spring device, hydraulic feed device or pneumatic feed device which feeds a power tool in to the work to be performed without human assistance.
5 claims 4 drawings assigned to High Precision Inc. Hamden CT

4,281,459 Sheet Metal Nibbling Tool:
Abstract: A hand held powered tool for the cutting of sheet metal. Able to cut irregular as well as straight and perfect circles. Cutting on the up stoke and thus not having a bulbous die retainer. Able to begin cutting in the center of a sheet with a very small hole.
12 claims 14 drawings Aug. 1981 available for license

4,294,013 Power Hacksaw, Blade Holding Device & Blade:
Abstract: A quick acting power hacksaw blade holding device and required saw blade.
15 Claims 13 Drawingsassigned to: Rule Industries & High Precession Jointly

4,252,481 Cutting Tool:
Abstract: A circular cutting tool for mounting on a grinder or sander, for the removal of stock from aluminum i.e. grinding of aluminum without the grinding device loading up.
1 claim 5 drawings Feb. 1981 available for license

4,078,698 Screw-on-jar-top with upstanding ears:
Abstract: A jar top with upstanding ears on opposite sides allowing a fork or butter knife to be utilized as a tool for opening said jar. Presently used forming dies can be used in manufacturing these new tops with only minor modification.
3 Claims 3 Drawings Mar. 1978 Available for license

4,340,804 Welding Nozzle:
Abstract: A welding nozzle for mounting on any MIG welding gun for fume elimination without interference to the shielding gas.
10 Claims 4 Drawings Assigned to Fab Tec, Colechester VT

4,788,027 Method and means for the removal of Stellite guide balls from (Nuclear) BWR Control Rods:
Abstract: A remote controlled under water punch that will remove the Stellite balls from the top of the BWR Control Rod and store same in a container for later removal and storage.
18 Claims 3 Drawings Nov. 1988 Available for non exclusive license including complete plans for construction available.

4,757,977 Universal Chain Guide for Orbital Pipe Cutters:
Abstract: a device that can be adapted to all orbital pipe cutters that ensures straight and true cuts, and correct tracking.
11 Claims 2 Drawings July 1988 Available for license

4,747,955 Velocity Limiter Shear for BWR (Nuclear) Control Rods:
Abstract: A Device that will cut off the Velocity limiter portion of the control rod (BOOR) under water and remotely. Such act through the shearing of both sides simultaneously, including automatic rotation for the second cutting.
4 Claims 2 Drawings May 1988 Available for non exclusive license including complete plans for construction available.

4,842,139 Cylinder Containment Vessel:
Abstract: A Cylinder containment vessel designed for the removal of gas cylinders containing toxic, poisonous and corrosive gasses which are leaking.
10 claims 2 Drawings June 1989 Patent infringed by German Firm.

4,873,902 Portable RR Rail Cold Saw:
Abstract: A portable power circular cold saw which utilizes the RR rail as the machine frame while cutting it. Separating into two components is power feed and can be driven by any power source providing rotational power.
8 Claims 4 Drawings Oct. 1989 Available for license

5,055,236 Method and apparatus for underwater remote controlled radioactive waste reduction (Nuclear) of BWR Control Rods:

Abstract: A machine operating under water which 1 removes the velocity limiter, 2 separates the control rod (X) into two (V) shaped objects. The Stellite balls having previously been removed by pat. # 4,788,027. (above)
7 Claims 6 Drawings Oct. 1991 Available for license.

Patented Products Available for License:

BWR Velocity Limited Shear, Stellite Ball Punch, Control Rod Crusher
Control Rod Disassembly Device.
Portable RR Rail Cold Saw
Portable RR Rail Cross Drill
3 Axis Hydraulic portable Milling & Drilling Machine

BIBLIOGRAPHY
and
RECOMMENDED READING
Listed by Author

Allen, G., *Conspiracy*

Allen, G. & Abraham, L., *None Dare Call It Conspiracy*

Atkinson, James, *The Edge of War*

Atkinson, R., *Treason at Maastrict*

Baret, R. J. & Muller, R. E., *Global Research*

Barnes, Harry E., *Perpetual War for Perpetual Peace*

Barnes, Harry E., *Genesis of the World War*

Bastiat, Frederick, *Economic Harmonies*

Bastiat, Frederick, *The Law*

Beard, Charles, *President Roosevelt and the Coming of the War, 1941*

Bennett, J. & DiLorenzo, T., *Official Lies*

Bohm-Bawerk, Eugene, *Capital and Interest*

Burnham, James, *Suicide of the West*

Burnham, James, *Congress and the American Tradition*

Carson, Clarence, *The American Tradition*

Castle, Eugene, *The Great Giveaway*

Chamberlain, William, *America's Second Crusade*

Chamberlain, William, *Appeasement – Road to War*

Chambers, Whitaker, *Witness*

Chesterton, A. K., *The New Unhappy Lords*

Connolly, B., *The Rotten Heart of Europe*

Council On Foreign Relations, The, *1995 Annual Report*

Crocker, George, *Roosevelt's Road to Russia*

D'Sousa, D., *My Dear Alex*

DeLove, Sidney, *Quiet Betrayal*

Douglas, Gregory, *Gestapo Chief*, 2 volumes

Dowd, Kevin, *Laissez-Faire Banking*

Ebeling, Richard, *Austrian Economics: A Reader*
Epperson, A. R., *The Unseen Hand*
Friedman, David D., *Hidden Order*
Friedman, Milton, *Capitalism & Freedom*
Friedman, Milton & Rose, *Free To Choose*
Funderburk, D., *Betrayal of America*
Funderburk, D., *Pinstripes and Reds*
Garrett, G., *The American Story*
Gilder, George, *Wealth and Poverty*
Glasstone, S. & N. A.Jordan, *Nuclear Power and Its Environmental Effects*
Golitsyn, A., *New Lies for Old*
Golitsyn, A., *The Perestroika Deception*
Greaves, Bettina Bien, *Austrian Economics*
Griffin, G. E., *The Creature from Jekyll Island*
Grigg, W. N., *Freedom On The Altar*
Hayek, F. A., *Road To Serfdom*
Hazlitt, Henry, *The Critics of Keynesian Economics*
Hazlitt, Henry, *Economics In One Lesson*
Horowitz, David, *Radical Son*
Hutt, W.H., *Keynesianism: Retrospect and Prospect*
Ikeda, Sanford, *Dynamics of the Mixed Economy*
Ingrams, Richard, *Muggridge: The Biography*
Jasper, W., *Global Tyranny Step by Step*
Jones, M., *John Cardinal Krol*
Kellems, Vivian, *Toil, Taxes & Trouble*
Kelly, B., *Adventures in Porkland*
Kelly, C., *Conspiracy Against God and Man*
Kessler, R., *Inside the CIA*
Kilpatrick, James J., *The Soverign States*
Kimmel, H. E., *Admiral Kimmel's Story*
Kincaid, C., *Global Bondage*
Lane, Rose, *The Discovery of Freedom*
LaPierre, W., *Guns, Crime, and Freedom*

Lax, Albert, *Consumers' Capitalism*
LeFevre, Robert, *The Philosophy of Ownership*
Locke, John, *Of Civil Government*
Madison, Hamilton & Jay, *The Federalist Papers*
Marx, Karl, *The Communist Manifesto*
McAlvany, D., *Toward a New World Order*
McManus, John, *Changing Guard*
McManus, John, *The Insiders*
McManus, John, *Financial Terrorism*
Mises, Ludwig von, *Human Action*
Mises, Ludwig von, *Socialism*
Mises, Ludwig von, *Bureaucracy*
Mises, Ludwig von, *The Theory of Money and Credit*
Morgenstern, George, *Pearl Harbor*
Morley, Felix, *Freedom & Federalism*
Mullins, E., *The World Order*
Nock, Albert J., *Our Enemy The State*
Nock, Albert J., *Mr. Jefferson*
O'Rourke, P. J., *Parliament of Whores*
Opitz, Edmund, *Your Church, Their Target*
Opitz, Edmund, *Religion: Foundation of the Free Society*
Palmer, William, *The Court vs. The People*
Palyi, Melchior, *Compulsory Medical Care and the Welfare State*
Phillips, *The Quest for Excellence*
Pombo & Farratt, *This Land Is Our Land*
Quigley, Carroll, *The Anglo-American Establishment*
Ray, Dixie Lee, *Environmental Overkill*
Ray, Dixie Lee, *Trashing the Planet*
Read, Leonard, *The Free Market and Its Enemy*
Regnery, Henry, *A Few Reasonable Words*
Roberts, A., *Victory Denied*
Robertson, Pat, *The New World Order*
Robison, John, *Proofs of a Conspiracy*

Rothbard, Murray, *America's Great Depression*
Rothbard, Murray, *Left & Right*
Rothbard, Murray, *Making Economic Sense*
Rothbard, Murray, *The Case Against The FED*
Sadat, Jehan, *A Woman of Egypt*
Sanera & Shaw, *Facts Not Fear*
Sauborn, F. R., *Design For War*
Sinkin, J. & A. Zelman, *Gun Control: Gateway to Tyranny*
Sklar, H., *Trilateralism*
Sowell, Thomas, *Ethnic America*
Stelzer, G., *The Nightmare of Camelot*
Stick, P., *Defrauding America*
Sutton, A. E., *America's Secret Establishment*
Tansill, Charles, *Back Door to War*
Theobald, R. A., *The Final Secret of Pearl Harbor*
Trilateral Commission, The, *1995 Catalogue*
Tuchman, Barbara, *The Proud Tower*
United Nations, *Charter*
U.S. *Bill of Rights*
U.S. *Constitution*
Vennard, Sr., Wickliff, *The Federal Reserve Hoax*
Walbert, M. W., *The Coming Battle*
Weaver, Richard, *Ideas Have Consequences*
Welch, Jr., Robert, *May God Forgive Us*
White, Andrew, *Fiat Money Inflation in France*
Woodward, B., *The Agenda*
Wormser, R. A., *Foundations and Their Power and Influence*
Zahner, D., *The Secret Side of History*

INDEX

A
Aachen, Germany 117
ABM 135
Abzug, Bella 83
Achtenberg, Anita 99
acid rain 62, 82
Afghanistan 102, 132, 133
Africa 43, 122
African continent 45
Alaska 44
All Souls College 194
America 114, 124, 128, 129, 142, 178, 179, 184, 196, 228
America 2000/Goals 2000 112, 109
American Chemical Association 196
American Civil Liberties Union (ACLU) 97
American Communist Party 145
American Constitution 96, 111, 164, 237
American Council of Churches 77
American Democrat party. 195
American Economic Association 196
American Far East Policy 182
American Federal Register, 103
American Govm'nt. Accounting Office 135
American History Association 196
American Indians 127
American Jewish Council 80
American people 212
American Psychological Association 196
American public schools 199
American Reform (Perot) Party 47, 48
American Revolution 127
American State Department 180
American taxpayer 35
Americans for Democratic Action (ADA) 165
AmeriCorps 162, 163
An American Dilemma 164, 165
Anderson, Arthur 163
Andreas, Dwayne 65, 66
Angola 43
Anschluss 179
Anti-Terrorism bill 133
Apparatchiks 119
Argentina 114, 115, 182
Art of War, The 131
Asia 142
Asuncion 114
Audubon Society, The 60
Australia 122
Austria 102
Austrian School of economics 147
Await, Johan 126
Axis powers 56
B
Bader Meinhof 128
Baer vs. Lewin 84
Balfour declaration 55
Balkans 127
Bank of International Settlements, The 153
Bank of New York 152
Bankers Trust 152, 212
Banks Involved in the Panamanian Deal 212
Barkett, Judge Rosemary 239
Basel Committee 154
Basel, Switzerland 153
Basque separatists (ETA) 132
BATF 199
Bavaria 218
Beatrice Webb House 64, 93
Beijing 83
Belgian paratroopers 136
Belgium 154, 178
Benelux nations 224
Berlin 192
Bernard, Prince of Holland 233
Between Two Ages 205
Bible in public schools 81
Bilderberger directive 144
Bilderbergers 113, 118, 120, 143, 144, 172, 173, 193, 196, 197, 203, 215, 221, 222, 223, 224, 226, 228, 229, 231, 232, 233
Bill of Rights 111
BIS 155, 156

Bismarck, Otto V. 199
Black Church Fire Hoax of '96, The 50
Black June 132
Black Panthers 51
Black September 132
Blair House 226
Blair, Tony 218, 222
Blitzkrieg 127, 179
Boer war 44
Bolshevik revolution 54
Bombing in Oklahoma City 133
Bones 113, 191, 197, 201, 202, 224, 233
Bones, Members of 201
Born-again Christians 80, 147
Bosnia 101, 132, 142, 222
Boudin, Kathy 198
Boudin, Leonard 198
Boudin, Michael 198
Bowman 180, 185, 188
Bradley, Bill 41
Brandt, Willy 172
Brazil 114, 115, 182, 228
Bretton Woods 153, 155
Britain 118, 142, 178
British 44, 54, 55, 181, 184
British Crown 199
British Government 55
British Home Secretary Herbert Samuels 55
British Institute of International Affairs 231
British Isles 117
British Labor party 64, 93
British Prime Minister 144
British sovereignty 221
Brooke, Roger Taney 105
Brown, Harriman & Co 194
Brown, Ron 37
Brown vs. Topeka Board of Education 1954 164, 238
Brown, Walter H. 194
Brussels 32, 113, 119, 121, 223
Brzezinski, Zbigniew 65, 204
Buckley, William F. 197
Buenos Aires 114
Buergerschtock in Switzerland 222
Bundesbank 119, 227
Bundestag 60
Bundy, William 194, 197, 199
Bureau of Land Management 61
Burma 184
Bush administration 35, 137, 225
Bush, George 32, 38, 65, 66, 137, 173, 222
Bush, Prescott Sheldon 194
Butros-Ghali, Butros 77, 134, 137
C
Caesar, Julius 117
Cairo 123
Cambodia 101
Canada 70, 114, 143, 153, 154
Capitalism 56
Capitalist economic system 58
Carnegie, Andrew 157, 158
Carnegie Corporation 165
Carnegie Foundation 159, 195
Carroll, Brazillia Reec 157
Carter, Jimmy 61, 173, 204, 210, 212
Catholic Orthodox 79
CBO 33
Ceausescu, Nikolai 93
Center for Democratic Renewal 50
Centralization of markets under govnt. control 58
Century Group 180
CFC 79
CFR Membership 174
CFR Study Groups 177
Chapter 322 191, 202
Charlemagne 117, 134
Chase Manhattan Bank 120, 152, 212, 214
Chechnya 102, 132
Chemical Bank 152
Chile 114, 115, 182
Chilean model 246
China 83, 113, 122, 125, 126, 128, 135, 182, 184
China town 75
Chinese industry 126
Chinese policy 210
Chopra, Deepak 65
Christian empire 117
Christianity 77
Christians 80
Church Fire Bill 51

Church-State issue 81
Churchill 184
CIA 131, 198
CitiBank N.A. 152
Civil Liberties Union (ACLU) 165
Civil War 105, 111
Clarke, Kenneth 218
Clean Air Act to be enforced by the UN 82
Clinton & Congress 49
Clinton administration 35, 137
Clinton, Bill 32, 38, 40, 48, 94, 135, 142, 149, 162, 173, 198, 210, 226, 238
Clinton, Bill & Hillary 29, 87, 147
Clinton Cabinet 36, 74
Clinton, Hillary 83, 99, 147
Cockburn, Alexander 82
Code Napoleon 154
Coffin, Henry Sloan 196
Coffin, Lewis C. 104
Columbia University 204
Common Market 218
Communism 200
Communist Manifesto 151
Communist Party 40, 106, 108
Communist Party (USA) 165
Communist USSR 242
Communists in the USSR and China 56
Concerned Women of America (CWA) 74
Congo 44
Congress 133
Congressional budget office (CBO) 91
Congressional gridlock 49
Conn. District Export Council (CTDEC) 225
Connolly, Ambassador 155
Coptic Egyptian 134
Cornell 196
Corporation For National Service, The 162
Costikyan, Granger Kent 194
Council of Economic Advisors 92
Council On Foreign Relations 113, 141, 156, 157, 162, 165, 170, 172, 173, 179, 180, 181,182, 183, 184, 185, 186, 188, 189, 193, 196, 197, 203, 208, 209, 213, 222, 224, 226, 233
Counsel of the Wise 66
Counter-4th generation war 130
Cox committee 157, 159
CPUSA 165
Cranston, Allan 65, 66
CS Holding 208
Cuba 57, 135
Cultural Jihad 49
Culture war 95
Cuomo, Mario 65
Czech 134
D
Dardanelles 124
Das Waffengesetz 103
Davis, John W. 187
Davis, Norman 180
Davison 194
Decline of America's standard of living 205
Deer Island 193
Democrat constituency 96
Democrat national platform 245
Democrat Party 87, 96
Democratic National Committee (DNC) 75
Dennis, Judge James 238
Denver, John 65
Department of Commerce 69, 225
Departments of Education, Energy, and Commerce 243
Depository Trust Company, The 152
Die Deutche Bundesbank 118
Die Nazional Sozialistische Partei (NSP) 56
Die Neue Zurcher Zeitung 68
Dikinsen, Andrew 192
Disadvantages of Being Educated, The 76
Dodd, Thomas I. 104
Dole, Bob 142, 226
Douglas, John 198
Douglas, Paul H. 198
DTC 152
Dulles, Allen 180
Dulles, John Foster 209, 232
Duma 40
Dunbarton Oaks Conference 187
Dutch 44, 118, 134, 184, 218
Dutch East Indies 184
Dwight, Timothy 192
E
E-B19 182

E-B26 182
E-B34 182, 183
Earls Court 232
Earth in the Balance 77
Eastern Europe 147
EC 31, 32, 37, 38, 41, 70, 88, 114, 117, 118, 119,
EC 121, 122, 144, 146, 169, 178, 182, 183, 189, 196, 206, 207, 224, 227, 228, 229
EC anthem 223
EC citizens 223
EC courts 223
EC parliament 223
Economic Bill of Rights 111
Egypt 123, 124
Eisenhower administration 59
Eisenhower, Dwight D. 113, 129
Endangered Species Act 66, 67
Energy Cartel by Norman Medvin 210
Engels, Frederich 147, 200
England 54, 64, 128, 129, 131, 147, 178, 179, 180, 181, 184, 196, 229
Engle vs. Vitale 96
Engler 29
English Labor party, 195
Environmental Overkill 79
Environmental Protection Agency, 34, 61, 72, 228
EPA standards 228
Esquire Magazine 194
Estate taxes 244
Ethiopia 179
EUC 207
Eurofascism 221
Europe 55, 114, 115, 116, 117, 119, 120, 124, 142, 184, 203, 208, 215, 221
European, Canadian, and American assets 231
European Coal and Steel Community 230
European colonial interests 185
European Common Market (EC) 114
European Court of Justice 223
European Economic Community (EEC) 230
European nations 230
European Organization for Economic Cooperation 230
European politicians 221
European Union 117
Evian, France 222
Executive branches 180
Executive orders 240
F
Fabian socialists 93, 205
Fabian Society 64, 93, 94, 195
Fabius, Quintus Maximus 93
Facts about the Bilderbergers 232
Far East 184
Far Eastern suppliers 182
Fascists in Italy 56, 242
Fatah (the Palestinian group) 132
Fate of the Forests, The 82
FBI 199
FDA 237
FDR 38, 111, 178, 180, 181, 184, 185, 186, 187
Federal Judiciary 95, 238
Federal Register 159
Federal Reserve Act 151
Federal Reserve Building 150
Federal Reserve System 35, 55, 97, 111, 116, 151, 152, 154, 156, 209, 224,
FEMA 240
Feudal society 168
Feudal system 121
Fifth-Socialist International, 172
Financial Monopoly 243
Fino 117
First Bank of Chicago 212
First National City Bank 212
First World War 54, 178
Fish, Hamilton 179
Flat tax 244
Flying Tigers 182
Fonda, Jane 65, 83
Ford Foundation 145, 159, 195
Ford, Gerald 157, 173
Ford, Henry 158
Foreign Affairs 177, 179
Foreign surrogate troops 105
Fortune magazine 87
Foundations 157, 160, 244

Foundations, Rockefeller and Ford 209
Founding Fathers 130
Fourth Generation War 113, 123, 126, 127, 128, 129, 132, 146, 186
France 118, 128, 131, 134, 153, 154, 155, 178, 179, 181, 184, 211
Franklin, George 232
Free Market 40
Free market competition 245
Free to Choose, Milton and Rose Friedman 111
Free Trade 37, 68, 70, 168, 169, 185, 214, 228, 243
Free Trade Area of the Americas (FTAA) 114, 115
Freemason 193
French Revolution 53, 93
Freon 79
Friedman, Milton 65
FRS 116
FTAA 114, 115, 121, 122, 182
Fumento, Michael 50
G
G10 154
G7 nations 120, 121, 154, 226
Gaia 77
GAO 135, 162, 243
Gardner, Richard N. 204
Garmisch-Patenkirchen 218
Gates, Bill 65, 66
GATT 31, 38, 120, 178, 227, 228
Gay 84
General Agreement on Tariffs and Trade 227
Geneva, Switzerland 178
Genscher, Hans Dietrich 65
Gentiles 194
German 116, 126, 134, 179, 183, 200
German Heer 134
German Wermacht 179, 181
German-made products 179
Germanic tribes 117
Germany 37, 53, 54, 60, 102, 118, 119, 129, 131, 134, 154, 178, 179, 181, 191, 218, 224, 245
Geyer, Georgia Anne 65
Gillman, Daniel Coit 192, 199, 200
Gingrich, Newt 226
Global Clearing Network (GCN) 153
Global Government 52
Global Green 60, 64
Global Paradox 135
Global System 203
Global Taxation System 207
Global Warming 52, 82
Globalization 53
GNP 119
Goals 2000 110
Goldman Sachs 226
Goldwater, Senator Barry 156, 202
Good-bye China 158
Gorbachev Foundation 64
Gorbachev, Mikhail 64, 66, 113
Gore, Al 65, 77
Gore, Tipper 32
Graham, Katharine 172
Granada 101
Grand Area, The 182
Great Britain 153, 154
Great Society. 96
Greater Asia Co-Prosperity Sphere 184
Greece 37, 231
Greek Ethnos 68
Green Cross International 64
Green Cross, The 60
Greenpeace 60, 139
Greens, The 60
Grosse, Karl Der 117
Guggenheim Foundation 159
Gun Control 101
Gun Control Act of 1968 104
Gun Control: Gateway to Tyranny 104
H
Hadrian 117
Hadrian wall 117
Haig, Alexander 113
Haiti 101, 130
Hamas 128, 132
Hammer, Armand 165
Handelman, S. 41
Hanoi Jane 244
Hansen 180
Harriman, Averell W. 194, 232

Harriman, Edward R.N. 194
Harvard University 196
Hassidic 80
Havel, Vaclav 65
Hawaii 83
Health and Human Services (HHS) 99
Healthcare industry 46
Heath, Edward 222
Hegel 90
Hegelian dialectic 28, 53, 93, 159, 165, 167, 199
Hegelian process 200
Hegelian thought 199
Heidelberg 191
Heine, Heinrich 200
Helvitians 117
Hesburgh, Theo. 65
Hess, Moses 200
High Frontier 40
Hillary Healthcare Committee 30, 46, 48
Hiss, Alger 135, 197
Hitler 28, 56, 102, 117, 179, 242
Holland 134, 154, 184, 224
Holy Roman Emperor 117
Homeless 214
Homosexual 84
Homosexual lobby. 74
Homosexual marriage 83
Hong Kong 125, 126
Hood, Charles 232
Horowitz, David 108
Hotel de Bilderberg 218
House of Representatives. 240
Housing and Urban Development 243
Hoveida, Amir 211
Hughes, Charles Evans 187
Hughes, Langston 158
Hull, Secretary 185, 187, 188
Hungarian Ambassador Ambaniaki 189
I
ICC 155
Iconoclast 194
Illuminati 145, 191, 193
IMF 154, 156, 186, 187, 222
Imperial Japan 242
Important CFR Personalities 174
Income Tax Amendment 244
India 128
Indochina 184
Indonesia 122
Inflation 43
Ingwell, L. 232
Innsbruck, Austria 222
Insight Magazine 61, 69
Institute for Foreign Policy Studies 145
Institute for Policy Studies (IPS) 165
Internal Revenue Service 159,
International Bank 186
International Chamber of Commerce 155
International Depository & Clearing 152
International Financiers 44, 55
International Monetary Fund 36, 154, 186
International Police Force 173
International Trade Commission 69
International Women's Conference 83
Iran 123, 124, 135, 210
Iranian Offshore Petroleum Co 211
Iranian Oil Consortium 211
Iraq 101, 124
Irish Republican Army (IRA) 132
Islam 77, 123, 124
Islamic fundamentalist state 123
Islamic Jihad 123, 128
Islamic law 124
Islamic nations 123
Islamic religions 80
Islamic social and religious thought 123
Isolation of Japan 182
Israel 124, 130
It Takes a Village 147
Italy 131, 134, 154, 179
J
Jackson, Andrew 235
Jackson, James E. 165
Jaeger Concept 126, 179
Japan 32, 34, 115, 121, 122, 179, 182, 183, 184, 185, 203, 208, 215
Japanese red army (Sekigun) 132
Japan's oil reserves 185
Jekyll Island 156, 209

Jesse Jackon's, "Rainbow Coalition" 214
Jewish homeland 55
Jews for the Preservation Of Firearms 104
John Birch Society 145
Johns Hopkins University 196, 199
Johnson, Lyndon 96
Joint Chiefs of Staff 141
Judaism 77
Judeo-Christian philosophy 147
Judicial Activism 238
Judicial Tyranny 49
Judiciary 49, 164, 237
K
Kennedy, Ted 29, 91, 156
Kennedy/Kassenbaum bill 47
Kennedy/Metzenbaum Health-care Reform 30
Kepel, Frederick 165
Key Bank 152
Keynes economic theory, 169
Keynes, John Maynard 90, 147, 153
Keynesianism 92
KGB 57
Khallid Muhammad 51
Khomeini, Ayatollah 211
Khruschev, Nikita 204
Kirk & Madsen 84
Kissinger, Henry 42, 113
KKK 80, 97, 145
Koppel, Ted 65
Koran, The 124
Korea 34, 115, 122, 134
Krol, Cardinal John 98
Kuhn & Loeb 54
Kulturkampf 95
Kurdistan 142
L
LA Herald Examiner 211
La Toia 221
Labor Party 87
Land Grant College Act 192
Lavaan Petroleum Company 210
League of Nations 169, 178, 179, 187, 230
Lebensgeschichte 28
Leipzig 199
Lend Lease 230
Lenin 54, 55
Letter to Colonel House 235
Liberia 135
Libertarian 109
Library of Congress 104
Lincoln, Abraham 192
Lindberg, Charles A. 150
Link, David 84
London, England 113, 146, 198
London Express 211
Lovelock, James 77
Lovett, Robert A. 194
Lowell High School 75
Luanda 43
Luce, Henry 197
Luxembourg 119, 154
M
M19 (Columbia) 132
Maastricht treaty 118, 120, 221, 223, 229
Machiavelli 131
Macedonia 130, 132
Madden, John B. 194
Madison Plan 99
Malaya 184
Mallory, Armstrong 180
Mallory, Walter 179
Managed Trade 71
Manchuria 179, 184
Manifest Der Kommunistischer Parti 146
Mao Tse Tung 56
Maquiladora plants 35
Maquiladora process 34
Marine Midland 152, 212
Mark, The German 119
Marshall, General George 230
Marshall Plan 169, 230
Martial Law 129
Marx, Karl 29, 70, 79, 90, 146, 147, 151, 200, 228
Marxist dogma 206, 210
Maximum term of 10 years for federal judges 239
McCarthy, Joseph 197
McGee, George 218

McKee, Judge Theodore 239
McLaine, Shirley 65
McLeach, Archibald 197
McNamara, Robert 172
McVeigh, Timothy 199
Medvin, Norman 210
Mein Kampf 28
Messersmith, George 180
Mexican bail-out, 1996 34, 212
Mexican government 31, 35, 225, 226
Mexico 36, 37, 38, 70, 71, 72, 114, 212
Mid Atlantic 152
Middle East
42, 44, 122, 123, 125, 210, 214
Mill, John Stuart 246
Miller, Nathen N. 187
Milliken & Co 69
Milliken, Roger 69
Milner, Lord 194
Milner's Round Table 194
Mineral deposits 125
Mitchell, George 65
Mohammed 124
Mongolia 44, 135
Montebello, Québec, Canada 143, 221
Mordita 35, 72
Morgan G.T. Co 152
Morgan, J.P. 232
MSAs (medical savings accounts) 46
Mulroney, Brian 65
Muslim nations 123
Muslims 80, 124
Mussolini 28, 56, 117
Mussolini's Lebensgeschichte 28
Myrdal, Gunnar 165
N
NAFTA 31, 35, 37, 38, 42, 68,70, 88, 114, 116, 119, 120, 146, 169, 178, 182, 189, 206, 224, 225,226, 227, 228, 242
Naisgitt, John 135
Napoleon 28, 117, 126, 134
Napoleonic France 53, 126
NASA 62, 78
National Center for Public Policy Research 61
National Committee of the Communist Party 165
National Economic Council 92
National Education Association (NEA) 109, 245
National Empowerment Television (NET) 189
National Lawyers Guild 145, 165, 198
National Origination for Women (NOW) 74
National parks being under UN protection 101
National Rifle Association (NRA) 109
National Securities Clearing Corp. (NSCC) 153
National Westminster 152
NATO 123, 124, 132, 134, 169, 178, 188, 189, 231
Nazi Germany 242
Nazi propaganda 147
Nazis 56, 106, 130
Nazism 200
NEA 245
Neo-Nazi Separatist Christians 80
Nesbitt, John 65
Netherlands 184
New Democrats 93
New Feudalism 168
New Radicalism 90
New World Army 134
New World Order 28, 42, 46, 53, 55, 70, 111, 137, 148, 167, 172, 183, 205, 222, 246
New York Bankers 35
New York City Teachers Union 108
New York Herald Tribune 157
New York Stock Exchange, 152
New York Times 157
New Zealand 122
Newfoundland 54
Newsweek Magazine 172
NFPA (National Fire Protection Association 50
Nicaragua 210
Nieman Fellowship 197
Nigera 135

Nixon administration 155
Nock, Albert J. 76, 86
North America 114, 115, 116, 120, 125, 215, 225
North and South America 182
North Atlantic 226
North Korea 57, 122, 135
NSCC 153
O
Oklahoma Bombing 133
Oklahoma City Federal building 198
Oosterbeek 218
OPEC 214, 215
Orthodox Jews 80, 147
OSHA 34, 72
Oslo 198
Ottawa 37
Our Enemy, The State 86
Outcome Based Education (OBE) 109
Oxford University 149, 194, 198
Ozone Hole 52, 62, 78, 79
P
P-B23 186
Pacific Rim nations 34, 42, 115, 120, 121, 122, 125, 226
Packard, David 65
Pakistan 131
Palestine 55
Panama 101
Panama Canal 210
Panama Canal give-away 212
Pantheism 77
Partial Birth Abortion 166
Partin, General 199
Partners for Peace (PFP) 189
Passing of legislation without a rollcall vote 241
Pasvolosky 185, 188
Patriarchs, The 193, 194
Paul, Ron 242
Pax Americana 185
Payne 194
Pearl Harbor 183
Percentage of Total World Trade, 1996 89
Perot, Ross 48
Perpetual state of emergency enacted by FDR 240
Peso Protection Fund 36
Peso purchases 35
Peterson, Pete 172
PFP 189
Philippines 122, 184
Playboy Magazine 95
Poland 41
Political Correctness (PC) 99
Portugal 43
Powell, General Colin 65
PRC 122, 204
PRC economy 125
President Buchanan 192
President Clinton 240
President Reagan 143
President Wilson 93, 151, 178
Presidio of San Francisco 64
Primakov, Yevgeny 40
Prominent CFR Participants 176
Promise Keepers 213
Prussians 126
Psychedelic drugs 166
Public Land Grant Act 192
Public schools 245
Punic wars 93
Q
Québec 143
Quigley, Professor Carroll 195
R
Radical Right Wing Christians 80
Radical Son, A Generational Odyssey, David Horowitz 108
RAF (red army faction) 132
Rarick, Congressman John R. 170
Ray, Dixie Lee 79
Reagan, Ronald 32, 40, 221
Reason Magazine 84
Red army brigade in Italy (RAB) 132
Reece Congressional Committee 157, 158, 159, 161
Reich, Robert 29, 58, 70, 88, 91, 92, 94, 148
Reichsgesetzblatt 102

Reichsgesetzblatt 102
Remove the tax exempt status 244
Republic National 152, 212
Republicans 36
Retinger, Dr. Joseph 231
Rhodes, Cecil 94, 195
Rhodes Oxford scholarship 94
Rhodesia 44
Rico Laws 107
Ritter, Karl 199
Rockefeller 157, 194
Rockefeller, David 120, 203, 204, 210, 214, 232
Rockefeller Foundation 159, 180
Rockefeller, John D. 158
Roe vs. Wade 96
Roman Empire 117
Romania 93
Romans 134
Roosevelt, Franklin Delano 111, 181, 184, 235
Rosenbaum, Ron 194
Rosewald Fund 158, 159
Rostenkowski, Dan 32
Rubin, Robert 36, 226, 227
Ruby Ridge 107
Rumania 134, 189
Rumanian ambassador Gezana 189
Russell, Bertrand 29
Russell, General William Huntington 191
Russell Sage Foundation 165
Russell Trust 191, 192
Russia 40, 54, 55, 120, 125, 128, 131, 134, 183, 222
Russian Jews 54
Russian Mafia 41
Russian Military 222
S
Sacs, Goldman 36
Sagan, Carl 65
Samuels, Secretary Herbert 55
San Paulo 114
Sandanistas 210
Saudi Arabia 131
Schmidt, Helmut 222
Schroeder, Pat 32
Schumer, Charlie 102
Scott, Dred 105
Scroll & Key 193
Second Amendment to the U.S. Constitution 101
Second World War 95, 122, 127, 134, 153, 171, 231
Secular Humanists 81
Security Council 137
Sekigun (Japanese Red Army) 132
Senator Aldridge 116
Senator Barry Goldwater 156, 203
Senator Bill Bradley 41
Senator Jacob Javits 223
Senator Ted Kennedy 49
Senatorial Review. 238
Sennholtz, Hans 151
Separation of Church and State 81
Sexual liberation 95
Sexual preference 84
Seymour: *Intimate Papers of Colonel House* 235
Shah of Iran 210
Shalala, Donna 83, 99, 162
Sheffield Scientific School 192
Shultz, George 65
Siberia 44, 122, 125
Sierra Club 60
Sikorski, General 231
Silicon Valley 43
Simikin, Jay 104
Singapore 122
Skull & Bones 191, 192
Sloan, Alfred 232
Slovak ambassador Lichaardus 189
Social Research Council 165
Social Security 33, 57, 245
Social Security taxes 99
Social Security Trust Fund 33
Socialism 37, 56, 57, 147, 200
Socialism's principal theorem 58
Sodomy 85
Solyom-Fekete, William 104
Somalia 101, 130
Somosa government 210

South Africa 42, 43, 44, 120, 125, 195
South African Communist Party (SACP) 210
South America 44, 116
Southeast Asia 184
Soviet empire 40
Soviet Union 222
Spain 128, 131, 221
Stalin, Joseph 56
State Department 181, 185
State Managed Trade 242
State Monopoly 68, 245
State of The World Forum 64
Steiner, Max 200
Stephanopoulos, George 94
Strong, Maurice 65
Students for Democratic Society (SDS) 198
Super Mandarins 233
Supreme Court 49, 164
Supreme Court decisions 96
Surrey, England 93
Sweden 147
Switzerland 153, 154, 228
T
Taft, William Howard 191
Taiwan 115, 122, 126
Talbott, Strobe 149
Tax advantage 157
Tax authorities 244
Tax exempt status 209
Terrorism 130
Thailand 122, 184
Thatcher, Baroness Margaret 144, 221, 229
The Group 194, 195, 196
The Order 172, 191, 192, 193, 194, 195, 196, 197, 199, 200, 201
Theocracy 124
Third Generation War 128, 181
Tibet 135
Time magazine 149
Time-Life 197
Toffler, Alvin 65
Tokyo 113, 121
Torrijos, General 212
Treaty of Rome 218, 230
Treaty of Versailles 178
Trich, Nhat Hanh 65
Trilateral Commission 113, 120, 121, 173, 193, 196, 197, 202, 203, 208, 210, 213, 214, 215, 222, 224, 233
Trotsky 54, 55
Truman Doctrine 230
Truman, Harry 32
Turkey 123, 124, 231
Turner, Ted 65, 66
Tutu, Desmond 65
Tyson, Laura D'Andria 29, 70, 91, 92
Tzu, Sun 131
U
UK 54, 87
UN army 134, 136
UN banner 105
UN Charter 137, 185
UN Department of Peacekeeping 135
UN force 101
UN Global Government 52
UN initiatives 136
UN military 134, 203
UN military incursions 90
UN NATO troops 132
UN Peacekeepers 136
Unanimous consent 238
Union Bank of Switzerland 208
Union Theological Seminary 80, 196
UNITA 43
United Church of Christ 80
United Jersey 152
United Kingdom 155, 229, 231
United Nations 83, 116, 130, 132, 134, 135, 136, 137, 169, 173, 178, 187, 207, 230, 231, 241, 242, 246
United States 54, 55, 70, 113, 120, 131, 153, 154, 178, 180, 181, 182, 183, 203, 208, 210, 230, 231
United States Department of Education 109
United States of Europe 230
Universal monetary system 205
University of Berlin 199
University of California 200
University of California at Berkley 92
University of Wisconsin 99

Uraguay Agreements 229
US aid to Russia 40
US armed forces 134
US Army Corps of Engineers 61
US Chamber of Commerce 109
US FDA (Food & Drug Administration) 61
US Federal gold supply 155
US Senate 104
US State Department 187
US Treasury 35
USDA 237
USDC 34, 37
USDE 109
USDL 72
USDT 237
USSR 40, 204
V
Value added tax (VAT) 99
Vandals 194
VAT 99
Venezuela 228
Vietnam 133
Vouliagmeni, Greece 218
W
Waco 107
Wall Street 35, 36, 212
Wall Street Journal 50, 208
Washington, Booker T. 98
Washington, George 58, 97, 105
Washington Post 157, 172
Wealth of Nations 246
WebbHouse 195, 205
Weekly Review 209
Weishaupt, Adam 145, 147
Wells, Secretary 185, 188
Wermacht 134
West Germany 172
Western culture 45
Western Europe 123
Western intelligence agencies 131
What's My Line 209
White, Harry Dexter 153, 186, 187
Wild Cards 123
Wilerson, Doxie 165
Wilson, Woodrow 111, 222
Wiseman, Sir William 232
With No Apologies 156, 203
Withholding tax laws 244
Wood, Judge Diane 239
Wooley, Knight 194
World Bank 116, 143, 154, 172, 173, 186, 187, 215, 222, 226, 227
World Council of Churches 77, 80
World domination 39
World Trade Organization 31, 38, 39, 70, 88, 120, 169, 178, 189, 227, 228, 229, 231, 242
World War I 95
World War I peace treaty 183
World War II 179, 183
Wundt psychological structure 199
Y
Yale 192, 193
Yale Divinity School 196
Yale School of Divinity 80
Yale University 191, 194
Yale University. 193, 201
York Masonic Rite 191
Young, Stephen Lord 194
Z
Zelman, Aaron 104
Zimbabwe 45
Zurich, Switzerland 54
Zwischengaener 143, 144, 168, 193, 196

"Albert Jay Nock's Mr. Jefferson, *is a superb biographical essay, beautifully written and penetrating in analysis; Mr. Nock understands Jefferson so well that one despairs of going at all beyond him."*

Richard Hofstadter
Columbia University

ISBN 0-87319-024-6
224 pages, Trade Paper, $12.95

Albert J. Nock (1870-1945) was a radical, in the venerable sense of the word: one whose ideas cut to the root and make you think again about things previously taken for granted.

ISBN 0-87319-041-6
224 pages, Trade Paper, $14.95